Oranges filled with Jelly

Fanchette

Galantine of Poulard, with Aspic Jelly

Gradins de Tartelettes de Poires

Pommes à la Pa...

...r Christmas Pie

THE
GREEDY
QUEEN

THE GREEDY QUEEN

Eating with Victoria

ANNIE GRAY

P

PROFILE BOOKS

First published in Great Britain in 2017 by
PROFILE BOOKS LTD
3 Holford Yard
Bevin Way
London
WC1X 9HD

www.profilebooks.com

10 9 8 7 6 5 4 3 2 1

Typeset in Fournier by MacGuru Ltd
Printed and bound in Great Britain by Clays, St Ives plc

A CIP catalogue record for this book is available from the British
Library.

ISBN 978 1 78125 682 4
eISBN 978 1 78283 273 7

To Matt, with love

In memory of my grandma, Brenda Gray (née Evans)

Contents

Acknowledgements

This book would not have seen the light of day without my agent, Tim Bates, who has been unwavering in his support and supply of beer, and my editor, Rebecca Gray, whose editorial comments were a delight, and whose patience in the face of endless toilet references has been awe-inspiring. Thanks also go to their excellent colleagues at PFD and Profile Books.

Many people have helped me with ideas or information while I've been researching *The Greedy Queen*, as well as allowing me access to archival material without which I could not have written a thing. Primary among these are the brilliant staff of the Royal Archive: Pam Clark, Allison Derrett and Lynnette Beech, along with Carly Collier in the Print Room. I am grateful to Her Majesty the Queen Elizabeth II for giving permission for the online publication of Queen

Victoria's Journals, and for the reproduction of some of the pictures included within this book. I would also like to thank the various archivists who took time to reply to emails, especially those at Staffordshire Record Office, Chatsworth, Bangor University, Hastings Museum, and Blair Castle. At (in some cases ex of) Historic Royal Palaces, I was encouraged by Lucy Worsley, and aided and abetted by Jonathan Scott at Kew, as well as Lee Prosser and Nigel Arch. At Kensington Palace, Deirdre Murphy talked to me about Queen Victoria's dress, figure and height, and Ian Chipperfield, costumier extraordinaire, also helped with matters of clothing. At English Heritage, Michael Hunter and Andrew Hann have been long-standing supporters, and the research I did for them on Osborne House forms the background to several chapters. Meanwhile over at Historic England, Steven Brindle showed me round the restored Windsor kitchens, and, along with Richard Williams of Windsor Castle, provided a very memorable morning. Richard Pollitt at Mansion House in York helped me out with particulars of the Queen's meals en route to Balmoral, as well as admiring with me the epic 100 Guinea Dish. My fellow historians, Richard Fitch, Marc Hawtree, Ivan Day and Sara Pennell, all pointed me in directions I'd not yet discovered, and I am also grateful to the various food people, historians and generally fascinating community I follow on Twitter. At the University of York, Kate Giles has supported my Research Fellowship, and I am grateful both to her, and the wider Archaeology Department, for enabling me to continue my association with York. *The Greedy Queen* was short-listed for the Jane Grigson Trust Award for New Food Writers in March 2016, which gave me a tremendous boost, and for which I thank the Trustees.

On a more personal level, I owe a huge debt to the team of *The Kitchen Cabinet*, both on and off-air, especially Jay Rayner, Tim Hayward, Rachel McCormack, Vicky Shepherd and Darby Dorras, and I'd like to thank them for their undying support and encouragement in the face of terrible pottage. I'd also like to thank the cast and crew of *Victorian Bakers*, in particular Peter Sweasey, Emily Thompson and John Swift, who have both encouraged me, and also given very specific particulars of gas ovens and anti-fart bread. Del Sneddon sent me a bottle of Lochnagar whisky so that I could carry out very important experiments in royal drinking, and the staff at Toppings bookshop in Ely fed me tea. Special thanks to Rebecca Harris Quigg for all the gin. My friends have been brilliant: Katharine Boardman, Rebecca Lane, Kathy Hipperson and Laura Gale, I salute you. Mike and Chris Grundy put me up (and put up with me) on repeated visits to Windsor, and saved me from certain death when knackered on the M25. The various people who have read drafts and commented, including many of the above, as well as Jess Smith, all deserve thanks, as do my family: Mike and Angela Gray, Kirsty Noble and Sean Griffin, Marion Howling, and Richard 'stop sending me stuff' Gray (who also looks after my website and makes elegant sense of my doodles). Last, but very much not least, I would probably still be thinking and not writing, were it not for my partner, the inestimable Matt Howling.

1

Introduction

n July 2015 a pair of extraordinarily large bloomers were auctioned in Wiltshire. They sold for £12,900, breaking the record for the previous pair of similarly generously proportioned underwear, which fetched £6,200 a year earlier, and the news of their sale was widely reported across the media. Embroidered with the letters VR, and verified as genuine by the auction house, they showed our continuing fascination with a woman who died over a hundred years ago. Bloomers of similar dimensions and provenance appeared as part of an online history course run by Historic Royal Palaces in 2016. Reactions were immediate and polarised, from those who peered at them in avid curiosity, seeing them as offering a rare personal insight into a distant figure, to those who found the whole thing sordid, and cried out for people to leave the poor woman alone. Her weight was her own issue, and we shouldn't be pawing over personal items in such an undignified way, even if she had given the items away as tokens of esteem, knowing that they would be treasured and kept for posterity – and, despite an initial interdiction to do so, eventually sold on.

Queen Victoria, who was, of course, the original wearer of the bloomers, was a complex, fascinating person, whose reign was, until 2015, the longest of any British monarch, and who was head of state during some of the most formative years of British history. A long and influential life has made her one of the best known figures from the past, and over 500 books have been written about her, with countless more about her children, her palaces, her influence and her legacy. This book is about her food.

When Victoria came to the throne, in 1837, she was a petite, elegant young woman, with what commentators called a fine complexion, though a lamentable tendency to pose, when resting, with her mouth slightly open. Very few people knew anything about her personality, which was barely formed at eighteen years old, and she was thrown into the maelstrom of court life with little experience of the world of politics, people outside her immediate circle, or fine dining. She was a party animal, eager for what she called dissipation, but equally ready to work hard. In recent years her damaging childhood and delight in becoming Queen has become better known in popular culture, mainly through films such as *Young Victoria* and the 2016 mini-series, *Victoria*. There has, however, been a tendency to dwell on her personal life and her marriage to Prince Albert while neglecting her very real political significance; although she was a constitutional monarch, she (and Albert, while alive) had a great deal of influence, both officially and unofficially, through the reams of letters they sent and their personal connections with heads of state abroad. The death of Albert, in 1861, plunged the Queen, in her mid-forties, into a black depression, and she mourned him for the rest of her life. Biographers have been inclined to refer to her as old from the 1860s onwards, which she certainly was not, and it's deceptively easy to divide her life too absolutely into pre- and post-Albert, whereas, as with anyone else, things were just not that simple. It is as a widow that she is best known, however, black-clad and growing ever larger as she turned to food for comfort. She was, too, increasingly sedentary, due to a knee injury that left her lame, and the most abiding image of her for many people, for a very long time, was a distant and forbidding figure in a donkey-cart.

Myths about Queen Victoria are plentiful, and largely unproven or taken out of context, from the 'not amused' comment, to the accusations that she slept with or even married John Brown, and image-searching Prince Albert at work is strictly for those who want to get sacked. Food myths, while not as well known, are equally entrenched: she liked a boiled egg for breakfast, she ate like a bird, she had Brown Windsor Soup for every meal, and she preferred plain food. Most of these crumble in the face of fact, and a far more nuanced story can be told: the only one which even vaguely stands up in examination is her liking for plain foods, but even that has to be seen in the context of someone whose habitual fare involved truffles and cream. In researching this book I did not set out to tackle every aspect of her life. I had no desire to explore the Queen's sense of humour, or her relationships with her family or her ministers, or her religion or politics or sense of social justice, or any of the other aspects which would form the basis of a conventional biography, and you will find barely a mention of a prime minister or a European crisis (unless there's food involved). Nor did I want to write a book about a woman and her weight, or make any kind of judgement about nutrition and health, which would project modern ideas and cod psychology back into an age with different ideas, and onto a person whom none of us can ever really know. Victoria undeniably had a complicated relationship with food: she used it to assert control as a seventeen-year-old fighting for her individuality, and she sought solace in it when she was abruptly widowed and thrown into mental turmoil after Prince Albert's death, but exactly what she felt and how that was expressed in her eating can only ever be based on guesswork.

The Victorian age was one of enormous culinary change. Many of the elements that were introduced or popularised had roots in the Georgian period, and still others took until the mid-twentieth century to really catch on. Things we associate with the Victorians, such as gas cookery, tinned food, raising agents, food moulds and the use of coal in cooking ranges, all pre-dated Victoria's accession in 1837, while others, such as chemical colourings, mechanisation, gas cookery (again), frozen foods, refrigeration and aspic in everything were as much features of the Edwardian period (and beyond) as they were of the decades before Victoria's death in 1901. Yet it is fair to say that the way food was produced, cooked and consumed altered significantly across the course of the 64 years she was on the throne, and that the eating habits of those living in 1901 were very different to those who were setting up home in 1837. In many ways the Victorian period saw the birth of modern food culture, complete with fad diets, worries about industrially produced foods, restaurant critics and heavily styled final dishes. Every time we worry about serried ranks of cutlery marching away at the side of our plate, we are being led by the late Victorians, and when we desperately search for novelty in food, while secretly craving a decent pork pie, we are echoing our nineteenth-century ancestors.

Victoria ate – obviously – according to the norms of the times. Her food, and the way she consumed it, showed more continuity than change, which is hardly surprising given that she had the power to eat the meals that she wanted, and her desires were hardly likely to go hand in hand with the latest gastronomic developments. But any meal is more than just its final form, and this book deals with where food came from, who prepared it, the kitchens it was cooked in, and the way meals worked in practice – elements which were often beyond the control of one individual. In doing so, it sheds light on Victorian food in general, for while the food of royalty only represents a tiny proportion of Victorian meals, the factors which went into preparing it are indicative of a much wider context. Victoria was influenced by this wider context, adopting – eventually – the new dining styles of the era, and eating new ingredients and types of cuisine. She in turn had an effect upon the world outside the palaces. Most of her subjects lived on or below the poverty line, so her direct impact was by necessity limited, but she provided a culinary figurehead. Her meals had to be lavish and luxurious, and eaten off gold – she was Queen, and one of her primary duties was to provide a focus for Britons to look up to. Reports on her travels, on her dinner parties, and on her receptions, filled the newspapers, and when she disappeared from public view in the 1860s, criticism was swift and severe, and included calls for her abdication. She was only a Queen because her people wanted her to be Queen, and acted towards her in the way that defined her as Queen. In return, she was expected to behave like one.

This book is, therefore, a book about food, and the Victorians, but seen through the life of a woman who ate a lot of one and defined the other. It is a sort of culinary biography, of a person who symbolised an age. Victoria was – and is – a polarising figure; many things to many people, often deeply contradictory. To some, she was a monster, but those who knew her usually adored her; to others she was emotionally unstable and uncertain, but she could also be stubborn, wilful and decisive; she was unable to cope without a strong man to support her, but unwilling to relinquish any power and always aware of her status as Queen; she was a terrible mother, but she doted on her children and did her utmost to give them the childhood she'd never had; she was clingy, she was independent; she did a lot for women, she hated feminism; she was sweet and feminine, and laughed at everything, she was humourless and horrible and bullied her son. People change over the course of a lifetime, and she was all of these and more. However, as this book will show, whatever she was, and whenever she was being it, she remained above all else, a greedy Queen.

2

Childhood

Victoria was born on 24 May 1819, at Kensington Palace. Her father, the Duke of Kent, described her as being 'as plump as a partridge'.[1] He had earlier declared that he did not mind whether his child was a girl or a boy; in the race to produce an heir to the British throne, a healthy child was enough. The Duke was one of a ragtag set of brothers, the eldest of whom was at the time Prince Regent, but would soon be George IV. George had no living children – his only daughter, Charlotte, had died in childbirth two years before – and, despite having been a womaniser in his youth, with a marital history worthy of a soap opera, by 1819 he was single, obese, and uninterested in producing another child. His heir was another brother, Frederick, who had followed in his elder brother's footsteps and was estranged from his wife. Next in line was William, Duke of

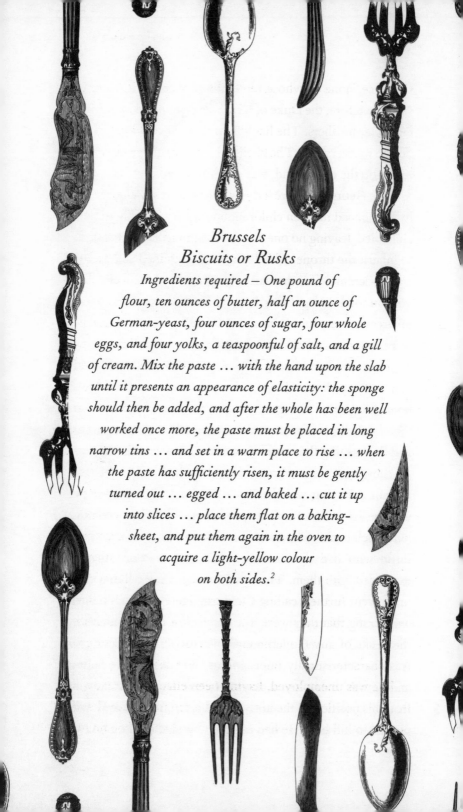

Brussels Biscuits or Rusks

Ingredients required — One pound of flour, ten ounces of butter, half an ounce of German-yeast, four ounces of sugar, four whole eggs, and four yolks, a teaspoonful of salt, and a gill of cream. Mix the paste ... with the hand upon the slab until it presents an appearance of elasticity: the sponge should then be added, and after the whole has been well worked once more, the paste must be placed in long narrow tins ... and set in a warm place to rise ... when the paste has sufficiently risen, it must be gently turned out ... egged ... and baked ... cut it up into slices ... place them flat on a baking-sheet, and put them again in the oven to acquire a light-yellow colour on both sides.[2]

Clarence, none of whose ten children were legitimate. In 1819, therefore, the Duke of Kent was 51, and had two childless older brothers. The likelihood that he would get to the throne was very low. The likelihood that his offspring would reign, on the other hand, was extremely high.

The Georgians were a dynasty of contrasts. George III had produced thirteen children, but in 1817 his only grandchild died, leaving no one beyond the immediate generation to inherit the throne. This led to an undignified and excruciating scramble for the various brothers – there were nine boys in total – to get married and have babies. Long-term mistresses were unceremoniously dumped, old scandals were dug out and circulated, and German-speaking princesses of any hue were scrapped over like valuable brood mares. They almost all had hideous reputations. Lord Melbourne captured the general opinion when he described them as 'wild beasts ... making love wherever they went and then saying they were very sorry, they couldn't marry ... they were, as it were, quite invincible'.[3] Their excuse for not marrying was the Royal Marriage Act, passed by George III in an effort to control his offspring's choices, but which backfired painfully for many of his children and those who had the misfortune to become romantically entangled with them. Thomas Creevey, a politician of the time, went further, calling them profligate and unpopular, and stating that they were 'the damnedest millstones about the necks of any Government'.[4] Victoria's father Edward was characteristically impecunious. His debts were huge, and he was unemployed, having been effectively removed from his position in the army after his troops mutinied and plotted to kill him. He had imposed harsh discipline on his men, but he also believed in self-discipline, and prided himself on his upright habits and on having the constitution of an ox.

That self-discipline didn't, however, extend to his lifestyle. He married his own German brood mare in 1818, settling on the widowed Princess Victoria of Saxe-Coburg-Saalfeld, proven to be fertile by the two children from her previous marriage. When she became pregnant with his child, he declared his intention to move back to England from Germany, where he'd been staying away from the critical British press, to ensure that the child was born on British soil. The Regent refused to pay for the trip, but, after hasty borrowings and wheedlings, the Duke raised enough money to come back. Wending its slow way from Leiningen to London came a bizarre circus of carriages and people. There were seven vehicles, containing the Duke, Duchess, the Duchess's daughter by her first marriage, maidservants, manservants, a governess, two doctors, several dogs and birdcages. There were also two cooks, and a man called Thomas Kingsthorn, whose role was to guard the Duke's silver, which travelled in its own caravan.[5]

They arrived at Kensington Palace a month before Victoria was born. There are no surviving records to show exactly what the weary staff made of their new home. It was infested with black beetles, and hardly the kind of royal palace they would have been used to back in Germany. Kensington had been built for William and Mary in the late seventeenth century, and was site of many a basic fish dinner for that fairly private and down-to-earth royal couple. By the 1810s, it had become a sort of repository for unwanted royals, living cheek-by-jowl in apartments carved out of the former staterooms and courtiers' accommodation. Victoria later recalled the constant ticking of the clocks belonging to another of the royal brothers, and the whole place must have had a rather forlorn feeling to it: a sad decline from its heyday as a baroque country retreat. The couple didn't stay there long. The state of the apartments was such that, despite spending a fair amount of money he didn't have doing them up, the Duke decided to decamp to the country, where it would be cheaper, and he could avoid the rest of his family.

The baby Victoria was the subject of intense press interest. While her father and his siblings were widely regarded as a waste of space, she was an innocent, and finally a potential decent heir to the throne. Excluding the late Princess Charlotte, Victoria was the first of a new generation, and could yet save the country from a whole line of dissolute old men, some of whom were even worse than those who had already reached the throne. Of course, nothing was guaranteed. Immediately above the Duke of Kent in the line of succession was the Duke of Clarence, who had rushed off and married his own German of childbearing age, Princess Adelaide of Saxe-Meiningen. She could well have children. Still, the press was thrown into a flurry, and, right from her birth, newspapers reported on Victoria with the almost proprietary interest in her life that was to characterise her whole reign.

Two days after Victoria's birth, *The Times*' daily bulletin read, 'The Duchess of Kent we are happy to say continues as well as can be expected in every respect…Her Royal Highness intends suckling the infant Princess.'[6] Breastfeeding, especially breastfeeding one's own child, was still enough of an oddity in the early nineteenth century to excite interest. The Duchess of Kent was an experienced mother and clearly well versed in the latest thinking on feeding young babies. The value of breast milk had been recognised by the eighteenth century, and, although children continued to be fed on animal milk or that seventeenth-century staple, pap and panada (breadcrumbs soaked in stock, milk or wine, and often flavoured with sugar or spice) right up to the time of Victoria's birth, most babies were fed breast milk. It just wasn't necessarily that of their mothers, who, if upper class, employed wet nurses instead. Over the next half-century, attitudes would change, influenced by concern over the habits and morality of wet nurses, and the idea that bad habits could be passed from nurse to baby along with the milk, but in 1819 this was not the case, and the Duchess's choice shocked the upper-class circle around her.[7] She wrote to her own mother, 'I am so very happy that I can breast feed her so well, I would have been desperate to see my little darling on someone else's breast ... everybody is most astonished that I am breast-feeding; people of the mondaine world are really very unhappy, how much genuine joie de vivre do they miss.'[8] The Princess was also vaccinated, again something which was in its infancy at the time, but would later be talked of with approval by the then Queen's early biographers.

Children in the late Georgian period were weaned at anything between six and eighteen months old, depending on the wealth of the family. For working-class families, the sooner a child could be fed on similar foods to the rest of the family, the better, but weaning could cause issues. The norm was to introduce foods such as beef tea, animal milk, broth, minced chicken and bread pudding, along with rusks and other biscuits. The poor couldn't afford most of these, and what they could afford would often have been adulterated, so infant mortality remained extremely high. Even among the upper classes it was relatively common: William, Duke of Clarence's wife Adelaide, as well as suffering miscarriages and a stillbirth, saw her only two surviving children die in their first few months. This was not the case for Victoria. Her mother commented on how large her appetite was as a baby, and when she was weaned at around six months old, the Duke of Kent wrote that she did 'not appear to thrive the less for the change'.[9]

For the whole Kent family, however, life was about to be thrown into turmoil. The move to the country took place on Christmas Day, 1819. On the 28th the Princess was nearly injured by birdshot, as a local boy out hunting missed his mark, but by mid-January local colour was the least of their worries. The Duke, so proud of his indefatigable constitution, had caught, and ignored, a cold. It rapidly worsened, and, as was the usual way in the Georgian period, the doctors brought in alternatively bled, cupped and applied leeches to their patient. Their tortures were in vain. On the evening of 19 January the Duke was seen to weep at the thought of yet more bleeding: by the 23rd he was dead. On the 29th George III finally died as well, making George IV no longer the Regent, but the King. Victoria and her mother were left stranded in Sidmouth with nothing apart from the Duke of Kent's debts.

Fortunately for the twice-widowed Duchess of Kent, her brother was already in England and in possession of a large government pension. In keeping with the excitingly incestuous ways of eighteenth-century European courts, he was the widower of Princess Charlotte, the daughter of George IV, whose death in childbirth had provoked that mad fraternal scramble to get married and procreate. Prince Leopold was one of the better of Victoria's fairly hideous cast of relatives (though he had his moments). She grew up to be very close to him and he supported her through some of the uglier moments of her childhood, although the relationship became distant when, as Queen, she took decision-making into her own, very ready, hands. Leopold moved the whole family back to draughty Kensington, and supported them financially. The Household became significantly smaller, although the Duchess seems to have retained the services of the cook, Charles Legleitner, a clear declaration of her desired status, as male cooks were expensive, and tended to come with hefty demands for modern kitchens and a wide range of equipment.[10]

At Kensington Palace the Kents occupied the apartments allocated to the Duke in 1798, spread over two floors of the south-east corner. The Duke had done a bit of work to them before he moved to Germany to get married, but they were still fairly basic by aristocratic standards. The palace itself was in a 'general state of decay',[11] with bulging walls held up by props and iron bands, dry rot endemic, and damp making many of the rooms uninhabitable. Cooking and service areas had been shoehorned in during the conversion of the palace to apartments, and often involved waiting staff scuttling between outdoor buildings to the main palace with no protection from the elements for them or the food they were carrying. The apartments were flanked by those of other spare royals, including the Duke of Kent's slightly disgraced sister, Princess Sophia. She quickly became a close confidante of the Duchess, who spoke very limited English, and was very isolated. Throughout Victoria's childhood, she was a staple fixture, often dining with the Duchess, or dropping in after dinner. Victoria's closest relationship during her childhood, especially after the marriage and subsequent departure of her beloved half-sister Feodora when Victoria was nine, was with her governess, Louise Lehzen (later Baroness Lehzen), who was reputed to like eating only potatoes, and chewed caraway seeds to alleviate bad breath.[12] This wasn't uncommon, and caraway comfits were widely available for that very reason. In many respects, this early part of Victoria's life wasn't drastically different to that of many aristocratic children. She was closer to her governess than her mother, she dined separately, on nursery food, and her main companion was a relative (Feodora) of similar rank. Despite her probable future as the most powerful person in Britain, she played with toys designed to inculcate standard female behaviours. She had a doll's house, where she could practice the required conventions of aristocratic girls. It still survives at Kensington Palace, and is typical of the toys deemed suitable for upper-class girls. It consists of a drawing room, set up for taking tea, and a kitchen, complete with mini charcoal stoves and a dresser laden with plates. Adelaide, Duchess of Clarence, gave her a child's tea set, which again was a fairly standard girls' plaything. Tea was intrinsically linked to femininity, and a woman at her tea things epitomised gentility and delicacy for many nineteenth-century writers. Victoria may have been set to be Queen, but she still had to adhere to the expected norms of feminine behaviour, among which skilled teapot manipulation was surprisingly telling.[13]

Of course, things weren't entirely as they were for others. All of this apparent normality was underlain with tension as to her future, and while it seemed that Victoria remained unaware of her status, she was clearly used to being fawned upon, and making demands, even when very young. She was at that point third in line to the throne, and not tainted by being an adult male Georgian. The public interest in her hadn't waned, and staged appearances helped to whet the appetites of those who glimpsed her. Later biographies, written while Victoria was on the throne, dwelt on the romantic aspect of her childhood in a tumbledown palace, behind wrought-iron gates. She was seen as a young child to take breakfast with her mother on the Kensington Palace lawn, attended by a single page. She rode a donkey around the grounds. She watered her feet instead of the flowers. She got stuck in apple trees and fell down scree slopes. All of these carefully culled anecdotes belie the fact that, as emerged later in Victoria's own writings and those of the people around her, by the time she was a teenager, a system had been put in place which was very far from carefree and innocent.

The Kensington System, as it became known, aimed to isolate the Princess, to ensure that she only socialised with a very select group, chosen by her mother and her mother's closest companion, John Conroy.[14] Conroy was, like the Duke of Kent, an unsuccessful soldier. He had entered the Kent household before the Duke's death, and, by the mid-1820s, the widowed Duchess was completely reliant upon him. She had previous form in relying on strong, but not altogether disinterested, men, having formed a similarly close relationship with a male advisor in Germany after the death of her first husband. The two were tied together by self-interest, and the awareness that, in Victoria, they had a tool that could ensure their success in the murky world of court and government politics, if only it could be handled right. They failed, but their attempts to shape Victoria into their creature were extremely painful, and at times downright cruel.

In later life, when Victoria looked back on her childhood her reminiscences were coloured by her experiences as a teenager, after Feodora had left, and the System tightened its grip. She recalled that 'we lived in a very simple plain manner, breakfast was at half past eight, luncheon at half past one, dinner at seven – to which I came generally (when it was no regular large dinner party) – eating my bread and milk out of a small silver basin. Tea was only allowed as a great treat in later years.'[15] That meal pattern, with those timings, was one she largely stuck to throughout her childhood. She also continued to eat very plain food. This was partly cultural: notions that a child's behaviour would be directly affected for the worse by strong flavours persisted well into the nineteenth century, especially for girls. Food science was in its infancy, but in general the concept that foods could be divided into groups (including the evocatively named 'flesh-formers'), and allocated according to gender, level of exercise, age and class, was well established. Likewise, the physical results of certain diets were pored over. Unsurprisingly, flatulence in particular tended to be noted as an undesirable trait in upper-class children. However, then as now, cultural ideas about foods played a large role in determining what was thought to be a 'good' diet. Meat was regarded as the mainstay of a healthy regime, especially mutton, along with eggs and vegetables. Sweet foods were reserved for bribery and treats.[16] However, the Duchess and Conroy seem to have taken this to extremes. Victoria ate like a child, kept to the nursery and fed the most basic of meals, for much longer than most of her class. Even after the age of thirteen, when children would generally emerge from the nursery and dine with their parents, many of her meals were still taken in her room. By the age of eleven Uncle Leopold was worrying about the effect on her nerves, 'I hear that you do not like over much to take exercise, listen to my advice dearest love, and force yourself. Though it may be a little tiresome, your health and state of nerves require a great deal of air and exercise and if you neglect it, you will materially suffer from it',[17] and it's clear that she developed a habit of eating too much, and very fast, whenever she got the opportunity: 'if I was to give you an opinion, I should say that a certain little Princess eats ... frequently a little too much, and almost always a little too fast. Eating too fast is particularly unwholesome, and should therefore be avoided as much as possible, because it lays the foundation of many a disease.'[18]

The regular large dinner parties Victoria refers to were another feature of life at Kensington. From at least 1828 the Duchess began hosting dinners, intended to impress and woo the assorted movers and shakers around the court. George IV was proving implacable on the subject of money, titles, status and all the other things that the Duchess and Conroy thought should be their due. With an eye to the future, when George would be no more, it was important to assemble a support network. If, in the years ahead, battle lines should be drawn up between the King and his eventual heir, the Duchess wanted to have as many people on her side as possible. After all, the Georgian monarchs had a well-established history of family rifts between monarchs and their heirs, so it wasn't as if she was doing anything radical or controversial.

The dinners held by the Duchess were glittering affairs. The kitchen was very well equipped, although badly set-up, and the Duchess repeatedly applied for money to make alterations. In the 1830s she finally succeeded in getting a new, state-of-the-art kitchen, with cast-iron ovens, a running supply of hot water, and hot closets to keep food warm, but before this her staff were working in a space largely unchanged from the days of William and Mary, and hopelessly out of date for the early nineteenth century.[19] However, it was supplemented by a confectionery and a still room (the housekeeper's domain, used for making jams and preserves, as well as distillations both for pleasurable and medicinal consumption), and there would have been no real limit to what could have been cooked there. The kitchen inventory for the Kents' apartments includes ice-cream-making equipment, cake moulds, jelly moulds and pastry pans.[20] The Duchess continued to employ a man as her head cook, and he would have been expected to produce meals to rival anything turned out by her aristocratic guests. The dishes would have been French-influenced, with complex flavours and a wide range of ingredients. Victoria would not, at this stage, have experienced all of those possibilities, however. She was not invited to the large dinners, merely paraded through the room before dinner and again after. Guests needed to be reminded of the reason they should support the Duchess, but that did not necessitate Victoria actually being present.

Victoria was also kept away from court as much as possible. George IV didn't seem unduly bothered by this, but when William, Duke of Clarence, acceded as William IV in 1830, he was rather more annoyed by the whole thing, blaming the Duchess for keeping his niece away from court, where she should have been gaining vital training for her role as Queen, and helping generate good PR for the tarnished image of the court. The young Princess was occasionally let out to see her very royal relatives and later recounted riding around in a carriage with a 'large and gouty' George IV at Virginia Water. At least as important as this recollection is the one which immediately followed it in her reminiscences: 'I afterwards went ... to the Page Whiting's Cottage ... here I had some <u>fruit</u> and amused myself by cramming one of Whiting's children, a little girl, with peaches.'[21] The love of fresh fruit was one that would never leave her, and her use of food to assert her authority was also an early indication of the way in which she would make clear her power in later years. As Queen, she dictated who came to dinner, and the style and pace of the meal, as well as who sat where, and she revelled in it.

At Kensington, in a domestic environment, the young Princess's culinary experiences were limited. Nevertheless, she showed an interest in food, and an adventurousness in taste, which would characterise her whole life. When the family holidayed in Ramsgate in 1825, she ate milk and cream fresh from the dairy and she would have been aware of where her food came from before it was transformed into finished dishes upon her table. Not far from the palace at Kensington were the royal kitchen gardens, with their pineapple and melon pits, as well as a peach house, mushroom house and cucumber frames, and there was also an ice house in the grounds.[22] As Victoria grew older, the Duchess recognised that, if the Princess wasn't at court, she still needed to be trained in how to behave as an adult and, in keeping with the practice of the time, Victoria was sometimes allowed to join her mother for dinner as a proper participant. While not attending big dinners until her mid-teens, she was certainly present at family dinners – the Duchess, Conroy and his family, and a few select others would be a typical party. The food would have been significantly more muted than the complicated dishes served at the dinner parties, not least because the household remained chronically short of cash. However, training her in dining etiquette would have been absolutely vital. One of the primary functions of a monarch was to facilitate social relations between politicians of all nations, as well as within the ruling classes of Britain. That meant hosting dinners, at which she had to be able to conduct herself with dignity and poise. Dinner was a key test of civility, and if she failed at that, she would fail at everything.

Despite the Duchess of Kent and John Conroy's increasingly draconian attempts to discipline Victoria, and to curtail the opportunities she had to be exposed to outside influences, they could not keep her to themselves completely. As she grew older, the King and his ministers put pressure on the Kent household to bring Victoria to court. The constant whirl of Drawing Rooms (formal social occasions at which the King would be present, and at which debutantes would 'come out', being presented to the King for the first time), dinners and balls at Windsor and Buckingham Palace meant that she had ample invitations, but the

Duchess preferred Victoria to go to nice, safe, outside events, such as the theatre, where she could be guarded and controlled. Nevertheless, in 1831 she attended her first Drawing Room, and before that she also danced, and presumably supped, at a children's ball hosted by George IV. These were regular occasions for the 'juvenile nobility',[23] though this particular one was in honour of Portugal's ten-year-old Queen, Donna Maria II. Charles Greville, a court official whose catty diaries provide endless anecdotes about the period, commented that, 'our little princess is a short, plain-looking child, and not near so good-looking as the Portuguese. However, if Nature has not done so much, Fortune is likely to do a great deal more for her.'[24] In contrast to these successful public appearances, the Duchess stopped Victoria attending William IV's coronation in 1831 after a spat about precedence. Victoria, fully aware of the jostling for position going on behind the scenes, was inconsolable.

In 1830 the Duchess and Conroy decided to ramp up the training of the Queen-in-waiting. The King was relatively elderly: three of his brothers were already dead, and there was a reasonable chance that he would die before Victoria was eighteen. If that happened, the Duchess was fairly certain that she would be made Regent. (The other obvious choice was another of the hated royal brothers, the Duke of Cumberland, who was even dodgier than the rest, and it was unlikely that the government would accept him.) She'd been a Regent before, for her son, Prince of Leiningen. She and Conroy now put all of their energies into establishing Victoria as a paragon of virtue, and her mother as her closest companion, without whom she would falter and fail. If their wishes came true, Victoria would be on the throne, but the Duchess and Conroy would control her. The first part of this new plan was to show off the Princess. This needed careful orchestrating, in order to expose her to the maximum number of people while not allowing her to spend too much time personally interacting with them, and to ensure that, at all times, she formed, to outside viewers, a solid unit with the Duchess and, where possible, Conroy. It was time to go on tour.

The Royal Progresses of 1830–35, as they've become known, were crucial in forging Victoria's early reputation, as well as in exposing her to a far greater range of food than she'd come across before. The first, which took in Stonehenge, Blenheim and Kenilworth, was billed as merely showing Victoria the sights. Those of 1832, 1833 and 1835, along with the 'holiday' in Tunbridge Wells of 1834, were much more serious. From 1832 almost until her death, Victoria kept a daily journal. It was, of course, read by her mother while she remained a Princess, so is rarely entirely honest, but as she grew in age and confidence, it became a sort of passive-aggressive form of communication with the Duchess, and, for all its omissions and later edits, remains a unique document.[25] It is quite clear from the beginning how important eating in public was, and how much the Progresses were built around it. The party, with assorted hangers-on, servants, pets and ponies in tow, sometimes overnighted at inns or hotels, but more often they stayed with members of the nobility. Even the inns would have put on a reasonable spread. They stayed at substantial places: the Blue Bell in Barnby Moor had stabling for 120 horses and 60 post boys,[26] while the Bull's Head in Meriden later became a manor house. They would almost certainly have employed male chefs, capable of serving high-end food, at the same time as having a more plebeian menu for the masses (and servants). John Farley, proprietor of the London Tavern in Bishopsgate, published his *London Art of Cookery* at the end of the eighteenth century, cashing in on the fame of the eatery to sell his book, which purported to be the book of the pub. The recipes reflect exactly the same mid-high-end cookery that his customers would have experienced at home (and in fact are largely plagiarised from the same recipe books that his customers' cooks would have been cooking from). Tavern dining wasn't exactly private, either, and on a number of occasions the royal party dined with the blinds up so that the general public could feast their eyes.[27]

At the various country houses at which they stayed, dinner was even more of a performance. Conroy took on the task of organising the tours, and they quickly established a routine, which maintained, as far as possible, regular hours and plain food: 'their Royal Highnesses would like to dine at seven ... The Princess may like to dine in her own room, the first day – with Baroness Lehzen. The Princess only eats plain roast mutton: but this depends on the Duchess finding her Royal Highness fatigued, or not.'[28] Most days, no matter where they stayed, they stuck to the same pattern as they did at home: breakfast around 8.30–9 a.m., lunch at 1 p.m., and dinner at 7 p.m. Unlike in Kensington, however, where Victoria only dined with her mother when there was no formal dinner party, she was expected to turn up and perform for at least one dinner at every place they stayed. She would have been used to the occasional dinner of a grand nature. She dined fairly regularly at Claremont, where Uncle Leopold employed a man-cook, Mr Hewitt; a confectioner of Germanic origins, Christian Steinhardt; and Hannah Parsons, a coffee-room woman, among others.[29] The Progress dinners were in a totally different vein, though. Instead of being treated like a child, Victoria was now the guest of honour, under enormous and unlooked-for pressure to perform. All credit, therefore, to the Duchess that the various witnesses to the Princess at dinner almost universally praised her behaviour. She ate in a wide variety of locations, from yachts to marquees, and mayoral mansion houses to episcopal palaces, eating an endless procession of cold collations for lunch, surrounded by eager, predominantly male, local dignitaries. The regional newspapers usually lavished extravagant praise on the catering, and there's little doubt that the hitherto limited dietary choices of the Princess were rapidly expanded, but it must quickly have become as monotonous as nursery food, especially with her mother and Conroy and the entirety of each town watching over her. In the journals, her relief when she wasn't on show and eating the best the local hostelry had to offer is palpable: 'we had a very nice luncheon in our carriage which consisted of sandwiches, and wine and water'.[30] She was also given gifts of food, including Shrewsbury Cakes, which were apparently gratefully received, and which she ate immediately, sharing them with her mother.[31]

Eating is conspicuously absent from the early journals. It was an everyday activity, and the foods themselves were rarely worth singling out. Yet when she does mention it, it is with a gusto which suggests that restraint was hard-won. Mutton was a particular weakness, and she took every opportunity to eat it. This rather gleeful journal entry from a trip on the Solent, is typical: 'Poor Mamma began to be dreadfully sick soon after, which was a great pity & was a great draw-back to my amusement. At about 1 I got some hot mutton chops which were very nice. It was very rough sometimes & poor Mamma suffered a good deal.'[32] Other specific food-based journal entries detail out-of-the-ordinary gastronomic experiences, and she was clearly adventurous when she could be. She was most enthusiastic about plain, hearty grub, as far removed from both nursery food and high-end French cuisine as it could be. She shared in naval rations while on board *The Emerald* in 1833, drinking grog, and eating beef and potatoes ('excellent') off wooden trenchers with naval cutlery.[33] Staying at the house of Lord Liverpool, whose daughter Catherine was a lady-in-waiting, and one of her few friends, the girls visited the dairy to watch butter being patted and then tasted the buttermilk.[34] Victoria was also an eager kitchen garden tourist. Many houses had 'public' areas in their kitchen gardens designed specifically for visitors, well away from the manure heaps, and which she would have been able to access easily. Her love of fresh fruit may have been a driver: she admired the mangoes at Walcot Hall,[35] and commented several times upon the quality of the fruit which was habitually served as dessert at formal dinners. Given the chance, she would gorge on it, eating gooseberries, grapes and cherries straight from the plants at Melbury Hall in 1833.[36] She also visited at least one kitchen, at Chatsworth, which she greatly admired.[37]

The dinners themselves varied in quality. While her own thoughts remained unwritten, the general standard at particular houses occasionally emerges through the writing of others. Wynnstay, for example, where she stayed in 1832, had 'wretched cuisine and nasty dinner[s]'.[38] A need for diplomacy is probably another reason why Victoria's comments on her dining experiences tended towards admiration of the endless gold plate, statuary and stained-glass windows. Alternatively, she may not have been terribly discerning. She certainly suffered through the sudden change in dietary pace, which had swung from limited and light to generous and rich with nothing in between. It's hard at a distance to diagnose past medical issues, but in her journals she complained of headaches, sickness, fatigue and loss of appetite, which occurred pretty regularly around the 16th to the 20th of nearly every month and which were almost certainly period related.[39] Some of her issues were of a more digestive nature. Dr Mason, who treated her at Plâs Newydd in 1832, kept a notebook, in which he detailed his diagnoses and treatments. The result is a gloriously personal account of Victoria's erratic bowel movements: on some days she pooed only once, and was treated with rhubarb pills, for constipation, but on others she went five times, sometimes 'copious[ly]'. He noted, 'I have reason to suspect some irregularity of the diet', and prescribed tincture of cinnamon and soda carbonates.[40]

As Victoria became a more public figure, the advice from well-meaning relatives came pouring in; her defects were analysed, and remedies suggested. She was 5 feet 1 inch tall, and seemed to have inherited her figure from her father's side of the family rather than her mother's. Uncle Leopold, now King of Belgium and married for the second time, increased his undoubtedly affectionate, but somewhat trying, campaign to get Victoria to eat sensibly in the face of

temptation, and take more exercise, as well as rather unhelp-
fully suggesting that she should try to grow taller. He
worried about her indigestion attacks: 'I was very sorry to
learn that you suffered from a bilious attack ... I shall take
the liberty of begging you not to eat too much at Luncheon,
or if you do, and feel a great appetite at that hour, not to take
violent exercise too soon after it, nothing is so certain to
derange the stomach. The dinner ought also if the luncheon
was considerable to be somewhat modified ... It is tiresome
to attend to these matters but at your time of life health takes
frequently the direction which it afterwards maintains',
adding a mildly bizarre postscript: 'the stomach is with us
poor human creatures often the cause of nearly all the diseases which plague us. Seagulls are better off in that respect,
they seem to have excellent stomachs and hardly ever to
suffer from indigestion.'[41] Victoria came back with a typically masterful, if rather pert, response: 'I wish you could
come here, for many reasons, but also to be an eyewitness of
my extreme prudence in eating, which would astonish you.
The poor seagulls are however not so happy as you imagine,
for they have great enemies in the country people here, who
take pleasure in shooting them.'[42] Meanwhile Feodora wrote
about her salt intake, 'I am certain it is very bad for you,
pray think of your older sister when you look at the salt
cellar with the intention of mixing so much of its contents
with your knife in the gravy, you have a peculiar quick and
expert way of doing it, sometimes in absence.'[43] There was
no escape from the criticism, even if it was well meant. She
had no privacy at the best of times: her mother had stated
that she was never to be alone, and she even slept in her
mother's room until she became Queen. To be examined

and critiqued by the British press and her family put intoler-
able pressure on her. She became acutely aware of other
people's figures and appearances and, unsurprisingly, grew
obsessed with her own weight, height and complexion,
comparing herself to others, and commenting in her journals on those she deemed pretty and thin.

By 1835 the pace was taking its toll. The atmosphere
back at Kensington and around the family in general was
increasingly febrile. Even in 1832 the Duchess was reported
to barely sleep through anxiety about the future, and from
her perspective things weren't going well. [44] Victoria refused
to co-operate with the Duchess and Conroy's System, and,
where she could, she was flexing her teenage muscles. She
wasn't as isolated as they wanted, and kept getting outside
advice (mainly from Leopold, but Lehzen was also firmly
on her side) which helped her to stand her ground when
Conroy tried to get her to promise to appoint him to her
Household when she became Queen. Behind closed doors,
Victoria and her mother were anything other than a close
unit, and she loathed Conroy and his family. When a Progress around Yorkshire was proposed, she said she wouldn't
go, and it took a mixture of threats and emotional blackmail
to eventually drag her out. In her journals for the trip she
was consistently sulky and emphasised how ill she felt. At
York she was, 'well tired'; at Wentworth she, 'could eat
almost nothing, I felt so sick'; and when the coach was
unhitched so that cheering townspeople could pull it through
King's Lynn themselves she was incensed. That all-important positive public perception was undented, however. She
was apparently, 'highly animated' at a ball for 300 people at
Burghley, and, 'much pleased with [her] reception' in King's

Lynn. Meanwhile she was back on the rhubarb ('nasty stuff'), and barely eating – all of which she wrote down for her mother to see.[45]

Matters came to a partial head at Ramsgate in October 1835. Victoria was seriously ill, though exactly with what it is hard to tell. Typhoid, tonsillitis and sheer nervous exhaustion have all been suggested. Conroy and her mother took advantage of her physical weakness and tried to force her to sign a document appointing Conroy as her private secretary. However, her mental resilience was stronger than they had anticipated. The incident destroyed most of the latent affection or respect between mother and daughter, and changed the balance of the Household as those who supported Victoria and those who wanted to break her became very obvious. Victoria grew up – fast. Conroy stood no chance against a newly determined Princess. Victoria later referred to him as 'the monster and demon incarnate'.[46]

She stopped writing in her journal for several weeks, and was treated as an invalid for much longer. In the weeks after her recovery, her joy in eating was heightened to the degree that her usual restraint left her in the pages of her journal and she listed all of the items she was able to eat. 'Took my luncheon at 12, which consisted of some potatoe-soup ... took my dinner at 5, which consisted of soup (crème au riz), and some little bits of excellent mutton with boiled rice, which I relished very much ... At 7 I had a glass of orange jelly with a Brussels Biscuit, which I liked very much.'[47] She ate classic invalid food: light soups, bread and butter, cocoa, chicken, rice and jelly. The Brussels Biscuits became a firm favourite. Leopold had them made in the royal kitchens in Belgium and sent over. She described them as, 'a sort of light rusk ... extremely good; they can only be made at Brussels'. One of her chefs when she was Queen published a recipe for them, calling them 'a superior kind of rusk ... well-adapted for the refreshment table at evening parties, or for the breakfast table', which suggests that she had retained a taste for them well after she became Queen.[48]

In the wake of her illness Victoria revelled in her new figure. She sketched herself looking pale and wan, and wrote to Uncle Leopold in proud terms, 'I am grown <u>very</u> thin and also a little taller and Dr Clark says I shall grow quite tall after this. I should be glad if that were the case, if only to please you, dear uncle'.[49] Eating was one of the few things she could control and, whereas before she had eaten too fast and too much, and obsessed over her figure without necessarily doing a great deal about it, she now put her considerable willpower towards refusing meals, including ostentatiously skipping dinner when she argued with her mother. In January 1836 she declared, 'I took no luncheon yesterday and none today, as I find myself so much better without it; I mean to take none for some time to come; I only take a little bread and butter.'[50] She largely continued this diet, varying it with rice and gravy, and except where official occasions got in the way, until March 1837.

The scare given to her family by her malaise focused their minds. There were a lot of different people with quite different interests swirling around Victoria, and, as she celebrated her seventeenth birthday, she found herself entertaining a procession of eligible young men, invited or foisted upon her as potential marriage partners. She was a very exciting catch, and at an impressionable age. The various royal princes of Germany and England each found themselves with backers. It was not unreasonable to hope that, while Victoria was the ruler in name, her husband would wield the real power. Picking a winner was of vital importance. Dinner was, inevitably, one of the tests for each, and various cousins were paraded around the dining table at Kensington. Victoria had by this point developed that habit of emotional over-reaction which was to characterise her adult years. Whenever she had visitors, on their departure she was utterly bereft and could barely cope. Not that she got a lot of support. A typical response from Uncle Leopold showed off his sensitive side in reply to one of her over-wrought letters: 'this, unfortunately, is the picture of life; all transitory except the thirst for happiness and bliss, which seems to indicate that in some future state alone it can be quenched'.[51] Victoria was, perhaps, rather overdoing it, but she had a vested interest in making sure that her future partner was at least someone she could vaguely fancy. When the future Prince Consort, Albert of Saxe-Coburg-Gotha, visited, on her birthday itself, she was aware that he was first choice for both Leopold and her mother. She set out to like him, despite what seemed a rather huge gulf. This was a girl who firmly stated that she was, 'fit for a great deal of dissipation, which unfortunately I have not had',[52] and would dance all night if she could. Albert, who was at the time overweight, and constantly beset by stomach problems, nearly fainted during her birthday dinner, missed several meals, and had to go to bed early.[53] On his departure he was taken in hand by those who favoured him in the marital stakes, and sent on a European tour in order to increase both his stamina and his worldly appeal to the sheltered – but adventurous – Princess.

Falling asleep and failing to behave in a confident, controlled manner at the dinner table was a minor failing in the etiquette of dining. There were worse things to do. Victoria was now regularly exposed to large, formal dinners inside and outside Kensington Palace, including dining with the King and Queen. She would have seen all of the highs and lows of aristocratic dining – and drinking, for which the English were renowned. The ugliest incident of a pretty unpleasant set of skirmishes between the Duchess and the King took place at William IV's birthday dinner in August 1836. The lead-up to the dinner was fraught. Weeks of petty squabbling and posturing had culminated in the Duchess of Kent snubbing an invitation to Queen Adelaide's birthday festivities in order to celebrate her own. On the day before the dinner, the King, visiting Kensington for the first time in ages, had discovered that the Duchess had appropriated some of the state apartments for her use. This had – probably – been approved somewhere by someone, but the King claimed it was all new and without his consent. He returned from the visit enraged, stormed into the Windsor drawing room and berated the Duchess. Inevitably, and probably under the influence of drink (the King notoriously disliked those who drank water at dinner), the King's birthday speech, in front of a hundred wide-eyed courtiers, turned into a rant. Greville reported the speech as told to him by one of those present:

I trust in God that my life may be spared for nine months longer, after which period, in the event of my death, no Regency would take place. I should then have the satisfaction of leaving the royal authority to the personal exercise of that Young Lady [pointing to Victoria], the Heiress presumptive of the Crown, and not in the hands of a person now near me, who is surrounded by evil advisors and who is herself incompetent to act with propriety in the station in which She would be placed ... I have been insulted – grossly and continuously insulted – by that person, but I am determined to endure no longer a course of behaviour so disrespectful of me.

It was strong stuff, delivered with what one guest dryly called 'singular tact'. Opinion was firmly on his side, in terms of the sentiment, but as Greville pointed out, 'such a gross and public insult offered to her at his own table, sitting by his side and in the presence of her daughter, admits of no excuse'.[54] Victoria, showing somewhat more tact, did not mention the incident in her journal at all.

Victoria turned eighteen in May 1837, with celebratory banners across Kensington Palace and a state ball in her honour, and the King got his wish, though he was by now very ill. As the hungry Princess waited in the wings, daily reports of his progress came to her at Kensington. The royal dining ledger for June 1837 graphically illustrates William's decline through the food he was served. On 4 June, he was present at 'Their Majesties' Dinner', along with Queen Adelaide and the usual thirty or so guests. They ate hotch-potch (a type of meat soup) and red mullet, braised ham and chicken pasties, veal tendrons, mutton escalopes, leverets, asparagus, plovers' eggs and set creams, among many other things. Yet there were some telling dishes, characteristic of invalid food: barley soup, soufflé and orange jelly. On the

5th, he dined alone, on beef tea, lamb ribs, venison, braised capon and roast fowl. His food became that prescribed for the very ill, or just weaned, the same dishes Victoria had eaten at Ramsgate in November 1835 and, further back, when she was a toddler, consisting of an endless diet of beef tea, chicken broth and chicken purée, with the occasional potted beef. On 16 June the Archbishop of Canterbury came to stay, listed at 'Her Majesty's Dinner', in preparation for King William's end, and Queen Victoria's beginning. On the 17th Victoria wrote in her journal that, 'the news of the King is worse today', and on the 18th, 'the poor King, they say, can live but a few hours more'.[55] On the 19th he ate beef tea, chicken broth and chicken purée. By the end of that day he was dead. The dining ledger for 20 June did not give menus for Their Majesties, or even Her Majesty. Queen Adelaide was now a widow: the ledger simply listed (much reduced) menus for 'Dinners at Windsor Castle'.[56]

3
Dining style

In June 1837, when Victoria acceded to the throne, what and how she ate was not her foremost concern. Neither the dining ledgers that record the meals eaten at the palaces, nor the supply books which list the produce purchased for the kitchens, show a marked departure from what went before. In the latter, the accounts were made up to the date of the King's death, and then continued until the end of the month, when they were made up again, as was the case for every month end. The ledgers only covered the monarch's official residences, so Kensington was not included, and, when Victoria finally made her first appearance at Buckingham Palace as Queen in July, her dinner was not markedly different to the last recorded full dinner served to King William IV two months before. The new Queen had other priorities. Young and politically inexperienced though she was, she had, as one of her ladies would later note, a 'vein of iron [running] through her most extraordinary character',[1] and she was determined to take control of her person before she did anything else. By the end of her first day as monarch, she had met with her main ministers, 'quite <u>alone</u>',[2] and held her first Privy Council. She had her bed moved out from her mother's room, and she slept in a room on her own for the first time in eighteen years. She also dined defiantly alone and, in the days which followed, made it clear that her relationship with the Duchess of Kent would now be dictated by her, and that never again would she be told what to do by her mother. This didn't stop the Duchess trying, but Victoria simply refused to see her in private, ignored the stream of pointed and bitchy notes, and made clear her intentions by denying Conroy and his clique any role in her new life. She also declared her desire to leave Kensington, and move to the not-quite-completed Buckingham Palace as soon as possible.

Victoria's behaviour won plaudits from nearly everyone, and there were a lot of people eager to comment. It was partly natural curiosity: she was a new monarch, and had rarely been seen up to that point. As a woman, however, she was a particular object of scrutiny. Britain didn't have a great track record with queens. Matilda had plunged the country into civil war; Mary I had been demonised as part of the great Protestant story of Britain; and Elizabeth had bankrupted the throne. Mary II could be safely sidelined in favour of her husband and joint ruler, William III; and Anne, despite a long and extremely significant reign, was largely written off as being ruled by her favourites. Victorian Britain – as it now was – was deeply patriarchal. Many

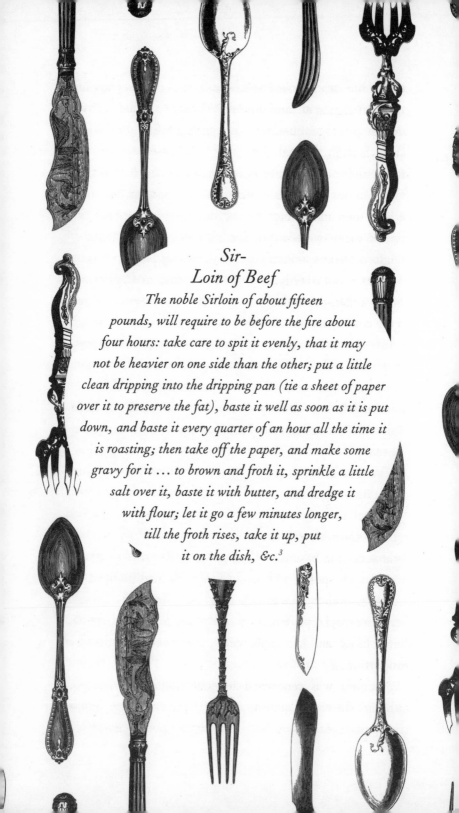

Sir-
Loin of Beef

The noble Sirloin of about fifteen
pounds, will require to be before the fire about
four hours: take care to spit it evenly, that it may
not be heavier on one side than the other; put a little
clean dripping into the dripping pan (tie a sheet of paper
over it to preserve the fat), baste it well as soon as it is put
down, and baste it every quarter of an hour all the time it
is roasting; then take off the paper, and make some
gravy for it ... to brown and froth it, sprinkle a little
salt over it, baste it with butter, and dredge it
with flour; let it go a few minutes longer,
till the froth rises, take it up, put
it on the dish, &c.[3]

other countries imposed Salic law, meaning that a woman couldn't reign at all, and the British aristocracy had its own version, primogeniture, which ensured descent of titles and lands through the male line only.[4] Women had very few rights, and social censure as well as the law restricted their opportunities still further. Moreover, the conduct expected of both men and women was becoming ever more restrictive. Women were wives and mothers first, politicians, religious leaders, military strategists and diplomats never, or at least, not overtly. A woman acceding as head of the church and leader of the country was a tense moment. Many of the comments about the new Queen, whether written in private diaries or in print, emphasised her femininity, neatly sidestepping the issues that her gender raised. They also dwelt upon her looks, not unreasonably given that she'd done very little to show her personality. Typical was Lord Holland: 'Though not a beauty, & not a very good figure, she really is in person, & especially in eyes and complexion, a very nice girl.'[5] A lengthier appraisal was published in 1840: 'her height measured precisely five foot two inches, "but small for a Queen", as Her Majesty has been known to remark upon herself; her figure was, or rather is (for but little alteration has taken place in her appearance since the period now spoken of), slight and well made, but sufficiently en embonpoint to indicate health and good humour; her bust especially is remarkably fine, the head being beautifully placed, and her arms, hands, and feet are exquisitely proportioned'.[6]

Victoria was renowned for her diminutive stature, although she wasn't quite as short as her modern reputation suggests. Contemporaries, including herself, universally put her at 5 feet 2 inches, but the only surviving bit of real evidence comes from the tape measure used by one of her portraitists to measure her height in 1837. This clearly shows that she was 5 feet 1 inch (just over 61 inches, or 155 cm).[7] The fashion was for flat shoes – she could have added an inch or two with heels, and she probably shrank a bit in old age. Height was a gendered issue. Women who were tall were seen as manly, and described as handsome, rarely pretty. Conversely, men were prized for their height, and if they were manservants, were usually paid more the taller they were. Being able to afford a tall footman marked you out as a person of taste and wealth – Victoria's were enormous. But it was also a class issue, and then, as now, height was related to wealth. Over the course of Victoria's reign, this last aspect would become even more significant, as living standards for the very poor declined, and average height with them. By the end of the reign, height restrictions for the non-officer classes of the armed forces were being revised downwards, as the traditional recruiting pool of poverty-stricken young men had lost inches due to poor diet. The difference in height between middle-class and working-class thirteen-year-olds in some areas was four inches.[8] Being short carried a whiff of poverty about it. But in 1837, and in Victoria's case, it was not necessarily a bad thing. For her, short meant unthreatening; it meant feminine. However, it also added to the sense of her youth, and meant that people were prone to regard her as a child. After all, she was only eighteen, and largely surrounded by older (and taller) courtiers and politicians.

The move to Buckingham Palace took place in mid-July 1837, and the first official royal dinner of Victoria's reign was duly entered into the palace's dining ledger on 13 July. Nineteen people were present at the Queen's table, including her beloved governess, now friend and confidante, Baroness Lehzen, and her mother, the Duchess of Kent. The menu, including the name of each course, was in French. They had a choice of soups: a thick soup of rice and chicken or a thinner spring vegetable soup. Then came fish: red trout, dory, whitings and soles, followed by the *relevés*: beef steaks, braised capon, roast lamb and baby chickens with tongue. Next up were *entrées*: lamb cutlets, fillets of sole, four different chicken dishes, sweetbreads, and pâtes à la reine, which were probably miniature puff pastry pies. There was a roast, or rather roasts, in the form of quails and another capon, followed by another set of relevés: German sausage and soufflé omelette. Then *entremets* of lobster salad, fricassee with jelly, garden peas and artichokes. The sweet entremets, served at the same time, consisted of a macédoine of fruit, wine jelly, raspberry cream, vanilla cream, biscuits, cherry vol-au-vent, a Chantilly turban (a moulded confection in the vague shape of a turban), German cake, sugar baskets and nougat.[9] Although not mentioned, as it was always taken as read, there would then have been a dessert of fresh fruit. Additionally, there was a sideboard with a sirloin of beef and a chine of mutton.

This seems, at first glance, to be a gargantuan amount of food, and a huge amount of work for the cooks. But the service style at this point was predicated on having vast quantities of food, cooked in myriad different ways. It was served *à la Française*, and the food itself formed the main focus on the table. It was served on the table, for all to see, with limited decoration besides. The style had developed for use in upper-class formal dining over several hundred years, and had become relatively fixed by the mid to late eighteenth century. Although at first glance there are many courses, the names are deceiving: they were a way of cate-gorising types of dishes, rather than indicating a properly separate course. The style at its peak consisted of just two courses, plus dessert. Diners would assemble outside the dining room, progressing in at a given signal, to find the first set of dishes already in place as they sat down. In this first course, and usually placed at either end of the table, were the soups. These would be uncovered and eaten first. In many cases, they would be served out directly by the host and hostess, seated at either end of the table, but in aristo-cratic contexts, waiters would be on hand, if not to serve out, then to hand the filled bowls to the assorted diners. Fish would already be present, sitting on hot plates with covers, and would be eaten next. Dawdling over the soup could mean slightly cool fish. Fish tends to lack something when tepid, and an alternative that was increasingly popular by the early nineteenth century was to replace it (and/or the empty soup tureens) with one or more new dishes. This was then known as the 'remove course' or, in French, *relevé*. With the fish safely dispatched, and the soup gone, the rest of the first course dishes, which were kept warm on the table on hot plates, of which the royal plate store had a large supply, could then be uncovered to be eaten at the same time as the removes. Again, the name of these differed. In English, they were called 'made dishes', and recipe books frequently had chapters called this. In French, they were *entrées*. There was an ongoing battle between French and English cuisine in the eighteenth century. Many classics of both culinary repertoires developed in the period, but French cookery was seen by the upper classes as superior. They employed French cooks, and called their dishes, and their courses, by French names. On the royal table, the French language, and a mainly French style of cooking, triumphed well before Victoria came to the throne. It was not only the perceived superiority of French: it was a far more universal language in Europe than English or German, so was rather more useful when guests at dinner could come from anywhere.

With the consumption of the entrées, the first course was over. Footmen would clear the table, emptying plates into waiting containers, and placing delicate crockery and silverware into padded boxes to be sent for washing up. Meanwhile, the second course would have been brought into an anteroom, which was often fitted out with warming tables or hot closets. In some cases, such as Ickworth House in Suffolk, a house particularly well equipped for entertaining, but with a main kitchen a very long way from the state dining room, a separate finishing kitchen was installed for putting the final flourish to delicate dishes. The second course would be laid out on the table exactly as the first course had been. Symmetry was key in *à la Française* dining, and when the table was laid out, it would have been with a set square and a ruler. Usually there was a central dish (or, at large gatherings, dishes), with plates then set around it at regular intervals. Each element was generally served on a different-shaped plate, and dinner services intended for *à la Française* included oval and square plates as well as those designed specifically to round off the corners. At everyday dinners every plate contained a different food, but they would complement and contrast with each other across the table, horizontally and diagonally from above, and provide each diner with a similar – yet different – dining experience. Recipe books at the time sometimes contained advisory ideal table plans, which make clear the complicated way in which menus were designed. A lobster might match, across the table, for example, a tongue (as both were red, long and a bit curved). A plate of small custard tarts might answer to a large moulded fruit jelly directly across from it, but diagonally there would be a large fruit flan, and in the remaining corner a set of small moulded blancmanges. At larger dinners, dishes were more often repeated at intervals along the table, generally flanking a central set of vases or something obvious in gold. With the meal in full flow, it could be hard to set out the second course, but there was no excuse. Footman's guides are full of admonitions, as well as tips, to ensure that everything is set out with mathematical precision. The royal footmen had no excuse for sloppy dish placement, for a team of men called table-deckers were employed specifically to plan and lay out the table – not to serve the food, but just to mark out where each element would sit. Again, the second course followed an order. The most prestigious dish of the whole meal was the roast, and it was this – or these – which were uncovered and tackled first. Again, host and hostess would often carve, and carving was seen as a great test of skill and gentility. However, in the most elevated social contexts, a butler would carve at a sideboard, and, again, footmen would be on hand to serve and pass dishes. As with the first course, the roast could be 'removed' with another dish or dishes, before the second course entrées, called entremets, were tackled. These were a mixture of small savoury items, vegetables and sweet dishes. The vegetable elements were akin to what would now be called side dishes (and could be called side dishes at the time – but only when they were literally placed at the sides of the table, with a central dish between them). They were a way to show off the skills of the cooking staff and usually involved sauces, garnishes, moulds, emulsions, jellies, pastry or sugarcraft, and were a sensory delight.

After this, cheese might be served as a separate course, or the second course might simply be cleared away and dessert brought in. Dessert was intended as a palate cleanser rather than a stomach-filler, and consisted of fresh fruit, nuts, and ices (both ice cream and water ices – what we'd now call sorbets), and sometimes sugarcraft confectionery. At the start of the eighteenth century, tables were sometimes laid with two cloths, so that one could be taken away after each course. Dessert would then be served directly onto the burnished tabletop, with the glitter of the candles reflecting and refracting off the glasses and the plate, as well as the silks and jewellery of the diners, to create a sort of personal fireworks display across the table. By 1837, this was no longer the case. However, visual overload was still achievable. When Victoria had been on Progress in the 1830s, she frequently commented on the proliferation of gold plate. Harking back to medieval buffets, with their proudly displayed gold and silver, some establishments still brought out their riches on special occasions. It was becoming less common: at the Mansion House in York the built-in buffets, which were shelves set in niches built into the walls either side of the fireplace, were covered by portraits in the early nineteenth century, but at Buckingham Palace and

Windsor the tradition continued. In pictures of state dining the gold plate is emphasised, and almost seems to glow.

Dinner services at the time were usually fairly plain, and, although the gold displayed on the buffet did include practical eating wares, the items on it were reserved for show, and included candelabra, vases and pieces that had fallen out of use. There was a gold – or rather silver gilt – service for state dining, put together by George IV, and which Victoria made full use of for entertaining.[10] Her everyday dinner services were more muted: she chose from a range of ceramics commissioned by George IV or William IV and which included all of the shaped plates necessary for *à la Française* as well as lots of round eating plates. For dessert, which was less showy in terms of food, the plates were more extravagantly decorated. One of the few big additions that Victoria made to the royal china store was a 116-piece dessert service that she bought from Minton's when it went on display just prior to the official opening of the Great Exhibition in 1851. It remained on show for the duration of the Exhibition, and Thomas Minton named it the Victoria service in honour of its first buyer. (She promptly swapped 61 pieces of it with the Austrian Emperor, who gave her a large carved bookcase, also at the Exhibition, in return.) As with most dessert services, it was highly coloured, in this case a vivid turquoise, with gilt edges and delicate paintings of fruit and flowers encased in mouldings, and with ceramic figures enacting bucolic scenes where there was room on the larger items.

There were other aspects of royal dining in the early years of Victoria's reign that emphatically looked backward, not forward. Written menus don't seem to have been provided until the 1870s, which was characteristic of service *à la Française*. In 1839, Lady Lyttelton, one of the ladies-in-waiting, wrote that, 'Yesterday at dinner the English servant who hands round the dishes, calling them by French names, offered me what he called "Fricasée de *Valets*" (*volaille*). I thought Lord Lilford would have died ...'.[11] She was lucky: in some versions of the style the servants were dismissed, and diners expected to know what dishes were as they served themselves and each other in a glorious free-for-all. At royal dinners, footmen brought the dishes round, reached for inaccessible items, and were generally on hand to serve and aid diners. *À la Française* looked very communal from the outside, but allowed for far more individual choice than the alternatives. Each diner could choose from the various dishes on offer and eat exactly what he or she most wanted. Even at some very formal dinners, guests would help themselves. One rare picture of people eating from this period, an image of a banquet held at London's Mansion House to commemorate Victoria's coronation, shows diners digging into jellies with gusto. The Queen was present, but the perspective puts her far away, and her own behaviour on the occasion is unrecorded. Its apparent communality and friendliness masked its real nature, though. *À la Française* wasn't an easy way to dine. Participants needed to know how to tackle each element on offer. They had to be aware of each other, and be able to share and not look greedy. Tales abound of unfortunates, not brought up to its intricacies, who failed at the dinner table. In one example from York, a young clergyman ate all of the dish placed in front of him, not realising that it was for all to share. He was the guest of honour, and 'his' dish, of ruffs and reeves, was a great delicacy. It had been carefully placed in front of him to indicate status, not that he could eat it all. Uproar apparently ensued when his mistake was realised.[12] (Both ruffs and reeves, and larks, another high-status dish of small roast birds, regularly appeared on the royal menus.) In other anecdotes, failure to show self-restraint in the face of so much food was the problem. Dr Johnson was known to grow red and sometimes weep at the sight of his dinner. Hardly the mark of a genteel man.

Victoria had been inculcated into the ways of *à la Française* dining, and in her early years very few people had anything negative to say about her habits at the table. But by 1837 the style had already started to change. There are pictures of George IV and Victoria's tables set out for very large dinners, which suggest that the norm for dinners once the number of guests crept beyond fifty or so was to have inedible table decoration along the centre flanked by dishes along both sides. Notoriously for the Prince Regent at Carlton House, an entire aquarium was once set up, complete with live fish. Meanwhile at Chatsworth, when Victoria visited in 1843, sugar castles were set up on the table, a type of display that first became fashionable in the 1760s, and continued as long as *à la Française* was used. By the 1850s the creep of decoration had reached a more domestic context, and Victoria was experimenting with fruit – the dessert course – displayed on the table before diners sat down and remaining there throughout dinner. This was a radical departure from the norm, and Eleanor Stanley, one of Victoria's ladies, commented that, 'we dine … with the dessert on the table, and it is really not so bad, or rather I am getting used to it'.[13] Known today as 'demi-Russe', this was a sort of transitional style, between *à la Française* and the full-blown sequential service that we associate with fine dining today. There were fewer dishes in each course, and, therefore, less food laid upon the table itself, as inedible decoration or the dessert course took its place. Victoria tried it at Osborne House, almost certainly because the kitchens there had a much smaller staff than those at Windsor or Buckingham Palace, and it was much easier for the cooks to manage. A full meal served *à la Française* at its peak would have been both a feast for the senses and the intellect. Mock dishes, including marzipan hams and meat melons were used to tease diners, who would have known that a ham served as a second course entremets was not a ham – because it wasn't the right place for it – but would not necessarily have known it was made of almonds. Georgian dining was a fantastic, awe-inspiring experience. Victorian meals, even in 1837, were a little more muted.

For Victoria, the new dining set-up was a joy. The royal kitchens had a staff of around 45 people, able to cater for any possible desire. For the first year of her reign, she had a fabulous time. She threw herself into the work, gaining praise for her desire to learn about the intricacies of ruling. She developed a strong relationship with her first prime minister, Lord Melbourne, and delighted in his company, especially at dinner. 'Her feelings ... are sexual, though she does not know it,' was Greville's comment upon the matter.[14] The illnesses that had plagued her as a teenager were gone, and in her journals she no longer complained of headaches and cramps on that tell-tale monthly basis. She also seems to have quietly dropped the bread-and-butter lunch habit, although the lunches listed in the dining ledgers indicate that often she and her court took their midday meal separately, and that it was much lighter than dinner. She wrote to her half-sister Feodora in October 1837: 'Everybody says that I am quite another person since I came to the throne. I look and am so very well, I have such a pleasant life; just the sort of life I like. I have a good deal of business to do, and all that does me a world of good.'[15] She also threw herself into the social whirl, balancing intellectual stimulation and that all-important dissipation she'd been craving. 'She is surrounded with the most exciting and interesting enjoyments; her occupations, her pleasures, her business, her Court, all present in an unceasing round of gratification. With all her prudence and discretion, she has great animal spirits, and enters into all the magnificent novelties of her position with the zest and curiosity of a child.'[16]

However, for all her private certainties, those outside her immediate circle became quickly frustrated with the new court over which she presided. The very reason that so many people had anticipated her accession with gladness – she wasn't a debauched old man – also made her court rather dull. Her mother and Conroy had exposed her to society, but on their own terms, and they had always been keen to emphasise that she was gauche and unfit to rule without their support. She had developed the habit of keeping her thoughts firmly to herself, and she was under significant pressure to impress much older and more experienced people. It's no surprise that when she first became Queen, therefore, she stuck to 'the smallest possible talk' on social occasions.[17] This contrasted with occasions in her childhood, when she'd been an inquisitive and considerate dinner companion. In Tunbridge Wells in 1834 one of the guests who dined with the Kents regularly for a few weeks in September was deaf, and used sign language. Victoria was fascinated by this, and wrote in her journal:

> Poor Mr. Isted has the misfortune to be both deaf and dumb; but he is a very pleasing, agreeable and intelligent person. He sat just opposite to me at dinner, and he asked me something with his fingers, which I almost understood, only that I was very much frightened to speak myself. He talked a great deal with his fingers to Mrs. Hobhouse who sat next him. He speaks also a little but in a very odd and unintelligible manner; the voice does not sound like a human one. He has a very pleasing countenance and appearance. Mrs. Isted (to whom he has been married 2 years) is a very delightful person … She talks immensely fast on her fingers.

By the time he left Tunbridge Wells she had obviously sought out instruction, and wrote proudly that, 'I took courage and said "thank you" to him on my fingers for his pretty drawing, and he understood me perfectly.'[18] By 1837, however, caution was in the ascendant as she worked out how to be a Queen. She was described as, 'timid and embarrassed, [talking] of nothing but commonplaces'.[19]

Dinner at court, as described above, was 'like any other great dinner',[20] but the etiquette was slightly different. In most households, the highest status man led proceedings, taking the highest status lady into dinner upon his arm, with the next highest status man taking the next highest status lady, and so on and so forth. Victoria outranked everyone, and the guests didn't always know each other, so, after all had assembled, a lord-in-waiting would appear to instruct them on who was accompanying whom. The Queen was usually late for dinner, which was, in 1837, nominally at 7.30 p.m., but more often served at 8 p.m., after she had appeared. Diners would be assembled in a drawing room: talking, but not drinking, as cocktails and pre-dinner drinks did not come in until the Edwardian period, and even then were regarded by most as a nasty American habit, designed to ruin your appetite. The Queen would enter, preceded by the Lord Chamberlain and gentlemen of the Household. She'd shake hands with the women, bow to the men, and the gathering would try to seamlessly sort themselves into order. They'd then all enter the dining room and be seated. 'Promiscuous seating', or man-woman-man-woman, had in the late eighteenth century replaced the earlier habit of having all the men seated at one end and the ladies at another. Greville, who had been desperate for a dinner invitation so that he could ogle the new Queen and see her relationship with Melbourne in action, recounted what happened after dessert had been served: 'The Queen sat for some time at the table, talking away very merrily to her neighbours, and the men remained about a quarter of an hour after the ladies. When we advanced into the drawing room, and huddled about the door in the sort of half-shy, half-awkward way people do, the Queen advanced to meet us, and spoke to everybody in succession.' He also recorded the conversation, which he remarked was 'a fair sample of a royal after-dinner colloquy':

Q: Have you been riding today, Mr Greville?
G: No Madam, I have not.

Q: It was a fine day.

G: Yes ma'am, a very fine day.

Q: It was rather cold though.

G: (like Polonius): It was rather cold, Madam.

Q: Your sister, Lady Frances Egerton, rides I think, does not she?

G: She does ride sometimes, Madam.

(A pause, when I took the lead, though adhering to the same topic)

G: Has your majesty been riding today?

Q (with animation): O yes, a very long ride.

G: Has your majesty got a nice horse?

Q: O, a very nice horse.

– gracious smile and inclination of head on part of Queen, profound bow on mine.

Dining at court was dull. Drawing rooms at court were dull. Victoria, while 'charming, cheerful, obliging [and] unaffected',[21] was highly conscious of her position, and always on guard. She felt most at ease with Lord Melbourne, who was almost always present and next to her at dinner, and with whom she secluded herself after doing the round of guests, after dinner. The court fell back on endless card games, and the tradesmen's bills for Buckingham Palace in 1837 and 1838 show packs of cards being purchased by the dozen. Light relief was provided only when the deaf Duke of Wellington was present, talking loudly about state affairs, or gossiping very audibly about other dinner guests. He was invariably stopped by the Queen, 'screaming out upon some other subject'.[22]

Underneath the stilted conversations and insistence on

etiquette, however, tensions were building. A year after her coronation, the novelty had worn off, and things weren't quite as altered as Victoria might have wished: 'This year I did not enjoy pleasure so much ... [I am] quite changed from what I was last year.'[23] Despite her attempts to distance herself from her mother, the Duchess of Kent remained at court, and Victoria was repeatedly told that any aggressive move to shift her would result in her being seen as unfeminine and cold. The Duchess simply didn't understand the depth of bad feeling that her treatment of her daughter had engendered. She continued to see her as a petulant child, and refused to go anywhere unless Victoria got married, at which point her husband could take care of her and manage her decisions. Conroy was still hanging about as well, demanding pensions and titles. Meanwhile, it was becoming apparent that he had mismanaged the Duchess's financial affairs, and that all of those Progresses and impressive meals had left her owing £55,000. (It got worse. Conroy and his cronies had lost or destroyed the financial records, and when the few accounts that remained were finally examined in 1850, it emerged that he had systematically defrauded both the Duchess and Princess Sophia of tens of thousands of pounds. In the murky world of courtly politics, he does seem to have been a genuine villain.) In addition to these ongoing annoyances, there were two well-publicised 'affairs', which soured the positive opinions that the press had hitherto had of Victoria. The first, the Flora Hastings affair, concerned one of her mother's ladies, who was seen at court with a visibly swollen stomach. The rumour put about, and encouraged by the Queen, was that she was pregnant. She wasn't: she had a tumour and eventually died in agony, but not before the poisonous atmosphere led her family to complain to the press. The Queen looked like a bully and an idiot. The second, the Bedchamber affair, concerned Victoria's ladies. In 1839 Lord Melbourne's Whig government faced defeat, and he resigned. His Tory opponent, Robert Peel, was duly asked to form a government and, not unreasonably, asked Victoria to swap some of her entirely Whig ladies-in-waiting for Tories instead. While women didn't have the vote, and couldn't enter politics officially, they could still hold influential positions. These ladies surrounded the Queen: they were potential friends and advisors. Yet most of them were married to prominent Whigs, and some were known to dislike Peel in particular. Victoria refused to change them, saying that she never discussed politics with them, and that they had no real power. Peel stood fast. She still refused. He told her he couldn't form a government with that kind of attitude from his Queen and resigned. Melbourne returned. Victoria now looked not only like a brat, unduly led by her emotional attachment to her prime minister, but one who endangered the constitution as well. In fairness to her, there was a great deal of miscommunication on both sides, and a lack of understanding of the need to balance personal feelings with political expediency. In later years, when a compromise was reached where only the most senior of her ladies, the groom of the stole, would be replaced at each change of government, she looked back at her teenage behaviour with embarrassment.

It's unsurprising, given her bouts of stress-related illness as a teenager, that under renewed pressure from her relatives, government and the press, Victoria relapsed. Life had been monotonous and predictable at Kensington. But it was the unpredictability of politics and public opinion that now caused problems. In the wake of the Bedchamber affair she was forced to face the fact that Melbourne would eventually be replaced, and that her new life would be one of constant change, especially in the people who surrounded her. She had had no real friends as a child, and now had to accept that, even if she could bring herself to trust anyone enough to fill that role as an adult, she would struggle to keep them with her if they held an official, and therefore political, position in her Household. Once again she complained of headaches and lethargy, and turned to food as a solace. Creevey remarked that, 'she eats as heartily as she laughs. I think I may say she gobbles.'[24] Melbourne didn't help. Victoria had come to rely on him, and was heavily influenced by his views and habits. He was a dedicated gourmand, as attached to mutton chops as the young Victoria was, and, according to onlookers, a great consumer of, 'consommés, truffles, pears, ices, and anchovies, which he does his best to revolutionise his stomach with every day'.[25] They bickered about her – and his – eating habits. In August 1839 she recorded that they had, 'talked of Lord M.'s being so well; my having no appetite; "I don't know what has happened to me," he said; "I began this morning by eating a cold grouse which I haven't done for a long time; and then I was so hungry again at 12 that I was obliged to have 3 mutton chops." And was he hungry again now? "I've eat[en] a great deal now," he said. I begged him not to eat too much.'[26] Meanwhile Victoria was under fire from him for exactly the same thing, which in her was seen as worse because she was a woman. Citing the example of her weighty paternal relatives, Melbourne told her off for over-eating, and for drinking too much beer. He told her that eating when she wasn't hungry was part of the issue, to which she responded that if she was only to eat when she was hungry it was fine: she was hungry all day.[27] Eleanor Stanley wrote ruefully, 'you know a great deal of eating always goes on at the Palace'.[28] It had an effect. By the end of 1838, it was suggested that she had, 'perhaps rather more appearance of a full habit of body than nice and nervous observers of health would quite approve'.[29] In December she was weighed and, 'to my horror weigh 8 stone 13!' She immediately shared her feelings with Melbourne: 'Talked of weight; my weighing near 9 stone, which I thought incredible for my size … talked of my fear of getting fat, and my Aunts being so; he said: "Why you have a good chance of being so" which made me laugh.'[30] He told her to take more exercise. She retorted that it made her feel tired and ill, and had her dresses let out instead.

By 1839, both Victoria and her ministers were feeling jaded. She was gaining the reputation of a party animal, most alive at 3 a.m., when browsing the stand-up buffet at a ball. Stand-up suppers were an innovation, replacing the earlier habit of a sit-down meal, served along similar lines as an à la Française meal, but with only one course, and predominantly cold food. Victoria's ball suppers were all about modernity, and shocked some of the older members of the court: 'The Queen stood to eat her supper. This shocked me greatly … there is not sufficient state in it. Even William IV, who was quite citizen King enough, always supped with his Queen in his private apartments with a select Party … it arises from her extreme youth but nevertheless I think it is a

great pity.'[31] She was working hard, but she was also partying hard, with balls and big dinners interspersed with trips
to the theatre and the opera. Bouts of lethargy and illness
contrasted with the grim determination with which she
threw herself into her beloved dissipation, but late nights
meant late mornings, and disrupted business. She became
irritable and angry when she wasn't being entertained, and
was impatient with others, including Melbourne, when they
didn't keep her amused after dinner: 'Lord M. fell asleep 3
times, was very silent, and I was cross, which is wicked –
when I saw that poor dear kind man looking pale and
exhausted and fatigued. Talked to him of bleeding, leeches,
cupping, &c. He said he was very tired, and was going
home.'[32] She had also fallen out with Uncle Leopold, who
failed to notice that she was no longer powerless and dependent upon him for affection and advice, but that she had new
allies and new responsibilities, which weren't necessarily
compatible with his desires. Her mother had repeatedly suggested that she wasn't mature enough, especially as a
woman, to rule without a Regent. By the end of the year it
looked as if she had a point.

There was an obvious solution. Albert of Saxe-Coburg-
Gotha had spent the last three years travelling around
Europe, studying hard and exchanging letters with Victoria.
In October 1839 he was due to make a return visit to
England, and had made it clear to his various relatives that
if he didn't come back to Germany engaged, then he would
consider the whole thing a waste of his time. Victoria herself
was resistant, unwilling to be told what to do, and aware that
the match wouldn't necessarily meet with universal approval
in Britain. She had, however, been conditioned from

childhood to favour Albert as a suitor, and she was disillu-
sioned, fed-up and permanently angry: 'if I were a private
individual, I should leave the country immediately, as I was
so disgusted by the perpetual opposition'.[33] Fortunately,
perhaps, for her mental health, and indeed that of the people
around her, when the Prince finally arrived, all of the pieces
fell into place. The new and improved Albert was slimmer,
more handsome and above all worldly-wise. He shared her
love of music and was a good dancer. It was enough. Victoria fell madly in love and proposed four days later; they
were married in February 1840.

The marriage was stormy, despite their mutual and
undeniable love for one another. They had very different
ideas about what their relationship would look like. It took
Albert several years to gain what he saw as his rightful place
as a husband and a man, especially one educated quite deliberately for the position that he now held. Victoria wasn't
about to hand over all of her hard-won power to a quasi-
stranger, especially one who wasn't British. She needed to
learn to trust him; and in fact she eventually came to rely on
him so completely that she could barely function without
him. He had to get rid of Lehzen, who was jealous of him
and caused problems with Victoria, and he had to persuade
her ministers to trust him. In time he rose to be highly influential and to instigate large-scale changes in the way in
which the palaces and their people functioned, and came to
influence policy within and outside the country. Closer to
home, he also started to change the dreary court dinners.

From 1840 to 1861, when the Prince died, courtiers
largely stopped commenting about the Queen's fast-paced
eating, or tendency towards greed, and she once more

stopped talking about food in her journals. She put on some weight, but given that she had had nine children and was in her forties by 1861, it's hardly surprising. The Prince had a painful relationship with his digestion: he had suffered from childhood with a dodgy stomach, which was prone to flaring up and causing severe pain if he was stressed or had eaten the wrong things. Like Victoria as a child, he fasted regularly, especially when he was ill. Unlike her, he regarded eating as a necessity, and not a pleasure, and would hurry through dinner to get it over with.[34] He still struggled with late hours, and the wild partying to which Victoria was addicted was not at all to his taste. She managed to keep going for a while, but by June 1840 it was common knowledge that she was pregnant, and she conceived again within weeks of her first daughter's birth. Pregnant ladies in the 1840s did not dance until 5 a.m. Even at concerts, Albert wasn't exactly encouraging company: 'The Queen took a more lively interest in it than the greater part of her guests did. Prince Albert slept. She looked at him, half smiling, half vexed. She pushed him with her elbow. He woke up, and nodded approval of the piece of the moment. Then he went to sleep again still nodding approval, and the Queen began again.'[35] Gradually Victoria calmed down, although she always remained more outgoing than her husband, and, while she stopped veering between over-eating and dieting, and stopped going to bed in the small hours, he also learnt that being the consort of a Queen necessitated the occasional late night, as well as the stamina to eat for hours.

Not only were mealtimes made more regular, but there were immediate changes in the tedium of the dinner ritual: 'We have, I begin to notice, rather a raised tone of conversation of late – many bits of information, and naval matters, and scientific subjects come up, and are talked of very pleasantly at dinner.'[36] By the 1850s, the Queen had stopped greeting everyone before they went in to dinner, and entered through a separate door. Moreover, the Household didn't habitually dine with the Queen and the Prince every night. If there were no invited guests, Victoria and Albert often dined alone, or with the Princess Royal when she was old enough to leave the nursery and join them as an adult. These were still substantial meals: on 8 June 1857, the three of them had Italian pasta soup and rice soup; mackerel and whiting; roast beef and capon with rice; chicken rissoles and asparagus; a baked meringue and filled choux buns.[37] As the children grew older, they lunched together as a family while the Household lunched separately, though on occasion, especially on holiday, the family atmosphere spread out to include the various attendants: '[Our] luncheons were quite in a new style. All together, Queen, children, Gentlemen & Ladies & the children's governess – this was an enormous novelty.'[38] This jolly picture went neatly together with a public emphasis on the Queen as a wife and mother, as Victoria was cunningly positioned to appeal to the middle classes amid pressure to extend the vote and fear of social upheaval. Press pictures of the family gathered around their Christmas tree, and commissioned portraits of parents and children relaxing together, surrounded by dead game and dogs, reinforced the happy family message. Albert even managed to engineer a partial rapprochement with the Duchess of Kent. Emphasising a division between Victoria as monarch, and Victoria as woman, proved a partial solution to helping the nation accept – and embrace – their Queen.

At formal dinners, meanwhile, the etiquette grew more rigid, not less, as Albert's influence grew. The dress code was strictly enforced, and those whose evening wear had been mislaid or wasn't correct were forbidden to come to dinner. *À la Française* service continued to be used for most meals, complete with a sideboard containing extra provisions, in the form of cold meats. By the 1850s, however, change was afoot in wider society. A new service style was being promoted, especially by chefs, for it made kitchen management much easier. Service *à la Russe* was a very gradual introduction, not adapted by most households until well into the second half of the nineteenth century. Victoria started to encounter variations in the late 1850s, and, along with her own experiments in that direction, found it was more and more common elsewhere. In 1861, while visiting Killarney House in Ireland, she commented, 'an excellent dinner, served à la Russe with merely dessert & fruits on the table, which was most tastefully arranged with nothing but China ornaments & quantities of cut flowers, chiefly dahlias'.[39] The new style was much more akin to a lengthy tasting menu at a high-end restaurant today. Each course was now served separately, entirely by waiters, and delivered onto diners' plates from large platters and the meal became completely sequential. Diners were still able to choose between types of soup and fish, and they could refuse dishes or potentially even skip courses, but choice was reduced significantly. There was a gentle but insistent gendering at work, with the dark or thicker soup aimed at gentlemen, and ladies showing their gentility by choosing the lighter version. On the *à la Française* table this had been reinforced by setting each soup in the appropriate place in front of the host and hostess. Now the question was left hanging, a subtle test of etiquette for each diner. Other dishes also carried gender assumptions, which again had been enforced by dish placement in the earlier style: farmed meats and fowl up the hostess's end of the table, game and red meats nearer the host. Of course, in both service styles each diner could choose as they wished in theory, but it was a bit of a minefield unless she or he knew the rest of the company well enough not to be judged for their choices. Written menus came in with à la Russe, and advice was available in the form of etiquette guides, but at an upper class level they were, frankly, useless. If you needed the book, you clearly weren't of the requisite class in the first place. 'Fin Bec', a nineteenth-century writer, dryly commented that, 'a manual of etiquette in the possession of a diner is virtually a pièce de conviction'.[40] It is impossible to draw conclusions about aristocratic dining based on books aimed at middle-class wannabes.

The Queen retained à la Française service for her meals until the 1870s. Even after Albert's death, when there were no guests she continued to eat separately to the main Household, dining with what passed for close friends, often one of her children. In the 1870s a new routine was established: there was now a Queen's dinner for Victoria and an invited group, often just her ladies, and a Household dinner for the rest, with written menus introduced for both. They were almost certainly now served à la Russe, or at least a version of it. The order of dishes in the written ledgers changed in May 1875: a small alteration that concealed a seismic shift for an establishment that had largely trotted along unthinkingly since before Victoria came to the throne. Now the meal was served sequentially as soup – fish – entrées, removes – roasts – entremets, and at a brisk pace which showed that Victoria had not lost the ability to gobble when she wanted to: one diner commented that 'the Queen ate of everything, even cheese and a pear after dinner. No "courses": dinner is served straight on, and when you finish one dish you get the next, without a pause for breath.'[41] There was sometimes a short break between the entrées and removes, denoting the change of courses under the old style. Dessert was served on stands on the table, along with flowers and candelabra present throughout the whole meal, and the Queen retained a sideboard, usually containing cold fowls, roast beef and tongue. The Household were further along the path of modernity, and their dinners did not include a sideboard. The full version of *à la Russe* banished all food from the room; it was portioned up in the kitchen, and in some cases even served onto individual plates before being exposed to the diners' gaze (although this last was more common in restaurants than large private houses). Although manufacturers were touting modern sets of crockery, suited for the service style, with bigger eating plates and the latest in graphic design and print technology, no one at the palaces felt the need to invest in new dinner plates, and the round eating plates from the existing services continued in use, now all at least 40 years old. They were also in use at luncheon, which was less formal, and still served in the older style. This meal was more disparate, and, although the Queen usually ate it in company, along with a formal Household Luncheon, ledger entries show that it was much less important: some attendants took it in their rooms, some were provided with a picnic, and others ate out if they weren't needed at that time.

Regardless of which style was in use for dinner, there was a great deal of food to be prepared. The Queen and her immediate Household needed feeding, but so, too, did hundreds of lower servants – the Establishment – and it was for this reason that the physical structures of the royal kitchens were enormous, and the staff in them plentiful. The royal table was the focus, but it was due to the people labouring in kitchens literally far below stairs, that Victoria got fed at all.

4

Kitchens

The way in which the Queen, her Household, and indeed her subjects dined changed greatly across Victoria's reign, but the physical surroundings in which her food was prepared and served changed rather less. At both Windsor Castle and Buckingham Palace, the kitchens had been set up or renovated by George IV, and so were as up to date as anything else which Victoria inherited. However, modern definitely didn't mean efficient, safe or pleasant to work in. The practical issues were immense, but they were compounded by a convoluted administrative set-up that took red tape into whole new dimensions. At times, the letters and official reports on the palaces read like a slightly far-fetched farce. After the marriage of Queen Victoria to Prince Albert in 1840, the Prince spent many years grappling with the intricacies of the system, in which supposed

tradition and very real inertia led to often dangerous situations being left unfixed for years, sometimes decades. The
official royal palaces of Windsor Castle and Buckingham
Palace were, on the face of it, architectural monuments to
the monarchy, but they were also places where people lived
and worked, and the challenges of running them were huge.
Nowhere was this more obvious than the kitchens.

The royal kitchens didn't just provide meals for the
Queen and her growing family: a huge number of people
were entitled to be fed at the royal expense. The dining
ledgers for the palaces listed all of the groups to be fed on
each day. Some groups numbered only one or two people,
such as ladies lunching in their rooms, or the provision of
picnics for travelling attendants, while others could be
counted in their hundreds, especially those eating in the
main servants' hall. Depending on the palace, and the year,
the kitchens catered for bishops and choristers, electricians
and workmen, nurses and doctors, military bands, policemen, governesses, tutors, and an almost infinite variety of
divisions within the upper and lower servant body. Eating
took place in tens of different spaces across the palaces,
from formal dining rooms to hastily decided-upon nooks
and crannies. Almost every class of Victorian was represented within the Household, and meals reflected that social
reality. A person walking through the palace would have
been able to witness everything from plain working-class
food, to middle-class aspiration, right up to the poshest food
imaginable, served to the Queen and her aristocratic attendants with all due ceremony. And if this wasn't enough,
state visits and extraordinary events such as balls required
that the cooks produce hot and cold buffets for over a

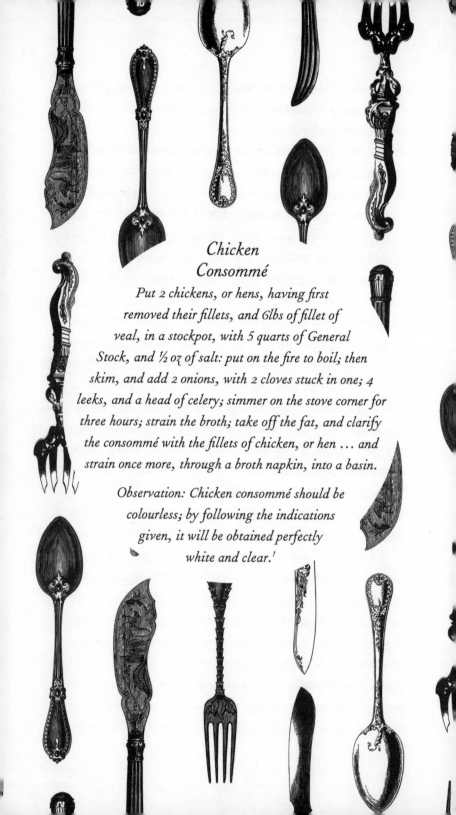

Chicken Consommé

Put 2 chickens, or hens, having first removed their fillets, and 6lbs of fillet of veal, in a stockpot, with 5 quarts of General Stock, and ½ oz of salt: put on the fire to boil; then skim, and add 2 onions, with 2 cloves stuck in one; 4 leeks, and a head of celery; simmer on the stove corner for three hours; strain the broth; take off the fat, and clarify the consommé with the fillets of chicken, or hen … and strain once more, through a broth napkin, into a basin.

Observation: Chicken consommé should be colourless; by following the indications given, it will be obtained perfectly white and clear.[1]

thousand mouths at a time, as well as catering to the specific dietary needs and desires of a multitude of guests from Britain and far beyond.

Cooking at the palace may have looked prestigious and interesting, but this was by no means finely tuned cheffing for a select group of discerning diners. It was mass catering on a factory scale. In March 1865 alone, 8,257 people ate food cooked by the royal chefs, and this was a fairly typical monthly figure.[2] The palace's population was divided into the Household and the wider Establishment. The Household was made up of Victoria and her family, along with the – usually titled – men and women who were her attendants. These were not people who fetched and carried. They were ladies-in-waiting, equerries, and occupiers of specific roles such as the Lord Chamberlain and Lord Steward. They all had duties, mainly organisational, but they also all had large houses and staff of their own. Some were permanent staff members, in which case they usually had London residences somewhere around St James's Palace, while some worked on rotation and had homes elsewhere in the country. All were entitled to rooms in whichever palace they were needed, as well as all of their meals.

At Windsor and Buckingham Palace, until 1861 the Household generally only dined with Victoria and, after 1840, with Albert, when they were entertaining specific visitors. Given their position in society, this was a pretty regular occurrence. The royal couple did, however, seek privacy when they could, eating together or, as the various children grew up, with one or more of their offspring. These private dinners were fairly muted: a mere snack of two soups, a fish, four entrées, two entremets and some cold fowl was served to them in July 1847. In June 1857, when Victoria dined with the Prince and their eldest daughter, the cosy threesome had soup au oeufs pochés (poached eggs), and a clear chicken soup; sole gratin and fried whitings; roast beef and capon with asparagus; vol-au-vents with béchamel sauce and grilled eggs; and an apricot flan and waffles 'mit creme'.[3] The clerk of the kitchen, who was responsible for writing out the menus, as planned by the chief chef and agreed by the Queen, was probably not a linguist, and a mixture of English, mainly correct French, and horribly garbled German was fairly typical. The meal also included the inevitable cold fowl on the sideboard and would have ended with fruit for dessert.

The rest of the Household dined separately, at the predictably titled Household dinner, at which numbers varied considerably. On the same day that the Queen ate the meal above, unusually, there were also only three people at the Household dinner. They had nearly the same menu, swapping the whitings for turbot; the beef for mutton; and adding mutton cutlets, chickens and veal noisettes. The waffles were replaced by plum pudding, and they also had roast pigeon and capons, plus ham toasts, citron madeleines and waffles. The food was of the highest possible standard: moulded, garnished, clarified, cut and finished off with extreme care and attention. The dining ledger from which these menus come lists quantities for some of the meat – the three members of the Household were expected to consume eight capons or chickens between them, an entire turbot, a lobster (which was in the sauce for the turbot), plus all of the other food. A roast beef joint was also provided, in case of sudden hunger between courses. Many of these dishes would have been served simultaneously as the service style was still *à la Française*. On this day specific meals were also provided separately for three of the older royal children, as well as for the nursery (roast lamb and roast fowl). The ledgers rarely give a lot of detail apart from that for royal and Household luncheons and dinners, so the various vegetable accompaniments and sweet courses for these aren't listed. However, they would have been there, along with the equally unspecified breakfasts for the family and Household. On this day, at that level of society, the kitchens also provided luncheons for the royal table and the ladies, along with a dinner for a spare woman of the bedchamber (Lady Barrington, who presumably missed the main dinner), and dinner for the equerries.

Beyond the Household was the wider Establishment. This consisted of everyone who did the actual work, and it was highly stratified. At the top were the private secretaries, tutors, governesses, clerks of the kitchen and high-ranking officials. They ate either in specific groups, or in the steward's room. Status mattered: the Household dined in the evening, around 8.30 p.m. Lower sorts dined around midday, emphasising the difference in rank. They also ate in small groups, but the bulk of them were fed en masse in the servants' hall. On this particular day the kitchens provided dinner for the night porters, upholsterers, singers, and the silver pantry, as well as a group of unspecified people eating in the coffee room, and the main servants' hall. Cooks and kitchen maids ate separately. There was also a ledger entry just for stock, which included large quantities of beef and veal, as well as a fowl for the soup.

The quantity of food cooked every day of Victoria's reign was stupendous, and the variety of preparations even more so. The kitchens had to be able to turn out the kind of well-presented, intricately flavoured dishes expected by the aristocracy, as well as catering for middle-class tastes and supplying bulk food for the masses. Unsurprisingly, the kitchens at the main palaces were huge, and operated on the same scale as a small factory. Even so, they couldn't always cope with the level of demand, and, on some occasions, outside caterers were used as well. This was consistently the case with bread, and often so as well with cakes and confectionery, especially at weddings and Christmas, when a large number of cakes were given away to friends, family and hangers-on. However, with the exception of these occasional forays into the commercial sphere, the kitchens provided everything.

Buckingham Palace was the first really royal palace encountered by the Queen. Kensington had once been a proud regal dwelling, but by the 1830s had been so hacked about and subdivided that it was hard to see the original layout. The Kents' kitchen there was quite a bit smaller than that at the average country house, while William III's original kitchen had been converted into a chapel. Victoria was desperate to move out, and, with the now Dowager Queen Adelaide still at Windsor, Buckingham Palace seemed like the place to be. True, it was still a building site, barely finished, hardly equipped, and didn't have any furniture, but it was a royal palace, and it was hers. She announced that she would move in as soon as possible, throwing her officials into an immediate panic, as it was not really fit for habitation. They pointed out its lack of carpets and fittings. She loftily stated that she had no need of carpets, or furniture: she could bring her own. She did demand a throne though, which she duly got. She moved in on 13 July 1837, and was utterly delighted with her new home. It was bright, garish, dripping with gilt and, to many people, utterly tasteless and reminiscent of the bad old days of George IV. Victoria, however, had a thing for gold and, now that she was out of dingy Kensington, she was entranced by its splendour. She was equally happy about the number of rooms, which meant that she could stable her mother at one end of the palace, and herself at the other, in her very own, private, rooms, with a new connecting door through to Baroness Lehzen's bedroom.

The palace was one of George IV's caprices. As at Brighton Pavilion, George had been determined to master-mind the construction of a palace that was truly fit for a modern monarch. Britain didn't really do decent palaces. St James's had sort of grown, piecemeal, around Whitehall, until a fire in the 1690s took most of it out of commission. Kew was ramshackle, with detached buildings of different periods making an impractical whole. Kensington was small and falling down. Hampton Court had been reasonable in 1540, but was now a mixture of styles, with Wren's massive extension sitting uneasily with the gloomy Tudor core. Where was the equivalent of Versailles, or the Winter Palace? Blenheim was the depressing answer, called a palace, but inconveniently not actually royal (and too far from London to have been of any use anyway). George IV was determined to change all of that. He presided over huge changes at Windsor, converted a seaside villa in Brighton into an exotic fantasy, and focused on an unprepossessing house in the middle of London – acquired by George III as a residence for his Queen – to convert into a palace that

Britain could be proud of. Poor George. It all went wrong at Buckingham Palace. From the start he didn't seem able to work out quite what he wanted, and his architect, the usually reliable John Nash, panicked under pressure and designed a bizarre building, criticised from the outset. His structural calculations proved dodgy; his building methods crazed; and, as the palace took shape, his budgeting was way out of control. He was eventually dismissed, but not before the new palace became a laughing stock. A particularly vicious – but brilliant – satire was published in one of the newspapers, purporting to be 'from a Frenchman':

I shall now give you an account of de royale palace, called here de Buck-and-Ham palace, which is building for de English king in de spirit of John Bull plum pudding and roast-beef taste, for which de English are so famous. It is a great curiosity. In de first place, de pillars are made to represent de English vegetable, as de sparrow-grass, de leek and de onion; then de entablatures or friezes are very mosh enriched with de leg of mutton and de pork, with vat they call de garnish, all vary beautiful carved; den, on de impediment of de front stand colossal figure of de man-cook with de large English toasting fork in his hand, ready to put in de pot a vary large plum pudding behind him, which is a vary fine plum pudding, not de colour of de black Christmas pudding, because de architect say it would not look vell in de summair time – it is vary plain pudding … On de wing of the palace, called de gizzard wing (de other wing was cut off), stand de domestique servant, in neat dress, holding de trays of biscuit and

tart ... Dere is to be in de front of de palace vary large
kitchen range made of white marble, vich I was told
would contain von hundred of goose at von time. De
palace, ven complete, will be called after von famouse
English dish, de Toad-in-de-Hole.[4]

The 'toad' was George IV. The pudding referred to a dome,
which originally peeped obscenely over the balustrade and
looked ridiculous, while the kitchen range was the marble
arch, intended as a triumphal entrance until someone
thought to see if the state coach would go through it. It
wouldn't. Food metaphors abounded. The pillars on the
front of the palace were criticised as being raspberry-
coloured, or, less politely, as resembling raw sausages.[5]

When George IV died, William IV refused to have anything to do with what Creevey called, 'this monstrous insult
to the nation, this cumbrous pile, this monument to reckless
extravagance'.[6] Proposals were circulating to turn it into a
national gallery, or a college, and when the Houses of Parliament burnt down in 1834, William delightedly offered up
Buckingham Palace as a replacement. Parliament, who were
aware of the state it was in, as well as the money pit it had
become, declined to take it on. Instead, the decision was
made to try to finish it. So much money had already been
spent that it seemed silly not to see the thing through.
However, with no pressure from the current monarch, by
1837 the palace was very far from a functional living space.

The kitchens at the time were under the main body of
the palace. In theory they had the usual full contingent of
main kitchen, scullery, pastry, confectionery, bakehouse,
larders and outdoor space. In practice not all of these rooms

appear to have been finished, and, as time went on, there were proposals to shift some rooms around and remove others. The fittings were fairly standard: ranges and charcoal chafing stoves, provided by the leading manufacturers of the day, including Jeakes, and Bramagh and Prestige. A lot of the fittings were also supplied by the new builder, Thomas Cubitt, who, with architect Edward Blore, who replaced Nash, took on the mammoth task of wrestling the palace into submission in the 1840s. These fittings were clearly subject to a hard life, and not entirely up to standard: in 1843 a list of alterations and improvements included installing an additional oven in the pastry room, filling in 'the opening in the pastry table', repairing the pastry sink, as well as the kitchen range and steam apparatus, and altering all of the windows so that they would open.[7]

The kitchens, like most of the palace, were gas-lit, though all of the cooking took place on coal or charcoal. Charcoal was odourless, smokeless, and, in the form of chafing stoves, highly controllable. The stoves were very simple in their design: just a metal grill, set into a brick surround, which held the burning charcoal while allowing the air to circulate and the ash to fall through. Cooks controlled the temperature equally simply, by raising or lowering the pan, using trivets where necessary to support it: primitive, perhaps, but far more instantly manageable than later electric or halogen hobs. The disadvantage was that they gave off carbon monoxide. They were entirely unventilated, and what little effort had been made to improve the issue – namely, opening the windows – was a 'disgrace to science'. Since the kitchen door was habitually kept open in a – futile – attempt to increase the air circulation, these fumes worked their way up the building and into the royal apartments. The ventilation debate continued, with occasional half-hearted attempts to tinker with the windows and install chimneys, concluding when an exasperated Lord Chamberlain wrote to the Commissioners of Her Majesty's Woods, 'with reference to the special works to be done at Buckingham Palace for the year ending 31st March 1847, I have the honour to state that great inconvenience as well as detriment to the health of the persons employed in the Kitchens at Buckingham Palace having been experienced from the fumes of the Charcoal used in the stoves not having proper means of escape, it is considered highly advisable immediately to construct hoods over the stoves with a communication to the ventilating shaft at present in use'.[8] The kitchen was described as, 'hot, unhealthy, and altogether unfit'.[9]

There were wider problems than those of ventilation. When the kitchens were being constructed, workmen excavating the foundations discovered a handy brick floor, which they left in place to form the floor of the kitchen. Any of them who were local would have known what it really was: a conduit which served most of the surrounding area as a sewer, and which turned out to have a somewhat porous structure. The consequences of this became apparent as soon as Victoria moved in. The kitchens were quickly described as, 'foul and offensive'. Raw sewage leaked from the floor and piled up around the walls while the cooks worked. To add to the anguish, the rooms next to the kitchen contained dustbins, 'filled with garbage of a very bad description', and urinals for the male cooks.[10] There were still workmen around, finishing off bits of the palace, and the mingled stench of urine, rotten food, glue and human effluent drifted upstairs and through the staterooms like a particularly noxious relative. And, in the palace proper, it got even worse.

Edward Blore was one of several people to prepare reports on the palace in the 1840s. He wasn't a fan. One particular gripe was – again – lack of ventilation. There were 200 fires in the palace, and they were notorious for smoking and refusing to stay alight. He attributed this to a closed system of air, which led to the fires pulling air from wherever they could, namely the water closets. While not every water closet actually worked – another cause for complaint – most were connected to some degree or other with the sewers. The traps leaked. The sewers stank. 'The emanations drawn into the palace were so powerful as to produce nausea, and feelings of sickness when we went close to the sinks.'[11] Furthermore, when people did manage to open a window, they were exposed to the area which surrounded the palace, and in which many of the lower servants lodged. Directly opposite was a street called Princes Court, 'which is used as a public urinal, the roadway through it is always drenched and covered with urinary deposits and others of a still more objectionable description. The walls on either side, saturated with urine, are falling to pieces the mortar being completely decomposed thereby ... all the buildings there being of an inferior description, and entirely without any drainage other than the open gutters of the unpaved streets ... the slops thrown out from the houses, cover an extent of many hundreds of square yards ... from which are constantly emanating exhalations of a most disagreeable and unwholesome character, and which during three quarters of the year are wafted by the south westerly winds right into the palace windows.'[12] Residents blamed a local gas works for the tarnished brass, and paint which blackened only hours after being applied, but no, it was just the effects of hundreds of people, all cooking and eating and defecating in the palace and its surrounds.

There were knock-on effects, too, on the neighbouring area. While plebeian turds were oozing up through the royal kitchen floor, royal effluvia were finding their way through the floorboards of the neighbouring houses. There was no effective sewage system in place for many of the surrounding streets, and residents complained about the devaluation of their houses due to the effects of the inadequate sewage systems of the new construction meeting the non-existent systems outside. If they'd stepped inside the palace, though, they'd have found human waste pooling in the courtyards, despite the best efforts of extra night-soil-men, who were employed to take it all away. They dumped it in the gardens, next to Albert's new summerhouse.

Security was an issue as well. Frequently, drunken soldiers or passing tramps had to be extracted from the palace gardens in the morning, and a couple of well-publicised break-ins scandalised a nation that assumed that its monarch was kept reasonably secure. On one occasion an obsessed silversmith was found a few yards from the Queen's bedroom, declaring that he had come to ask Victoria to marry him. And on four separate occasions between 1838 and 1841 a boy called Edward Jones gained entry through open windows or gaps in doors. On the first occasion he was found, covered in soot and grease, wearing two pairs of trousers, and with various stolen objects, including ladies' underwear, hidden about his person. On the second, Lehzen and Mrs Lilly, the Princess

Royal's nurse, dragged him out from under a sofa while a rather useless page looked on. On the third and fourth, he came in, established that the security had not been improved, went home to get a meal, and came back again the next day. Questioned in court he admitted to having helped himself to 'victuals in the kitchen', leaving fingerprints in the stock. On the final occasion he was found with cold meat and potatoes, which he'd filched, wrapped up in a cloth.[13]

The place was a shambles, both physically and administratively. A large part of the problem lay with the ridiculously complicated administration of the palaces. Over hundreds of years, structures had evolved which simply did not work. In addition, both high-ranking officials and lower-down servants had grown used to playing the system. Notorious abuses eventually came to light, including ordering candles for rooms which had been gas-lit for years, and ordering wine for people or purposes which had long since become obsolete. Looking back, one book from the end of the period commented that: 'The perquisite system was in full force, and wine or candles, and other imperishable items which had been produced for any particular occasion and had remained untouched, were calmly annexed by certain officials and their underlings, although perfectly fit to be brought forth again. Those were the days when scores of people outside the palaces lived in luxury on the proceeds of robbery and waste within.'[14]

By 1837 it had become virtually impossible to get anything done. Examples of confusion included window mending: a broken kitchen window required a requisition signed by the chief cook, countersigned by a clerk of the kitchen, signed by the master of the Household, and then authorised by the Lord Chamberlain's Office before being passed to the Department of Woods and Forests for the actual work to be scheduled and – eventually – carried out.[15] Another was fires. Again, different departments were responsible for laying fires and lighting them. Even Victoria herself struggled to get any sense out of her officials, and her complaints, via the inevitable chain of officials, that the dining room was damp and cold, were met with excuses rather than anything as useful as actual fire-lighting. The problem wasn't so much that no one knew who was responsible for various tasks: more that there were so many competing interests, and no cross-communication, that nothing ever got done efficiently. Guests complained that there was no one to show them to their rooms, and that when they did get there, if they left, they could never get back again. One man spent the night sleeping on a sofa after failing to relocate his room after dinner. The housemaid who found him called a policeman, assuming he was a random drunk. Servants cleaned guests' shoes in their own rooms as no boot room had been provided amid the ongoing building works, and if they managed to provide water for guests for washing, it invariably arrived cold, due to inadequate plumbing provision, and filthy, thanks to the general atmosphere.[16] Victoria either didn't notice, or was prepared to ignore it all. In her early years she was far more preoccupied with partying and politics than dusting and drains. She put Baroness Lehzen in charge of running the Household on a day-to-day basis, and forgot about it. However, the situation had become so farcical that it required a wholesale reorganisation, something that Lehzen had neither the power, nor the inclination, to carry out.

In 1840, however, Prince Albert had arrived, and was raring for a challenge. He was frustrated by Victoria's refusal to trust him with confidential political documents, and her determination to retain absolute authority as Queen, despite the fact that she now had a handsome and accomplished husband. Victorian men did not expect to play a subservient role to their wives, and Albert had entered into his marriage with a certain trepidation about Victoria's wilful character and the efforts he would have to make to achieve a harmonious relationship. Harmonious, to Albert, meant that he was not sidelined as a wife would be, but able to play a significant role as Victoria's advisor, as well as being a significant figure in his own right. One of the sticking points was Lehzen, who was jealous of the Prince, and deliberately caused trouble between the couple. It took him two years to prise Lehzen out of her privileged position as the Queen's closest confidante, but at the end of 1842 she was persuaded to retire on an annual pension of £300, and shipped off to Germany. With her departure, Albert was able to take control, both of Victoria, who became increasingly reliant on him now that no one else was around to support her, and of the internal running of the creaky royal household. Much to her outrage, Victoria was also pregnant for large swathes of her early married life, and repeated bouts of related illness, postnatal depression and confinements wore down her early determination to always do everything alone. Together with Baron Stockmar, his advisor, personal secretary and friend, Albert systematically investigated the various departments, and instigated reforms. He caused outrage by removing long-held perks and rooting out abuses of the system that were costing significant amounts of money. He slashed the salary bill, both by tweaking the number and type of office-holders, and by simply reducing wages or associated extra payments. He properly delineated the responsibilities of the Lord Chamberlain and Lord Steward's departments, making the political appointees largely honorific positions, and giving the master of the Household the real responsibility for ensuring that things got done. It wasn't perfect, but by the time he had finished, it almost resembled a working administration.

One of the most pressing aims of the newly streamlined royal Establishment had to be sorting out the Buckingham Palace kitchens. By the late 1840s, Victoria and Albert had decided that the palace was too small for their ever-increasing family, and didn't provide proper reception space for state occasions. Albert disliked central London living anyway, and, as he and Victoria gradually stopped having ferocious rows, and his influence upon her grew, she started to agree with him. Their main preference was for the intimate environment of Balmoral or Osborne, but they weren't ideal for attending to government, or entertaining ambassadors and heads of state. Where possible, they used Windsor, but Buckingham Palace still needed a revamp, and in 1851 it finally got it.

Money, as usual, had been one of the stumbling blocks, but Victoria and Albert devised plans that would mean that the upgrades would cost the nation practically nothing. They were both careful housekeepers, in stark contrast to Victoria's predecessors. Part of the money for the rebuild came from the sale of Brighton Pavilion, which, despite her love of the garish, Victoria hated. Some of the furnishings were, however, transferred to Buckingham Palace and reused, notably in the Chinese breakfast room. The glorious Brighton kitchens, however, were left on site, being part demolished as the town council converted the building for new uses. The new kitchens at Buckingham Palace were not a patch on those at Brighton, though they were vastly improved. They were bigger, with all the auxiliary rooms fully planned for, and decently ventilated. They were also better positioned in the building, under a new ballroom and entertaining space. The ballroom had central heating, gas lighting, and was huge. The kitchens also benefitted from gas lighting, but otherwise made a lot of use of the fixtures and fittings from the old kitchens. This made sense: they were, after all, less than twenty years old. This time around they were connected to working chimneys and drains. The new kitchens had decent hot-water apparatus, a state-of-the-art roasting range (the spit mechanism is still there), and enclosed water closets. Despite this, there was a certain sense of déjà-vu. The fit-out was completed in October 1852. Already by June 1853 the kitchen passages were being labelled as dark, gloomy and unventilated. A memorandum written on the 25th urgently called for better circulation of fresh air, in order to stop tainted air in the larder coming into contact with joints and other articles of food.[17]

Another key area to be addressed by Albert's reforms, both at Buckingham Palace and at Windsor, was food waste.[18] The kitchens got through enormous quantities of food. In October 1842 up to 90 loaves of bread per day were consumed across the Establishment, along with 24 rolls, 6 cottage loaves and 6 fancy twists. The standard loaf was a quartern, which weighed four pounds. Several suppliers were used, as was also the case for the 36 pounds of butter per day, and over 800 pounds of Cheshire Cheese that month.[19] Although supplies were recorded in detail, as they were purchased, there doesn't seem to have been anyone keeping much track of them after they were cooked. *À la Française* service was predicated on supplying gargantuan amounts of food on the table, and much of it was eaten. It was a more physical age, and everyone needed more calories than modern dietary advice recommends. Plus, from Melbourne to the Queen herself, there were some notoriously big eaters at the palace at every stage of Victoria's reign. Leftovers were an integral part of the system, though, especially cold roast meats, as they could be transformed into a huge range of puddings, soups and stews (hashes) for the rest of the Household (or breakfast, lunch or nursery teas). Even left in the state in which they came off the table, roast meats from the aristocratic table provided cold meals for servants across Britain, and the royal Establishment was no different: 'If the servants could not have a little cold fowl or turkey for supper they felt they were very badly treated indeed.'[20] This wasn't a question of petty pilfering: it was built into the system. The upper servants, those who ate in the steward's room, ate a sit-down supper after the Queen's dinner had finished, at 9.30 p.m., when the uneaten dishes would be transferred from the upstairs dining room to the downstairs steward's room, ready for a rather tepid feast. Nevertheless, there were still leftovers, and still more general waste from cooking. Peelings and scraps could go for pig slurry, but prepared dishes were effectively part of the social welfare system, which at the time was based largely on philanthropy and a strong sense of duty towards the poor, and which formed the basis of upper-class education, particularly for women. Most country houses had developed a sort of edible almsgiving system, based on cooked food waste, which aimed to provide basic sustenance to those members of the local community who were unable to provide for themselves.[21] At the palaces, the poor would queue up in the hope of receiving food, but it was open to abuse, as there were no checks in place to ensure that would-be diners were actually in need. A new structure was put in place, therefore, which ensured that food would be distributed, not to hopeful individuals, but via designated charities who could send representatives on a rota basis. In December 1855, the palace ledgers recorded that 650 'poor of Windsor' were fed, and, where numbers were recorded, they are all in the hundreds.[22] This worked so well that when, in 1902, the coronation feast of Edward VII had to be postponed due to an emergency operation, rather than panicking about what to do with the food for 250 guests, the more perishable dishes were seamlessly – but discreetly – used to feed the poor of Whitechapel. It was presumably the first and last time most of them ate immaculately clarified pheasant soup, or woodcock stuffed with foie gras.[23]

By the late 1850s, with decent sewerage being installed, and the kitchen rebuilt, Buckingham Palace was almost habitable. However, Victoria and Albert increasingly spent most of their time when they were needed in London at Windsor Castle. In 1849 the Slough–Windsor branch line opened, so the whole journey into central London could be made by train, which was easy and convenient. The vast majority of state visits were conducted at Windsor, and

Buckingham Palace became the unloved site for vast balls, drawing rooms, and fleeting stays when it was otherwise unavoidable. Windsor was bigger, with more accommodation for the Household and Establishment alike; it was easier to get away from, for trips to Osborne, or the south-coast ports; and it had much, much better kitchens.

The Windsor Castle kitchens are iconic. Even under Victoria, they were a must-see attraction for her attendants, and lords, ladies, statesmen, their wives and underlings all visited them. The structure dates back to the medieval period, when the Great Kitchen was constructed as a massive, barn-like space, edged with roasting ranges and brick-built charcoal chafing stoves, and it remained largely unchanged until the 1820s. There were significant building works to repair the kitchens under Elizabeth I, by which time they had disintegrated to the point that they were unusable, and under Charles II, who added a second kitchen and reworked all of the auxiliary rooms, especially the bakehouse. Many of these changes were in turn swept away under George IV, who employed Sir Jeffry Wyatville to rebuild most of the upper ward (the highest part of the castle, housing the staterooms and royal apartments), creating the interiors that are still in use today. Wyatville also created the kitchens that Victoria would have known. Completed in 1828, they were both an unsubtle homage to fine dining, and a practical working space. They were fitted out with a vast new batterie de cuisine, in gleaming copper, with each piece crested and numbered. There were pans of every description, including specialist fish kettles, plain saucepans and huge stockpots. There were culinary moulds for jelly, cake and blancmange; along with dariole moulds for making tiny, exquisite moulded puddings and cakes, and all of the other highly specialised equipment which high-end French-style cookery demanded. There were bain maries for sauces, baking sheets for pastry, and waffling irons, pancake pans and all the rest. There was a confection-ery, a bakehouse, a pastry room and extensive larders, all kitted out to the highest level. That meant not only the obvious things – hot water on demand from a cistern on the roof, steam-heated hot tables and warming closets, boiling coppers for large joints and puddings, brick ovens with cast-iron doors – but also a level of ornamentation and design which was decidedly not the norm. There were gothic-style cast-iron bases for the chafing stoves, which were moved from sitting against the walls, where the fumes wafted gently into the kitchen, and installed instead in place of some of the roasting ranges, neatening up the whole kitchen by streamlining the edges, and giving them direct ventilation up the chimneys. The remaining ranges were refitted with modern smoke-jacks: spit mechanisms driven automatically by the draw of the fire, which turned a fan positioned a short way up the chimney and which was then connected to a system of cogs and pulleys, with ornate has-teners (roasting screens) in front of them. They, and the fireplaces they screened, had their own battlements. The floors were spread with sand, which was replaced several times a day, ensuring that all scraps and spills were captured and cleared efficiently. Gas lighting was installed, along with lantern windows in the ceiling to maximise light. Whitewash and tiles replaced bare stone and wood. Gabriel Tschumi, who worked in them for many years from 1898, described his first impression of them as being like 'a chapel, with its high domed ceiling, its feeling of airiness and light, and the gleam of copper, well-worn and burnished, at each end of the room'.[24]

In 1855 one of the Queen's dressers, Frieda Arnold, went on a trip to the kitchens, an obligatory experience for servants and served alike. She was awed by its size, saying she got, 'quite lost in it'. She went on:

There are twelve ranges, with a huge iron table in the centre which is heated from below, and on which the dishes are set. On both sides are huge fires over which roasts are suspended on spits, with great iron chains driven round constantly by a machine. On one of these fires alone five zentner [approx. 250kg] of charcoal are burnt every day. At Christmas a whole ox weighing 400lb was roasted here; it was brought to the table: that was indeed a roast beef. I saw a Welsh capon in the kitchen which weighed 24lb – everything here is on this scale. But the greatest calm and order reigns, as if nothing was happening.[25]

Even the newspapers got in on the act. The *Illustrated London News* published a picture of the kitchens in 1850, accompanied with a description: 'Large fires at both ends of the kitchen look enormous, and, with the viands slowly revolving on the spits, present a wonderful picture. On either side there are charcoal stoves for the more delicate cookery – for the chefs d'oeuvres of French invention – aided by certain mysterious utensils used in the process that sadly bewilder the uninitiated, whose astonishment is moreover excited by the great size and number of the culinary

vessels displayed ostentatiously round the huge fire-places.'
The master cooks all worked on their own preparatory
tables, which surrounded a steam-heated hot table. As they
finished each dish, they placed it on the central table in the
position that it would occupy in the dining room upstairs,
ready for the footmen to collect. The dishes demanded
intense concentration, which was reflected in the atmosphere: 'The scene in the kitchen is one of great order; no
bustle, no confusion; all the details, even of the largest
dinner, being so subdivided and arranged that each person
has his own part to attend to, and, in consequence, there is
no disorder. The quiet is remarkable.'[26]

The quiet was relative, especially for a journalist almost
certainly writing from second-hand accounts. There was
little talking, but the noise of cooking made for sensory
overload, as this account from 1897 makes quite clear:

> Under the brilliant glare of numberless gas jets, the two
> great open fires roar up their wide-throated chimney,
> while all before the fierce blaze two score of glistening,
> juicy joints, all crackle and splutter. White-clad cooks
> hover round monstrous coppers which fill the air with
> the hum of their bubbling. At his desk the storekeeper
> checks the quantities of food in course of cooking, or
> sends messengers flying to the storeroom for supple-
> mentary supplies. With the monotonous jangle of the
> endless chains that turn the spouts, mingles the noisy
> stoking of the many different fires and the clang of the
> oven doors as they are sharply open and shut ... the
> bain maries hiss forth a most savoury steam of appetis-
> ing sauces, while before their particular blaze, fat

chickens frizzle contentedly under the attentions of a
roasting cook and his basting ladle.[27]

The book from which this is taken, *The Private Life of the
Queen*, was banned on publication. It was probably written
by a servant to one of the maids-of-honour, and is very
detailed on the fabric of the building, the paintings, ceramics, and contents of the storerooms, but it's quite clear that
the author was not part of the Household, and had never
dined with the Queen. She or he was confused about salaries
and numbers of staff in the kitchens, but knew the contents
of the China Room extremely well. As a guide to the work-
ings of the kitchens, however, it is invaluable. As with
almost every visitor to the kitchens, the roasting ranges
clearly made the biggest impact, but a smaller range, used
just for cooking the Queen's daily cold roast fowl, is also
noted. The cook's room is described as well: 'a cosy apartment, furnished with a chest of drawers, washstand, table
and a most comfortable armchair. There is also a writing
desk. Above the fireplace, which faces the window, hangs a
china plate, mounted on a velvet plaque. It is emblazoned
with the royal arms, and was presented to the Queen some
years ago by the Cook's Guild. The wide window-sill is
piled up with blue-paper covered books, in which the Royal
and Household menus are daily entered.'[28] There was also a
room specifically for the master cooks, at least in 1843, when
it was re-carpeted, but the chief cook always had his own
place of quiet contemplation, where, according to one
architectural guide at the time, he could 'consult his authori-
ties'.[29] Even the most advanced cook needs a reference
library. Pictures from the 1860s to the 1890s show that there

was also a small octagonal table with a couple of stools in the main kitchen. This is probably the storekeeper's seat described above.

Visitors to the kitchens rarely ventured beyond the main space. There were sculleries and storerooms galore, many occupying Charles II's second kitchen, which had been subdivided into an absolute maze of rooms. Frieda Arnold described the confectionery room and pastry kitchen as 'very interesting', but said no more. These were both quite separate to the main kitchen, with their own staff, and own responsibilities. The confectionery in particular was a specialist area, 'a most fascinating apartment, and the variety and beauty of the shapes and moulds to be found there, the charming little ovens and stoves which go almost all round the room, and the dainty appliances for "piping" and the more delicate parts of confectionery would delight any woman who is possessed of a "sweet tooth"'.[30] Confectionery had a long history of association with women, especially gentlewomen, and in the sixteenth and seventeenth centuries it was regarded as one of the ladylike domestic arts to which upper-class women should aspire. However, by the Victorian era it had been professionalised and Frenchified, and its practitioners were largely men. That didn't stop sugarcraft, with all its connotations of purity, delicacy and whiteness, continuing to have feminine associations.

The Windsor kitchens remained the hub for royal dining for the whole of Victoria's reign. The confectionery and bakehouse in particular were not readily replicated elsewhere, and, although other palaces had such facilities, they were not on the same scale. Windsor was used as a catering facility, supplying cakes, bread and biscuits to all of the other palaces several times a week, where necessary. It made logistical sense: the royal kitchen gardens were consolidated at Windsor after 1850 – another of Albert's reforms – and so deliveries were heading off in other directions anyway. The kitchens didn't change much. There were minor repairs, and occasional additional installations, but nothing substantial until after 1901. Although some sources – though never anyone with experience of cooking in the kitchens – mention gas stoves in addition to the charcoal ones, it doesn't seem as if gas was actually installed at Windsor for cooking during Victoria's reign. Many large houses continued to cook on coal and charcoal until well into the twentieth century and, although gas ranges were installed at some of the wealthier clubs and hotels from the 1840s, they were much rarer in upper-class domestic environments. By the 1890s, therefore, the kitchens were pretty much as up to date as they had been in the 1830s, and just as impressive to those who went round them.

Windsor was by no means beset by the issues that dogged Buckingham Palace, but it did have a few problems, including paralysing cold in many parts of the castle. Again, sewerage was inadequate, and, again, there was a large forgotten underground sewer, this time under part of the boundary wall, which was found to be slowly washing away the foundations in the 1820s. The main complaint about Windsor from an Establishment point of view was that it seemed to consume dusters, which led to a mildly hilarious flurry of letters in the 1850s. It was clearly very serious for those concerned, mainly housemaids, but also silver room staff, table-deckers and anyone else who felt the need for a stout linen cloth – which would have included the kitchens.

'This duster business' culminated in the loss of 24 dozen dusters, and a stern warning to the housekeeper, whose department was deemed responsible for most of them, that 'if the matter is to be gone into again, as it should be, I should recommend that all the dusters should be issued, and accounted for, by a man'.[31] With such pressing concerns at the forefront of their London life, it is perhaps no wonder that Victoria and Albert sought somewhere to retreat to which was new, fresh, and not ruled by the myriad customs of the official royal Establishment. In 1844 Victoria wrote to Uncle Leopold, 'Windsor is beautiful and comfortable, but it is a <u>palace</u>, and God knows <u>how willingly</u> I would <u>always</u> live with my beloved Albert and our children in the quiet and retirement of private life and not be always the constant object of observations, and of newspaper articles.'[32] Life in the Isle of Wight and the Highlands beckoned, not only for the royal couple and their children, but also for the Household, and the Establishment, including the cooks.

5
Cooks

Dishes don't cook themselves, and the vast and occasionally stinky kitchens at the various palaces were inhabited by a permanent staff of men and women. They occupied a bewildering variety of positions, named according to an archaic structure unique to the royal Establishment. There were between 35 and 45 cooks, but around them was a range of other people, employed in departments such as the cellar, the pantry, the silver room and the coffee room. In all, and excluding those who worked in the gardens, filling the stomachs of the palace residents provided direct employment for around 70 people in 1841, with the number rising slightly by the end of Victoria's reign. They were all lumped under the heading of the Lord Steward's Department and kept firmly below stairs. Hidden deep within the palaces, cooking for thousands of people each month, they

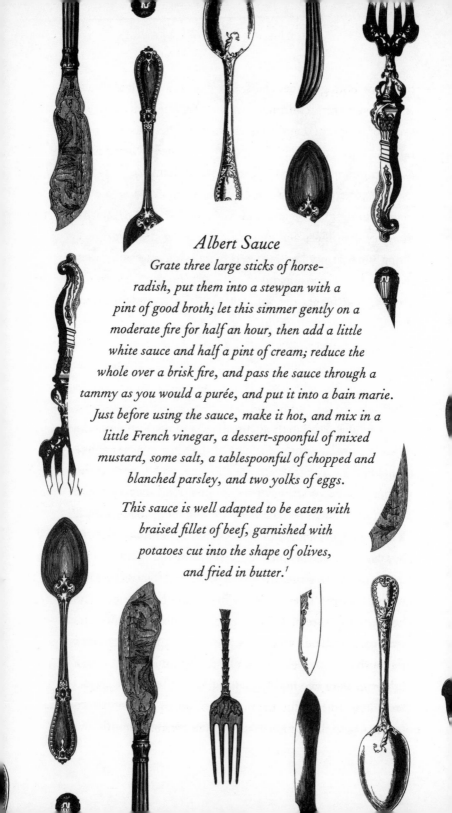

Albert Sauce

Grate three large sticks of horseradish, put them into a stewpan with a
pint of good broth; let this simmer gently on a
moderate fire for half an hour, then add a little
white sauce and half a pint of cream; reduce the
whole over a brisk fire, and pass the sauce through a
tammy as you would a purée, and put it into a bain marie.
Just before using the sauce, make it hot, and mix in a
little French vinegar, a dessert-spoonful of mixed
mustard, some salt, a tablespoonful of chopped and
blanched parsley, and two yolks of eggs.

This sauce is well adapted to be eaten with
braised fillet of beef, garnished with
potatoes cut into the shape of olives,
and fried in butter.[1]

had to be both gourmet chefs, catering to individual tastes, and mass caterers, churning out meals for hundreds or thousands of people at one sitting. It was a unique place to work, bound by traditions which sometimes seemed as antiquated as the buildings that on occasion housed them.

The structure of the royal kitchens had developed over many hundreds of years, and was peculiar to the palaces. Many of the offices and departments had medieval origins, though modernity had intruded in individual form by 1837 in the form of gas apparatus men. Within the Lord Steward's Department, the kitchen was the biggest section, though it was itself divided into kitchen, confectionery, pastry and bakery (this was sometimes included with the pastry division). There was also a 'ewery' (responsible for table linen), the silver pantry (which also included all the gold), the cellar (wine and beer) and the table-deckers. Those who worked in these divisions formed the bulk of the department, but they had a staff of middle managers above them. For the kitchens, this was a set of four clerks of the kitchen, above whom was a Clerk Comptroller. His job was to plan the menus, send them up to the Queen for approval, fill in the ledgers and, with his deputies, order food and supplies and ensure the smooth running of the whole thing. Above them the structure grew hazier and less inclined to definable work. There was the inevitable committee, The Board of the Green Cloth, which had existed since the medieval period but which by Victoria's reign largely looked after disputes, as well as administering the payroll. Even higher up were two highly salaried political appointees, the Lord Steward and his deputy, who wisely left all of the nitty-gritty to the administrators below them.

Beyond the Lord Steward's Department were others, including the Lord Chamberlain's Department, with which there was a great deal of crossover, for this included house-maids and serving staff; effectively front of house. The duties of everyone concerned were published for the wider public in one of those typically detailed, dry and utterly fas-cinating books in which Victorian Britain specialised. *Sketches From Her Majesty's Household* (1848) was lavish in its praise of Albert's household reforms, painting a picture of a newly reorganised Establishment, where everyone now knew their role, and no one took advantage of the system, or claimed perks to which they weren't entitled.[2] It was a bit premature, for the Prince's reordering took up most of the 1840s, and its repercussions were still being felt in the early 1850s, when the Buckingham Palace kitchens were finally rebuilt.

In the kitchens, reforms had been ongoing for a while prior to Victoria's accession. Many of the roles had been renamed over the previous 50 years – the Georgian children of the kitchen and boys of the kitchen (all adults, despite the names) had disappeared, while the turnbroaches of an earlier era no longer actively turned spits, and were now roasting cooks. Nevertheless, the full list of positions remained satisfyingly archaic. Top of the pile was the chief cook, occasionally also known as the maître d'hôtel. In 1837 this was William Bale, with an annual salary of £250. He was also entitled to apartments in St James's Palace. There was very little inflation in the nineteenth century, and even in 1897 the chief cook's salary had only risen to £300. Below him came two master cooks, on £150 and £220. Two yeomen of the mouth (by 1869 renamed as third and fourth master cooks) and two yeomen of the kitchen followed them. There were two roasting cooks, four apprentices, two scourers (scullery maids in any other world, but these were scullery men, and dignified with a different title), a woman cook and a kitchen maid. The kitchen staff in 1837 was completed by four non-cooking positions: a larderer, a storekeeper, a green office man (vegetable peeler) and an errand man or messenger. Meanwhile, the confectionery had two yeomen and two assistants, and the pastry had one yeoman and one assistant. Over the 63 years of Victoria's reign, all of these roles shifted, as the emphasis on certain areas increased or declined. Already by the 1840s they had been joined by two more scourers, plus three assistant cooks (one was actually the renamed larderer, and the others were promoted apprentices), a baker and his assistant, and two gas apparatus men. More women swelled the ranks as well, as another kitchen maid and another pastry assistant were added to the wage lists. They were the lowest paid workers in the kitchen, earning £30 to £58 per year.[3] The upper kitchen staff, including the clerks of the kitchen, also benefitted from extra allowances, including the £150 fee paid by parents to the kitchens for taking their children on as apprentices. Staff also received 'vails', gifts of money left by visiting dignitaries as tips, which were divided up according to seniority. Lodgings were provided, and full board when the royal family was in residence.

This structure remained largely unchanged throughout Victoria's reign, along with the wages for each position. More women came in to fill the lower positions, which, invariably, underwent a hasty name change, in a cunning move to save money, for women could be paid about half as much for the same job that a man would do. The first women had joined the kitchens in active cooking roles during the Regency *or* in the 1810s, but they remained a minority. After Albert's reforms in the 1840s, 8 out of 39 kitchen staff were women. By 1900 the figure was 8 out of 35.[4] They all occupied subsidiary roles, whether within the kitchen proper, the confectionery or the pastry. This was normal. Large country houses, hotels and other wealthy establishments employed male cooks, ideally French male cooks, as a preference. Wages at country houses were usually in the region of £120–150 p.a. for a French male cook, with a slight decrease for an English male cook. Women, meanwhile, earned around £50–60 a year for the same job. Women had only entered the professional kitchen in the seventeenth century, and, despite a steady increase in the number of female cooks, were still regarded as inferior.

The cooks were a disparate group of people, from across Europe and occasionally beyond. They had to be ready for anything, from dealing with the appalling conditions of the Buckingham Palace kitchens in the 1840s, to cooking in a none-too-brilliantly converted stable at Osborne House. Every cook had to be prepared to work in any or all of the Queen's palaces. As with country house staffing conventions, they moved with the family, and only a skeleton staff was left in each palace when it was vacated. However, if they did spend an occasional night without the main staff, they got an extra allowance, board wages, to cover eating expenses. Some cooks would usually be sent on ahead to the next palace to prepare for the descent of the full Household, while others stayed behind to clear up. In later years, when the Household was at the new, private palaces of Osborne and Balmoral, the staff divided entirely, some going with the Queen, and some remaining at Windsor, sending goods out as needed. Edible gifts winged their way across the world, especially at Christmas, while all of the stupendous iced wedding cakes that were produced for the weddings of Victoria's many children, wherever they were held, were baked and decorated at Windsor. Victoria's own wedding cake was made at Buckingham Palace by the then confectionery chef, the impressively named John Chichester Mawditt.

Mawditt had been in the service of the Duke of Clarence, and transferred to the royal Establishment with him when he became William IV. He became head of the confectionery in 1835, remaining until 1850, and his name appeared regularly in the newspapers of the time. Confectionery was a true art form, centred on sugar, and regarded as a separate branch of cookery. Mawditt was lauded for his creations: for the christening of the Prince of Wales in 1842 he produced a christening cake which was,

ornamented round the bottom with a neatly-executed border of the rose, thistle and shamrock. On the sides of the cake were placed, alternately, medallion portraits in silver of Her Majesty and Prince Albert, with the arms of England over them, and the Prince of Wales' feathers with the arms of Wales over them; the whole surmounted by a neat scroll in dead sugar work. Above were three tiers, each environed by smaller scroll work, surmounted by silvered princes' feathers; and on the summit were pedestals supporting sugar figures of Ceres, Fortune, Plenty, Britannia holding the infant

Prince, Clio, the goddess of history, and St David, the titular saint of Wales. In the centre of the group was a representation of the royal font; and several small vases, with flowers, surrounded the figures. The tout ensemble presented an elegant and chaste appearance.

Mawditt also contributed to the dessert course at the dinner which followed, with, 'several pieces of the most exquisitely prepared confectionery … from the profusion of flowers with which they were decorated it seemed as if a gay parterre had suddenly sprung up among the other gay illusions of the scene'.[5] Ornamental – yet theoretically edible – sculpture was a popular element on the *à la Française* dessert table. For Albert's birthday in 1842, Mawditt made two sugarcraft columns, which, 'more resembled elaborately executed pieces of sculpture in marble, than being fashioned from the frail material of sugar'. They came complete with statues, bas-relief representations of battles and military trophies, 'tastefully grouped … in appropriate colours'.[6]

Many of the newspapers of the time had a *Hello*-magazine-like tendency to heap praise on the doings of the royal family. Criticism of Victoria and Albert and, later, their children, for their political choices, was common at various times, but weddings and christenings were rarely attacked. There were telling exceptions, however, and the royal wedding cake was one. Most reports followed a pattern, describing the cake in detail. It was composed of 'the most exquisite compounds of all the rich things with which the most expensive cakes can be composed, mingled and mixed together into delightful harmony by the most elaborate science of the confectioner'. It weighed 300 lb, with a circumference of 3 yards, and on top were foot-high sugar models of Britannia blessing Victoria and Albert, 'dressed somewhat incongruously in the costume of ancient Rome'. The happy couple were surrounded by symbols of fidelity, love and a large number of cupids.[7] So far, so good for Mr Mawditt. *The Morning Post*, however, took a different view, and gave more details. The 'Queen's own cake', intended for the Queen's wedding breakfast, was indeed made by the confectioners at the palace. But there were also a number of others, made by professional confectioners. The most well known firm of confectioners in Britain was Gunter's, on Berkeley Square, and they supplied the cake for the state banquet. *The Post* described it as 'a piece of elaborate architecture built up so proudly as to out-top all other dishes and be the envy of surrounding ornaments'. Gunter's also supplied fourteen cakes to be sent out to friends, relatives, foreign ambassadors and the like, across the world. Another well-known confectioners, Waud's, provided eighteen more. They make Mawditt's efforts sound somewhat lacking: 'There is no gilding or "gingerbread" about any of them – no allegorical nonsense, no chubby cherubs, no colours, no muslin, no silver-leaf, no white mortar-work executed by trowel and hod! All is naturally and delicately fanciful ... [they have] one serious defect – they are too pretty to be eaten!' Amid all this hyperbole, the description of Mawditt's cake is stark: 'as plain as a sugar-loaf in its exterior, so that nobody need feel any hesitation in demolishing it. Its proportions are, indeed, so cheese-like that all the poetic effect of the allegorical figures on the top, and the elegance of Mr Yates' artificial flowers around the sides cannot carry off its clumsiness. But no matter. The shape is orthodox. The wreaths and roses are made to be pulled to pieces and carried off as souvenirs, and the cake itself to be cut to pieces and eaten; and so it shall fulfil its destiny.'[8] Mawditt's skills must have been up to the job in some respects, or he would presumably not have remained in place as long as he did. However, when scrutiny of the kitchens increased in the late 1840s, he was found to be somewhat lacking, and was dismissed in 1850. (He then seems to have gone freelance or set up shop with his nephew, listed with him as a confectioner in Marylebone in the 1861 census.) The papers were obviously being kind, or perhaps the journalists simply didn't get close enough to see the flaws.

The royal kitchens struggled to recruit and retain really top-notch chefs. In the main kitchen, most started low down the ranks and progressed upwards, never really experiencing life outside the decidedly unique atmosphere of the palaces. The confectioners were the consistent exception, as the job was so specialist that it required training elsewhere. They were paid the same as the chief cook, and the position was a rare one in private houses, unless their incumbents were exceedingly well off. Sir John Cowell, the master of the Household from 1866, wrote ruefully to the Queen about the problems of recruitment: 'There are very few houses in which confectioners are kept, so that the large Pastry Cook's Establishments are almost the only places where they can be found.'[9] As a result, they were often poached from Gunter's or one of the other big firms. Confectionery was not perceived as a particularly English talent: the granddaddy of French cuisine, Antonin Carême, had been its most famous practitioner, and the French and

Italians continued to lead the profession. Around half of the male royal confectioners were of French or Italian origin. Mawditt left in November 1850, and the position was vacant for a month until he was replaced by Jules le Blond, a Frenchman, who lasted six years. His replacement, James Hankinson, who'd been the head confectioner at Gunter's, completed his trial period of three months, and wasn't taken on. It was a demanding job. Constant Emilie Pagniez, who started as the second yeoman to the confectionery when Edward Thomas was promoted into Hankinson's place in 1857, made head confectioner before he retired in 1869.[10] He'd been suffering from vertigo and fits during his last year in service, and died in 1871, aged 48, of a cerebral haemorrhage.[11] His replacement, Samuel Ponder, was again from Gunter's, and had almost certainly worked in the kitchens as an extra hand during the visit of the Sultan of the Ottoman Empire a couple of years before. He remained in position until after the Queen's death. Meanwhile, Giuseppe Califano, who was the second yeoman under Pagniez, left shortly after Ponder started. He went on to run his own small shop in Eton, and was renowned for his short temper:

> Califano ... invited the shortest of visits. I have said that Webber made no Neapolitan ices. Califano made all ices well, Neapolitan ices best of all. But, except for the consumption of ices, his was not a shop in which to linger. It was not possible to converse with Califano. He knew very little English, and in the English conversation to which he was accustomed he was always on the look-out for one particular topic. He saw it coming

afar off, and made sudden and obvious preparation. It was a question, and to the best of my belief I never heard it asked; indeed, there were very good reasons for that. Califano was believed to have held at one time a high position in the kitchen at Windsor, and to have vacated the position suddenly. He would not allow this episode in his past life to be the subject of any inquiry, however polished; and it was asserted that if the fateful sentence, 'Cally, why did you get the sack from the Castle?' were ever completed, the questioner immediately found himself being pursued down the street with a carving knife.[12]

Despite the schoolboy inferences, Califano wasn't sacked. He managed ten years in royal service, and received a royal pension, so it seems more likely that he just didn't get on with his new boss, or that he resented being passed over for promotion.

In contrast to all of the goings-on at the top of the confectionery department, from 1839 until 1878 the first assistant to the confectionery was Jane Elgar. Elgar joined the royal kitchens in 1828, when she was seventeen, one of a very small number of maids working in a very male-dominated environment. She outlasted nearly everyone, above and below her in her own section, as well as in the main kitchens, and retired at the age of 67, with a pension, to her native Kent. She had earned £40 a year for nearly her entire time in service: less than a quarter of the salary of the five heads of department she'd worked under during her career.

Jane Elgar was exceptional: her length of service, at 50 years, was long, even by royal standards. The maids were the fastest changing group of people in the kitchens. They tended to leave to get married, or shortly after marriage. Some stayed single, though, and remained in the job, usually with one promotion, for 20 or 30 years. With only two or three maids in any one department, prospects were limited, though it was clearly a job for life, with good behaviour. A pension was automatically awarded after ten years of service, which, in Victorian Britain, was a huge boon and well worth staying for. The criteria were quite clear: 'Every servant who serves in Her Majesty's Household for 10 years, and is incapacitated for further service, is entitled to a pension, and the same at the expiration of their service with any member of the Royal Family, if the servant is trans-ferred at your Majesty's desire, after serving your Majesty for 10 years. If a servant left your Majesty's service in order to better himself ... he would probably not be entitled.'[13] Possible promotion elsewhere would rarely have been worth losing the chance at a pension, especially for a single woman, whose prospects would in any case have been limited by her gender in the male-dominated world of nineteenth-century professional cookery.

The male cooks, on the other hand, could expect steady promotion up the entire kitchen career ladder as long as they stayed healthy and, like the longer-serving maids, many stayed for their entire working life, and retired with good pensions. Both men and woman were usually recruited through existing links. In the 1870s, kitchen maid Mary Kinner was the daughter of one of the royal policemen; fourth master cook George Dessaulles was the son of a page of the presence; and the third master cook, Gottlob Waetzig, was the British-born son of a Swedish bandmaster. Most of the English staff were born in London or the Home Counties, often in the area around St James's Palace, in Windsor, or near Kensington Palace or Hampton Court, and the Scottish kitchen staff hailed from around Balmoral. When Gabriel Tschumi's cousin Louise was trying to get him a job as an apprentice in the 1890s, she was told that, 'all of the apprentices are English lads, recommended by relatives already amongst the Household staff'.[14] The higher-ranking cooks were sometimes appointed from elsewhere, if those below weren't quite ready to be promoted, but they were still found through word of mouth and personal recommendation. Eugene Thion, who started as third master cook in around 1858, came from the establishment of the master of the Household, Colonel Biddulph, who wrote him a reference stating that he was, 'perfectly honest, sober, chaste, intelligent and … a very good cook'. He went on to make the point that although Thion led his kitchens, he was only cooking for ten to twelve people, and was unused to catering for the vast numbers present at the palace. Thion, as with all new staff, underwent a three-month trial before being confirmed in the position. He rose up the ranks: second master cook in 1861, then first master cook and finally chief cook in 1869, a position that he held until 1888.[15] His replacement, Arthur Feltham, had been one of a gang of new starters in the middle of the turmoil of the 1850s reforms. After 30 years in the kitchens, he had worked his way from apprentice to chief cook. He had been surrounded for most of his career by the same people: Charles Jungbleeth, in service from 1847 to the late 1880s, John Mountford (served 1829–80), Gottlob Waetzig (1838–76), George Dessaulles (1838–81), Jane Whiting (1836 to c.1860), Emma

Johnson (1857–77) and Thomas Hollis (1848–91). Most employees stayed for well over the ten years required for their pension, and in many cases clocked up over 30 years in royal service. The lengthy list of pensions, as well as medals awarded for long service, show just how loyal the staff were. Whether they were more devoted to Queen and country, or pensions and a comfortable life, is debatable.

The individuals listed above formed the backbone of the kitchen for the whole of Victoria's reign. They joined in their mid-teens, progressing with predictable regularity up the career ladder, one position at a time, until retiring in their fifties or sixties. The upper staff all seemed to end up in Battersea, living with their families. Wherever they had started on the social scale – and with relatives in royal service it was usually lower middle class – they ended it several rungs higher up, invariably employing a servant of their own. Frequently their surnames appeared elsewhere on the staff lists, as the nepotistic recruitment methods of the royal Household continued for at least another generation. Inevitably, many people also married partners from within the Household: pastry cook Alphonse Gouffé's son married the clerk comptroller William Cullen's daughter, Eliza Sophia, while Arthur Feltham's wife Annie Rawlins was one of the Queen's sewing maids. The whole thing seems rather like a deeply exclusive boarding school, where names are entered at birth, and scholars never leave. A couple of Feltham's cohorts – George Malsch and Alfred Manning – did venture outside for a few years, but returned, and duly clocked up their long service medals in the 1880s.[16] Others left for good, such as Alexander Thévenot, who left 'of his own accord to better himself', in 1860, successfully reintegrating himself into life outside and developing a fairly standard career.[17] Conservatism over serving style and a resistance to culinary change may have originated upstairs, but it was doubtless echoed downstairs, where routine was paramount.

On occasion, outsiders did come in, though they hardly seem to have shaken up the unchanging habits of decades. The pastry department, too, was somewhat apart from the main kitchens. Alphonse Gouffé headed it up for most of Victoria's reign, entering service in 1840, directly as head pastry cook, and staying for 41 years. He had been in the UK less than two years when he got the job, and may have been recruited in part due to family reputation. His father had been a pastry chef in Paris, and his brother, Jules, had trained under Carême, and by the 1840s was rapidly acquiring a European-wide fame. In the 1870s, Jules wrote a number of very well received cookery books, including the weighty *Royal Cookery Book*, which Alphonse translated into English. *The Spectator* commented on it that,

> in the advice to beginners with which the author commences his course of instruction, he tells the incipient pastrycook what qualities he must bring with him in order to insure success; they are qualities which would probably make him the master of any other art which he might be desirous to acquire – quickness, intelligence, a lively and inventive fancy, a love of study, patience, perseverance, and artistic feeling. Armed with these requisites, he is recommended to have an elementary knowledge of drawing, sculpture, and architecture, and to devote eight or ten years to the

practical study of pastry! Who would have thought that all this was needful, in order fitly to provide baked meats even for the tables of kings?[18]

He was probably the closest to a celebrity that the royal kitchens ever employed, apart from the properly famous Charles Elmé Francatelli, who cashed in on his year-long sojourn as chief cook for the rest of his life, without ever quite mentioning its rather unfortunate end.

Francatelli was recruited in 1840, recommended by the then Lord Steward. At the time, he was cook at Crockford's, a well-known gentleman's club that prided itself on employing the best chefs in Britain. They were almost always French. Francatelli was an exception: he was of Italian extraction, but thoroughly British himself. He had trained under Carême, which immediately marked him out as special in the eyes of the culinary establishment. The top of the kitchen hierarchy was undergoing what, for the royal kitchens, counted as seismic change at the time, as the effects of the new regime began to be felt, and reorganisation got underway even before Prince Albert really got his teeth into it all. Several new men came in to fill the top two or three positions, before hastily leaving again. One of them was Louis Chevassot, whose entry onto the payroll on 20 June, the date of Victoria's accession, suggests that he was probably the cook to the Kents at Kensington, being found a position as the two households amalgamated. First master cook when Francatelli started, he left three months later. The new chef caused problems. He had a fierce temper, as well as an ego, which he presumably felt was entirely justified, given his fame. He left at the end of December 1841 (though was paid until March 1842). There is no record as to whether he left voluntarily or was dismissed. However, several newspapers carried the same report, of a 'fracas at Buckingham Palace'. Dramatic stuff: 'Francatelli ... has kept his department in continual broils, which have been the cause of many dismissals and numerous complaints to the Lord Steward. On Monday last Mr Francatelli took the opportunity of insulting Mr Norton [the Clerk Comptroller] in the presence of all the Pages and about forty others, when high words ensued, which ended in a policeman being set to take Francatelli into custody, but he managed to make his escape before the officer arrived. The result of the investigation was the suspension of Francatelli until the matter shall be laid before her Majesty and Prince Albert, when there is no doubt that measures will be adopted to prevent a recurrence of such disgraceful proceedings.'[19] Disgraced he might have been, but Crockford's welcomed him back with open arms and a massive salary increase. Indeed, given that he was probably earning in excess of £1,000 there, versus the standard £250 at the palace, there were definite benefits to leaving. And taking into account the unreformed, sewage-laden state of the Buckingham Palace kitchens, and the general administrative mess within the royal Establishment at the time, it becomes quite easy to sympathise with his position. He remained within the world of gentleman's clubs and hotels for the rest of his life, attracting lavish praise as well as complaints about his arrogance, until his death in 1876. He published four cookery books, each advertised as being by a former chief cook to Her Majesty, and by his death was known both as 'the greatest artist who is catering, at this present writing, for the gourmets of London', and as a man who 'truffled his dishes not wisely but too well'.[20]

Not everyone got on in the royal kitchens. The early Establishment lists show that dismissals were not infrequent, though, as with Francatelli, they don't give reasons why. After Albert's death in the 1860s Victoria became more directly involved with the lives of her servants. She had always seen them as individuals: her unedited journal entries often named her dressers, and showed her interactions with them and her other servants. Her youngest daughter, Beatrice, who went through all of the entries before allowing them to be seen, removed many of these references, giving the impression that her mother rarely gave any thought to anyone below an aristocratic level. Nothing could be further from the truth. In the 1860s, James Penny, one of the staff attached to the steward's room, where the upper servants dined, was caught, 'carrying provisions out of the house in considerable quantity'. Colonel Biddulph, the master of the Household, recommended he be dismissed. The Queen wrote back, terribly worried, and expressing the view that the man was elderly (he was in his fifties); that no one knew the circumstances; that he might be in dire need, or ill. The affair escalated. Despite Biddulph's plea that, 'this old servant has abused your Majesty's kindness', Penny was listed as receiving the Queen's Bounty in the 1870s.[21] The Queen evidently won. Indeed, Victoria seems to have been seen as something of a soft touch. It became quite difficult to get sacked, and not simply 'retired'. Even drunkenness didn't always do it – and it wasn't an uncommon problem. There was an 'intemperate' confectioner in the 1860s, who did get dismissed, as did George Ward, the fourth master cook in 1860 ('dismissed for drunkenness').[22] However, by the late 1860s, it was more of a grey area. One of the cellar men, Robert Albertanson, was already seen as unfit for any promotion in 1867, but by 1868 he had reached the point of no return. Previously, he may well have simply been sacked, but now the Queen, 'wished him long ago to be moved from a place which led him into temptation, but she thinks he ought <u>not</u> to be <u>entirely</u> dismissed – he could not well be appointed to any place of <u>trust</u>, but there are small places, comparative sinecures, to which he might surely be appointed, and another trial given to him, without turning him <u>entirely</u> off with so small a retirement, that he would almost starve ... Barker the Gentleman Porter was removed for similar offences and has been perfectly steady ever since. R. Albertanson has a very nice wife and for the sake of her and his family the Queen would wish some small place to be found for him.'[23]

Working in the kitchens certainly took its toll on the health of its inhabitants. While many reached a ripe old age, others dropped dead at their posts. Mary Timms, an assistant in the confectionery, joined the kitchens in 1859 and died in service in 1872, aged 44. Her death certificate gave cause of death as albuminuria and apoplexy: kidney disease, often associated with diabetes and extremely painful, terminating in a stroke. Jane Whiting, meanwhile, a kitchen maid from 1836, was listed as a recipient of the Queen's Bounty for sick or impoverished staff in 1861–62, before retiring in 1862. Meanwhile, Thomas Hall was taken on as a roasting cook in 1875 and was dead by the end of the year. John Kraufslach, one of the 1850s intake of apprentices, died of heart disease in 1880.[24] Some positions were unhealthier than others: the roasting cooks were in front of the fire for most of the day, and in 1872 the first scourer was passed over for promotion to the lower ranks of roasting in recognition that, at 50, the heat of the fire would be too much for him (he was given a salary increase of £20 to compensate).[25] The master cooks were at risk as well. They were most likely to spend time preparing delicate French-style sauces over badly ventilated charcoal chafing stoves. Respiratory failure due to carbon monoxide inhalation was a common problem among cooks, especially those in upper-class kitchens, which demanded lots of French sauces cooked on a charcoal stove, as were more generalised ailments such as fallen arches due to hard stone floors, and joint problems due to the frequently repetitive and very physical graft. With fire being one of the biggest killers of the period – especially for women, where it was second only to childbirth – the risks of the kitchen were manifest. But there were perks, as well. Apart from reasonable salaries, guaranteed pensions and, by the late 1860s, a tolerance of behaviour that would lead to dismissal elsewhere, the men were allowed to grow facial hair. Gabriel Tschumi commented, 'though liveried servants had to be clean-shaven, it was not thought necessary to extend this rule to cover the chefs and cooks on the staff. As a result, all those when I joined sported magnificent moustaches and there were even one or two small beards. There was a certain amount of bitterness on the part of the liveried servants who occasionally came to the kitchens that they were not allowed to follow the fashion of the time for whiskers.'[26] Photographs taken of some of the senior staff in the 1860s demonstrate a certain dedication to the growing of sideburns. Whether this made up for carbon monoxide poisoning is a moot point.

One of the other benefits of long service was access to the Royal Bounty, a system of welfare provision that was in place from 1782 until 2002, and which was designed for emergency aid in cases of extreme need. As with Jane Whiting, extraordinary payments were made to cover illness. In addition, regular pensions were paid from it, to dependants of dead staff members who could not work, and would otherwise be destitute. The records are bald and unsparing: Ann Bonmar, the 74-year-old widow of one of the grooms of the wine cellar, was described as, 'out of health for ten years, without any employment. Her last husband (Bonmar) left her nothing but debts, which she paid. Has two sons by her former husband (Stokes), one deranged in an asylum, the other a surgeon.' Caroline Barnard, widow of one of the grooms of the kitchen, was in similar circumstances, 'in 70th year – crippled in hands by rheumatism – has one child (26) afflicted with fits, entirely dependent upon her. No ... income beyond the Bounty.'[27] The Bounty also paid out to a variety of other individuals, such as struggling artists, religious refugees and a number of others. In the days before a government-sponsored welfare state, one of the duties of large houses was to provide some means of support for the poor of each dependent parish. Charitable endeavours and volunteer work were a vital part of the lives of upper- and middle-class women in particular, both in rural and urban areas. Edible alms were part of the way in which leftovers were managed, but food wouldn't pay the rent. The royal Household led by example, therefore, not only with the distribution of leftovers, but also, as here, with direct financial help.

Dropping dead while performing a job was a concern, especially when it occurred in public. In 1869, after two footmen had died while on duty, a hurried memo was sent round instructing that bodies shouldn't be taken to a hospital or workhouse, but to the palace. This was deemed especially necessary for upper servants, male and female, and footmen, who would 'be sure to be recognised'.[28] After 1861 Victoria developed a morbid fascination with death, and became something of a death rites junkie. She was able to indulge herself to a large extent with a series of deaths among her family and attendants in the 1870s, throwing herself almost gleefully into mourning, and describing herself as 'never depressed at a funeral'.[29] Gatecrashing her servants' funerals was a step too far, but she wrote to her officials regarding the arrangements being made for them, and kept memorial cards, which can occasionally be found stashed away within the archives. When a housemaid died while the Household was on holiday in Grasse in 1891, she organised, 'a sort of funeral service in the Dining Room, the coffin in our midst not even screwed down'. Marie Mallet, one of her ladies-in-waiting, commented, 'I admire the Queen for taking such a lively interest in her servants, but it is overdone in this sort of way and it is very trying for the Household.'[30] She also sometimes 'happened upon' services, such as this one, in 1878: 'Her Majesty and Princess Beatrice walked and drove this morning ... and witnessed the funeral pass of Her Majesty's much-regretted head gamekeeper, Mr Land, who had been seven years in the Queen's service.'[31] It was probably a little disconcerting for his relatives.

At times it seems that Victoria spent more time worrying about her servants, and harassing the master of the Household, than she did on her official duties. Food and dining routines particularly concerned her, and there was a flurry of correspondence in late 1865, when the Queen became concerned about the quality of the food in the steward's room and servants' hall. Under pressure from above Colonel Biddulph investigated, supplying a list of dinners which shows how well the servants ate. The upper servants' meal was equivalent to a reasonable middle-class dinner in a domestic context: soup, roast beef, saddle of mutton, mutton cutlets, French beans, potatoes, omelettes, tarts and puddings, cheese, dessert.[32] Meanwhile, the hundreds of lower servants ate significantly better than the vast majority of the working-class population. Every day they ate meat, usually mutton or beef, both boiled and roasted, and every day they had 'potatoes and other vegetables'. On Sundays they also had plum puddings. His conclusion was that, 'the food is plain, but is varied almost as much as plain fare can be, the only thing which appears not to be always as good as it might be is the potatoes, and these are difficult to get good'.[33] Debate evidently ensued, with the Queen lobbying for the addition of soup to the menu. Eventually, more puddings were added, three times a week. The old pewter plates that the servants had been eating off were replaced with crockery at the same time, marked with the names of the space (servants' hall, coffee room etc.) in which they were to be used.

Concerns about below stairs dining didn't go away, however, and in early 1868 Biddulph's replacement, Sir John Cowell, was exchanging equally exasperated letters with his

monarch about dining times and whether the servants had
to wait for their meals. He pointed out that those upper servants who habitually consumed leftovers from the
Household table for their supper would always be fine: 'The
supper is placed upon the table within five minutes before or
after 9.30. But as this must always depend upon the time that
your majesty's dinner is over (since the dishes have to be
taken from the dining room to the Steward's Room), those
who wait at your majesty's dinner are never likely to be late
at the supper & in fact are there as soon as it is upon the table
properly arranged.'[34] A more serious and longer running
furore blew up in March 1868, when the Queen got wind of
the bewilderingly complicated system of seating at dinner,
and immediately took umbrage on her personal attendants'
behalf. 'The Queen wishes that <u>all new</u> pages of the back-
stairs, should <u>not sit above</u> her <u>2 personal</u> and confidential
servants, Lohlein and Brown, at meals, but either in the first
place, on the <u>opposite side</u>, or <u>below</u> them on the same side
… it is would not be <u>proper</u> or <u>becoming</u> that [they] should
go over the heads of these <u>confidential</u> servants, who are
constantly in <u>personal</u> attendance on the sovereign, and in
far more important positions than any of the pages. In this
way they will be placed in a similar position to the Queen's
Dressers, which is what they should be.'[35] This one rumbled
on and on. In 1883 the personal servants were finally granted
a room in which to eat separately (though with the same
wine allowance as men in the main steward's room).

Spats over precedence and the division of the Establishment into ever-decreasing groups for dining reflected a
wider obsession with who did what and whether that made
them more important than others. The cooks were, to a

large extent, isolated from the rest of the servants, for their tasks were not easily stopped for meals, and, unlike most of the others, they were physically confined within a clearly defined set of rooms. Within the kitchen staff, there were two theoretical dining options: with the main body of the servants in the servants' hall, and with the senior staff in the steward's room. In practice, some cooks always remained in the kitchen, keeping an eye on the fires and any stocks or other concoctions which were in progress, and the kitchen maids usually ate separately, again needing to be on hand and flexible depending on what was cooking. In December 1837, 118 people ate in the servants' hall, 54 in the steward's room, with 10 people remaining in the kitchen, and 15 maids eating somewhere else.[36]

The rigid hierarchy extended into the kitchens themselves and dictated the dishes upon which every cook worked. The apprentices circulated between the master cooks, the pastry and the confectionery, but once qualified, they would have found themselves part of a system set up to emphasise status, arguably at the expense of efficiency. The system was based on that which would have been found in any establishment serving *à la Française*. Because it relied on many different items being ready at the same time, each cook worked exclusively on one or two complete dishes. In the Royal Archive is an undated menu for a Household dinner, probably from the mid-1870s.[37] Unusually, not only does it list the dishes, but also who was responsible for each, and is almost certainly an example of the menu that the master of the Household used to keep by him at dinner, making notes on the quality of the meal and who had done well that day.[38] Thion, then chief cook or just below, cooked the most prestigious dishes, the entrées, while Thomas Hollis, first yeoman, dealt with soups, and Malsch, first assistant, with the next level down. William Eaton, probably the second roasting cook at the time, covered off the roasts. The chief cook would have prepared only the most difficult items, while also 'passing' everything made by the rest of his staff, especially the master cooks and yeomen working on the high-status dishes. The kitchen maids were almost certainly responsible for the general servants' food, while the assistant cooks, just above them, looked after the fare for the steward's room, as well as the occasional more elevated dish. This worked very well most of the time. On big occasions, though, extra staff, both men and women, were taken on, especially in the pastry and confectionery.

With the advent of service *à la Russe*, this set-up, which was replicated on a smaller scale in stately homes across the country, started to change. The modern-day brigade system was established at the end of the nineteenth century, and is usually attributed to Auguste Escoffier, the early twentieth-century equivalent to the hallowed Carême, although it was to a large extent just a development of existing structures. Under the new system, the cooks were divided into teams, sometimes of just one man each, responsible for different types of dishes. There would be a fish cook, an entrée cook, a sauce specialist and so on. Lower-ranking chefs would put together basic preparations to be passed up the chain and be made part of other dishes, rather than just preparing meals for servants. This change, which was adopted in most of the large hotels, if not in country houses, which often resisted *à la Russe* as ferociously as did the Queen, seems to have bypassed the royal kitchens. Indeed, despite the length of

Victoria's reign, very little changed in the kitchens. The apprenticeship scheme was tweaked: from the 1870s the Queen paid the fees, rather than parents. Some roles were renamed. A new chief cook, Louis Chevriot, started in 1897, the first to be brought in from outside since the ill-fated experiment with Francatelli over 50 years previously. However, the first master cook, his immediate subordinate, was George Malsch, who had started as an apprentice nearly 40 years earlier, and whose son Frederick was now an apprentice in his turn.

At the end of the period a certain sloppiness set in. By the autumn of 1900, it was apparent that Victoria's long reign was drawing to an end, and, that with it, the closed system of the kitchen would be ripped apart. A new monarch was waiting, with his own cook, and his own preferences for food. Footmen now openly smelt of booze, while the cooks gave every impression of merely going through the motions while the Queen's life ebbed away. It had been 64 years since the last regime change, and 60 since the last attempts at kitchen reform. The men and women now slaving over hot stoves were a completely different crew to those who had worn dents in the floor in 1837, and, as the new century began, their futures were, for the first time, uncertain.

6
Private palaces

When Victoria married Albert in February 1840, she was deeply in lust. She had been secluded from the outside world, especially eligible men, and carefully groomed to prefer Albert above all others, but she was nevertheless aware of male attractions. As soon as she was married she was free to discover the joys of sex, and, like so much in the young Queen's life, she did so enthusiastically. The journal entries for her wedding day and the morning after bubble over with joy, despite the nervous headache she suffered in the evening after the ceremony. Indeed, the first lines of the morning after have more than a hint of gloating about them: 'When day dawned (for we did not sleep much) and I beheld that beautiful angelic face by my side, it was more than I can express! He does look so beautiful in his shirt only, with his beautiful throat seen.'[1] Love, however,

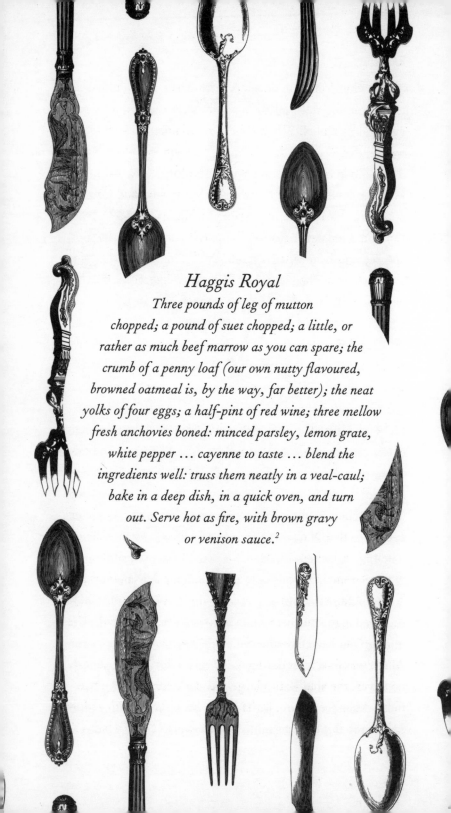

Haggis Royal

*Three pounds of leg of mutton
chopped; a pound of suet chopped; a little, or
rather as much beef marrow as you can spare; the
crumb of a penny loaf (our own nutty flavoured,
browned oatmeal is, by the way, far better); the neat
yolks of four eggs; a half-pint of red wine; three mellow
fresh anchovies boned: minced parsley, lemon grate,
white pepper ... cayenne to taste ... blend the
ingredients well: truss them neatly in a veal-caul;
bake in a deep dish, in a quick oven, and turn
out. Serve hot as fire, with brown gravy
or venison sauce.[2]*

took a while longer to develop. As she had made quite clear right from the start, Victoria was fiercely determined to do everything 'alone'. When Albert complained that their long weekend in Windsor was hardly a honeymoon, she admonished him in no uncertain terms: 'You forget, my love, that I am the sovereign, and that business can stop and wait for nothing ... it is quite impossible for me to be absent from London. I am never easy a moment, if I am not on the spot, and see and hear what is going on.'[3] The idea that Albert would share her bed was enthusiastically embraced, but that he should in any way share her power was very far from being acceptable. Albert, who was every inch the Victorian male, and who had married Victoria conscious, but by no means accepting, that he would be in an anomalous position, was not particularly enamoured with this situation. He set out to change it, and, though the marriage was always volatile, and his path to being Victoria's inseparable business companion as well as lover was by no means easy, he did, eventually, achieve his desires.

Albert was three months younger than Victoria. They had been delivered by the same female doctor and were first cousins – the Duchess of Kent was Albert's father's sister. They both lacked a parent for most of their childhoods, with the remaining one being less than ideal, as parents go. Albert's father wasn't a bully, but rather a constantly indebted egocentric and an inveterate skirt-chaser. His mother had been exiled from court and her children when Albert was five, after daring to have an affair herself. There, however, the similarities largely ended. Albert was an aesthete. As a second son, he had been brought up with a view to his probable marriage into British royalty, with a fallback position being marriage into somewhere else's royalty. The gaucheness that he exhibited on his first visit to London in 1836 had been firmly educated out of him in preparation, but he was hardly an enthusiastic socialite. He could dance, and was trilingual, as was Victoria (French was de rigueur for the upper classes, with German and English, unsurprisingly, being their other languages), but he was quiet and studious. He was an avid self-educator, loved art, architecture and, an interest he shared with his bride, adored music. He was not, however, a fan of food. When he was in Italy, his routine was to rise at 6 a.m., have a light breakfast, study, and dine at the unfashionable hour of 2 p.m., 'a simple dinner, which he hurried as much as possible', saying that, 'eating was a waste of time'. He'd play music, sing, go walking, have a light supper at 7 p.m. and be in bed by 9 p.m. This was in 1838, when Victoria was revelling in going to bed, exhausted, at 2 a.m. after dancing and eating all night.[4] The Queen of Great Britain was a brilliant catch for him, a two-bit noble from a minor German duchy, and a lack of obvious compatibility was not an obstacle. He was well aware of the differences between them, writing after his engagement that, 'I think I shall be very happy, for Victoria possesses all the qualities which make a home happy, and seems to be attached to me with her whole heart. My future lot is high and brilliant, but also plentifully strewn with thorns. Struggles will not be wanting.'[5] Marriages among royalty were rarely love matches, and there were plenty of examples, his own parents among them, of things going very badly wrong. But there were also plenty of good examples, and of marriages where initial ambivalence turned to genuine mutual love and respect. That this was the case for Albert and Victoria is well known, although that is not to say that it was as harmonious in reality as it was in Victoria's memory after he was dead. There's no doubt that Albert saw power as his due as a husband, and a highly educated man, and that he was extremely frustrated by Victoria when they were first married. He wrote angry letters, complaining that he had no role, and felt emasculated. He had blazing rows with Victoria, which usually culminated in her storming off in tears, and his writing notes to her, in much the same way that her mother had set out to manipulate her as a teen. Both parties had their faults, and they both behaved appallingly at times, but they were only in their mid-twenties, had barely spent any time together before their marriage, and neither had any examples of functional relationships from which to work.

By 1842, she and Albert had largely ironed out their early differences. Lehzen had gone, and could no longer express her jealousy of the Prince by making mischief. Melbourne was out, and the Queen had realised that she would have no real friends except her husband. Meanwhile, two pregnancies had forced her to delegate, and Albert had proven himself not only willing but also very able to aid her. While she remained confined after each birth, ill, irritated and 'suffering so from lowness',[6] he represented her at council meetings, read documents and worked out ways to negotiate, by carefully worded letters, thorny issues connected to European and domestic politics. He could not fully deputise for her at public appearances, but he did slowly manage to carve out a niche for himself as a public figure, mainly connected to agricultural reform and the promotion of trade. The letters that the couple exchanged when

Albert was away are genuinely tender and, for all that he clearly did set out, quite deliberately, to create the position he felt was due to him, there is little doubt that they were deeply in love. There are, to the modern eye, distasteful elements, however. Victoria later claimed that Albert had 'tamed' her, and, after his death, she looked back on her early years on the throne with mild horror. In the authorised biography of the Prince, written under the guiding influence of the Queen when she was desperately memorialising and deifying Albert in the 1860s, her feelings are made clear: 'It will be seen that those late hours in the morning, of which the Queen speaks with such regret, were gradually improved under the influence of the Prince – an influence which was further evident in the judicious and well-regulated division of the hours and occupations of the day.'[7] Whether the natural ebullience of a teenager just freed of a restrictive upbringing needed to be so drastically improved was not something she was willing to consider. After Albert's death, Victoria was desperate to emphasise her self-abasement with regards her husband. While she was notoriously stubborn, it took her a long time to regain confidence in her own abilities, and she used her gender, and the supposed weakness of women, as an excuse for her seclusion in a way which showed how far removed she was now from her younger self. Immediately after his death she wrote that without him she, 'did nothing, moved not a finger, arranged not a print or photograph, didn't put on a gown or a bonnet if he didn't approve it'.[8] If this was true, it would not only be a terrible slur on his taste, as she had notoriously little dress sense, but also a damning indictment of their relationship, which has usually been seen as relatively balanced. (Indeed, her dependence would be worryingly close to some of the examples given as part of the new psychological abuse law, passed in 2016.) However, she wrote this when she was in the first paroxysm of grief in 1861, and was certainly exaggerating. Albert, unlike Victoria, did not keep a journal, and wasn't as given to from-the-heart outpourings in his letters. This means that any view of their relationship will always be seen mainly from the point of view of the heart-broken widow, desperate to emphasise how lost she was without him. They still had ferocious rows right up to his death, and in the late 1850s she complained regularly that she didn't see enough of him as he was always working: this is hardly a picture of a man constantly on hand to disapprove of hat choices.

Victoria's relationship with food was affected by her marriage. When she first acceded as Queen, she revelled in it, making up for lost time from her childhood. At times of stress, she over-ate, piling on the pounds very quickly and, with the royal kitchens entirely at her disposal, she was never short of supplies. Yet she was not at all overweight at her marriage. She was described as plump, and by the standards of the time, with malnutrition rife, she was not thin, but her surviving gowns, designed to go over corsets, indicate that she easily achieved the desirable figure of the time until well into her forties. Her weight fluctuated: 8 stone 11 pounds in 1838, dropping to a proudly noted 7 stone 2 just before her marriage in 1839.[9] (To put it into modern and rather meaningless perspective, this makes her BMI at that point 18.8, which is almost underweight.[10])

Albert wasn't fond of the pomp of court dining, and throughout the marriage, relatively light and private meals served separately from the main Household were held whenever practical. He struggled with the level of scrutiny: Victoria may have increasingly found her husband to be perfect, but the British press, and indeed the Household, were less convinced. Lady Lyttelton, who headed up the nursery in the 1840s, veered between thinking him humourless and stiff, and finding his affection and love for the Queen and his children charming, and his conversation learned and interesting. She exposed the disparity in the royal relationship, even while she picked out amusing incidents to relate to her family: 'The Prince advised her (on her saying, like a good child, "what <u>am</u> I to do another time?") to behave like an opera dancer after a pirouette, and always shew her teeth in a fixed smile. Of course, he accompanied the advice with an immense pirouette and prodigious grin of his own, such as few people could perform just after dinner, ending on one foot and t'other in the air.'[11] The press, meanwhile, had drawn its own conclusions, and the public, insofar as opinion was reflected by the popular newspapers of the time, were not big Prince Albert fans. Yet another German, yet another relation. When the engagement was announced, one satirical verse that did the rounds read:

> He comes the bridegroom of Victoria's choice,
> The nominee of Lehzen's vulgar voice;
> He comes to take 'for better or for worse'
> England's fat Queen and England's fatter purse.[12]

Public opinion didn't really change until the huge success of the Great Exhibition, which Albert largely masterminded, and even then there was always a background of negative feeling towards him. Victoria grew increasingly defensive, and anti-press, and, with the growing aversion to London which the couple were developing, it's not surprising that they spent more and more time at Windsor. Smelly drains and unending internal wrangling followed them wherever they went, though, and, inspired after a visit to France in 1843, they finally decided to strike out on their own.[13]

The first of the independent royal residences was Osborne House, on the Isle of Wight. In January 1844, Victoria wrote to Uncle Leopold, 'Every year I feel less and less desire for the so-called "worldly pleasures", and if it were not my duty to give receptions and banquets, I should like to retire to the country with my husband and children.'[14] By the end of the year they were in the middle of buying Osborne, and by the middle of the next, rebuilding it. The estate was ideally positioned, at around three hours from London (if you happened to possess private stations at both ends and guaranteed transport links, as did the Queen: it was a longer journey for those not travelling with her, who had to use public transport). Three hours was a pretty established distance for royal retreats: the same approximate distance outside London that Hampton Court had been in the sixteenth century, for example. However, the existing house was a fairly generic Georgian box, with limited service facilities and nowhere near enough rooms for even a much-reduced royal Establishment. The kitchens were so under-equipped that the pastry cooks had to make use of the ovens at Wheeler's bakery in East Cowes, paying for the privilege ('8 days' use of oven, fuel and attendance' is recorded in March 1854), in the same way that a working-class family with limited domestic facilities would pay for space in their local baker's oven.[15] The couple owned Osborne themselves, and were free of government restraints, so when they decided to rip it down and start again, work progressed much more quickly than anything publicly funded. By autumn 1846 the new house was ready, and they moved in. Albert had played a large role in designing it, working with Thomas Cubitt, whom he later also used as the master builder at Buckingham Palace. For the Prince, it was a much-needed chance to do something tangible, and put some of his many ideas about architecture and design into practice. Inevitably, some people criticised it, as much because of the Prince's involvement as because it was badly designed, but it set up a new and much-copied architectural style, especially on the island itself, and others, including the Queen, loved it.

Osborne was always intended to be low-key, a family home, not at all set up for state entertaining. Yet, despite being enthusiastically embraced by later generations as a sort of middle-class Queen, Victoria remained entirely upper class, and never relaxed her work ethic or forgot that she was the monarch of an ever-expanding empire. The house was designed as a rather brilliant compromise: a central pavilion which was a cosy, family home, by the standards of the filthy rich with many servants; and a double-winged adjoining block which was essentially a grand hotel, and stabled all of the various royal-hangers-on, and some of the wider Establishment. Gentlemen attendants were lodged in Barton Manor, an entirely independent house a few minutes away, and which was renovated at the same time that Osborne was rebuilt. The servants,

meanwhile, slept everywhere. There were bedrooms scattered around the main living quarters for housemaids and
personal servants, with further provision for the maids
above the remodelled service wing. A lot of the male servants, including the cooks, lived out of the house, spread
across various outbuildings and cottages and coming to
and from the house in carts and carriages depending on
their status. In 1850 Albert oversaw the construction of a
new dormitory block, designed specifically for the male
servants, with extra provision for the various valets waiting
on members of the Household. It was extended in the
1880s, to provide separate accommodation for the newly
arrived Indian servants. In the 1890s a further, smaller
block was added for female servants, mainly to accommodate the household of Princess Beatrice and her family. It
remained rather ramshackle: servants had no means of
accessing the main house except by dashing through the
not infrequent rain. Covered passageways to the dormito-
ries weren't provided until the 1890s. Even for more senior
servants in the main house, conditions were noticeably different to those in the main palaces: 'As space is in general
limited here, we have very small rooms. The beds are not
very big either, and thus a bigger one had to be arranged
for me, so that I can lie full length.'[16] On the other hand,
it didn't smell of urine like Buckingham Palace, and it
wasn't bitterly cold like Windsor: 'Our first night in the
new house is well past. Nobody caught cold or smelt paint,
and it was a most amusing event the coming here. Everything in the house is quite new, and the dining room looked
very handsome. The windows, lighted by the brilliant
lamps in the room, must have been seen far out to sea.

After dinner we rose to drink the Queen's and Prince's health as a housewarming.'[17]

Dinners at the new house were deliberately less elaborate than at the official residences. The chief cook didn't habitually accompany the Household, remaining in London. Rooms were provided in the new dormitory for three master cooks, a pastry cook, an indeterminate number of roasting cooks (probably two), and up to four apprentices. That a much-reduced cooking corps was the norm can be confirmed by the 1861 census, as although the royal family was in residence, only seven cooks were listed as being present: two master cooks, two assistants, the pastry cook and two apprentices. There were also two kitchen maids and two scourers, or scullery men. The chief cook at the time, Jean Aberlin, was ensconced with his children – and own servant – back in his St James's apartments. The rest of the staff also remained in London, including, on this particular night, the roasting cooks, who were at home with their families. Indeed, the first roasting cook, Edwin Godfrey, and the first assistant cook, Charles Watson, were taking advantage of the Queen's absence from London to have a get-together. There was clearly pressure on the clerk comptroller to keep the numbers to a minimum: in the 1870s, the then comptroller, William Cullen, wrote to the master of the Household to tell him that the number of cooks at Osborne could be reduced, but that it would be rather unfair on the apprentices, as they needed to learn.[18] In the 1860s eleven cooks went off to Osborne, rising to sixteen in the 1880s and 1890s: still far short of the full contingent.[19]

The kitchens in which the cooks worked were also far short of what was provided at Windsor and, working conditions aside, at Buckingham Palace. The kitchens in the original Osborne had been under the house, so when it was demolished, they went too. New kitchens were, therefore, a matter of some urgency, and in 1845 a new set of rooms were wrapped around the existing stables and brewhouse. The stables formed three sides of a rectangle, with the west side open and a paved yard in the middle. The new kitchens went in on the north range, stretching along the long outside wall of the stables. North-facing kitchens were common, as it helped to keep them cool. There were three main rooms: a kitchen, a scullery and a separate roasting kitchen, which was lit from above. There was also a confectionery, cook's room, larder and game larder, all of which had separate entrances and were accessed from an exterior corridor that ran alongside them. It had a roof, on ornate iron columns, but was still a draughty and occasionally damp way to access the rooms. The same somewhat half-hearted solution was applied to the short distance between the kitchen block and the main house.[20] These initial rooms were deeply unsatisfactory: there was no decent storage space, the kitchen was tiny, there was no outside access to the scullery, and the juxtaposition of horses and food preparation was not ideal. In 1861, therefore, the stables were resited completely. The former brewhouse and all of the horseboxes on the north side of the now empty block were converted into kitchen offices: a new scullery, larders and a cooks' sitting room. The kitchen could now be expanded into the former scullery space, and, even more excitingly, an internal corridor was built to access the confectionery and meat larders (the outside doors were replaced with windows). At the same time, a huge new servants' hall was installed in the south

wing, with a separate scullery and a room for the upper servants to eat in. Upstairs, the hayloft was converted into
bedrooms, and at some stage a servants' smoking room was
added. The outside loos were replaced at around the same
time, moving indoors. They still survive and are rather luxurious Doulton Waverley porcelain toilets with generous
mahogany seats. Water closets were by no means rare in
country houses, though their provision and quality could be
decidedly erratic, depending on their owners, but the majority of the country still relied on chamber pots or earth
closets with fixed benches, so this was pretty high life below
stairs.

Conditions were still not ideal for cooking the kind of
high-end food expected by the royal Household, but, with
no big occasions to cater for, it was manageable. There was
almost certainly no proper pastry room, and the pastry cook
had to make do with a marble slab set into a decidedly cosy
niche which doubled as a short corridor leading from the
main kitchen to the roasting kitchen, but the cooking facilities were new and, after 1861, more modern than those at
either of the official residences. The main kitchen had coal-
fired ovens when it was built, but these were replaced in the
1861 revamp with gas ovens, which had become established
– but not widely installed – in the 1840s. In a remarkable
move, the charcoal chafing stoves were replaced with gas
hobs, and gas lighting was also installed in all of the detached
buildings. The supply was always problematic, however,
and when the royal family was in residence, the surrounding
neighbourhood found that their own lighting suffered. As
with so many below stairs aggravations, it took years of
letters and complaints to eventually find a solution: the pipes

were enlarged in the 1870s, and new stoves installed, with an entirely new gas main, all to no avail. In 1880 the latest round of letters to the East Cowes Gas Company claimed that the gas 'has caused constant complaints for many years by the Queen's principal cooks', and that they were forced regularly to, 'fly to extemporised measures to prevent the spoiling of the Queen's dinner'.[21] Another new gas main was installed in 1880 in response. Osborne was the only palace which kept pace with the times in cooking technology terms, though the new was adopted slowly and piecemeal, and the old was retained if it did a good job. In around 1874 the kitchens were immortalised in a set of photographs which are almost a visual metaphor for the whole period, and clearly show the juxtaposition of changing Victorian culinary technology: knobs on the gas hobs, a coal shovel by the range. The works accounts tell a similar tale, with boiling coppers in the scullery sitting side by side with potato-steaming equipment and game-singeing apparatus.

On a day-to-day basis, the kitchens were able to provide all of the required meals: the Queen's breakfast, luncheon and dinner; the Household meals; separate provision for anyone leaving early or just arrived; the main servants' hall; steward's room and the same plethora of different groups that characterised eating at the other palaces. They were not, however, able to deal with large-scale events. The annual local fêtes, held to celebrate Prince Albert's birthday or, by the end of the century, harvest festivals (and two Jubilees), were catered for by local hotels. Cakes and other confectionery produce, including Princess Beatrice's wedding cake in 1885, were sent over from the kitchens at Windsor. People still ate all over the place, despite the spanking new servants' hall (there was a second servants' hall over in the new stable block as well, presumably for the outdoor servants). Status was as strictly maintained at Osborne as anywhere else: the Queen's table-deckers accompanied her to ensure that her table and sideboard were properly and beautifully laid out. They had their own service room in the basement of the pavilion, below the royal dining room, and slept in the men's dormitory along with the cooks. The various dining rooms helped to enforce status through their decor and tableware. The royal dining room was hung with family portraits and glittered with silver and fine porcelain, while the Household dining room had neutral landscapes upon the wall, very much the mark of the middle-class dining room in a broader social context: portraits were generally reserved for those with family members who had been rich enough to commission them, and elevated enough for their descendants to want to acknowledge them. Meanwhile the servants' hall had long, communal tables with white, plain tablecloths laid with old-fashioned horn beakers and basic cutlery, and flanked by plain wooden benches, just in case anyone forgot where they were in the Establishment hierarchy.

The royal couple adored Osborne, furnishing it with their own furniture, and according to their own tastes (which ran largely to marble sculptures of bits of children and rather lavish celebrations of human nudity). They settled into a regular pattern of visits: a short break in March or April, another in May, a longer summer holiday in July, and a pre-Christmas jolly in November or early December.[22] The Household tolerated it, in the main, though there were grumbles about it being so far from London, and the difficulty of getting there. Some were more enthusiastic. Frieda Arnold, one of the Queen's dressers, echoed her royal mistress when she wrote to her family that, 'everything is designed to enchant the senses ... here one only wishes to revel in the enjoyment of art and nature ... everything is so lovely, so bright and cheerful, everything smiles at one'.[23] It was very much a family home, which made it inevitable that after Albert's death Victoria's usage of it would change. After 1861, she could no longer bear Christmas at Windsor, as it reminded her too much of her loss, so she decamped every year to Osborne instead. The summer visit remained, but spring was dropped in favour of other excursions, including, eventually, to the south of France. The occasional formal engagement was also now hosted at the house, including the visit of a group of Maori chiefs in 1863, and eventually the Indian-influenced Durbar Wing was added, specifically to enable large gatherings to be held inside the house, rather than in marquees on the lawn. The house was not ideal for winter living, and, as Victoria insisted on keeping the windows open and eating outside as much as possible, it soon gained a reputation for being as glacial as Windsor. When, as a child, Princess Beatrice was asked what windows were for, she remarked feelingly, 'to let in wind',[24] and in the latter part of the reign, the December stint quickly became a source of much Household moaning.

The court got off lightly, though they weren't aware of it at the time. For many people, the next step in seeking royal privacy was almost a step too far. Between 1842 and 1847 Victoria and Albert visited Scotland three times, the first royal visits since George IV's vaguely bonkers trip in 1822 (during which he insisted on wearing a kilt, but found it too revealing, so stuck flesh-coloured hose on under-neath). Victoria and Albert absolutely adored it, seeing the whole country through a veil of Walter Scott, and buying completely into his romanticised view. They spotted an enormous potential for their much-desired privacy, not least because the various lochs and mountains made some areas highly inaccessible: Albert crowed delightedly that Ard-verikie, where they stayed in 1847, was, 'an uncome-atable place'.[25] The royal physician, himself a Scot, advised them that the Scottish air was some of the best in the world, though some areas were better than others. Then, just as they started making serious noises about buying a second private residence, in Scotland, in May 1848 they were offered – sight unseen – the chance to buy the remaining lease on Balmoral Castle, in the very area of the Highlands that the royal doctor was currently advising they consider. They took it, commissioning pictures in order to get a vague idea of what they were letting themselves in for, but not visiting in person until September 1848. The Queen recorded in her journal that,

> it is a pretty little Castle, in the old Scotch style ... In front are a nice lawn & garden, with a high wooded hill behind, & at the back, there is a wood. The hills rise all around. One enters a nice little hall, & comes to a bil-liard room & Dining Room. A good broad staircase takes one upstairs & above the Dining room is our sitting room ... We lunched directly & then walked up to the top of the wooded hill, opposite our windows, where there is a cairn, from which there is a pretty winding path. The view was beautiful ... It was so calm

& so solitary as one gazed around, that it did one good & seemed to breathe freedom & peace making one forget the world & its sad turmoil. There were some slight showers, but nothing to signify ... Albert was going to try his luck with some stags, which were lying quite close to the house, as they come down of an evening, – but he was not successful.[26]

Food, views, a sense of escape, and shooting the local wildlife were to be running themes in the royal relationship with Balmoral.

As at Osborne, the house was too small. Criticisms abounded, even from the usually peaceable Lady Canning, one of the Queen's favourite ladies-in-waiting: 'It would be comfortable for a few people and due proportion, but now with eight at dinner everyday, besides the three children and their governess, there are 60 servants.'[27] The rooms were even smaller than those at Osborne, and there was endless moaning, from personal attendants and politicians alike. One minister complained that 'the rooms are so small that I was obliged to write my dispatches on my bed and to keep the window constantly open to admit the necessary quantity of air, and my private secretary ... lodged some three miles off. We played at billiards every evening, the Queen and Duchess [of Kent] being constantly obliged to get up from their chairs to be out of the way of the cues', but the couple couldn't have cared less, and the minister admitted that 'nothing could be more cheerful and evidently perfectly happy than the Queen and Prince, or more kind to everybody around them. I never met a man so remarkable for the variety of information on all subjects as the latter, with a great fund of humour.'[28] It brought out the best in both of them, and even Greville conceded that they were happy, commenting only slightly acerbically that, 'they live there without any state whatever: they live not merely like private gentlefolks, but like very small gentlefolks, small rooms, small establishment'. There was a notable lack of security, ostensibly because the place was so isolated, although it seems that journalists still thronged about the borders, leaping from beds of nettles to catch a glimpse of the royal party off excursing.[29] By 1852 Albert was getting itchy feet. Osborne was largely finished, and he was fresh from the Great Exhibition and wanted a new project. He worked with a local architect, William Smith, son of 'Tudor Johnnie', who was responsible for the current, decidedly Jacobethan house, to design and build Balmoral mark II: bigger, better and filled with a lot more tartan.

As with Osborne, the rebuild was designed to allow the royal family the illusion of total privacy, while simultaneously having enough rooms for all of the various attendants, ministers, relatives and staff. The new house was not as obviously divided as Osborne into 'them', 'us' and 'the servants', but it nevertheless relied upon a totally separate service wing, containing not just the kitchens, but also many of the rooms which were in the basement of the main house at Osborne, notably the linen room (which was also a space for dining), and various other spaces for the care of the frequently muddy and sodden clothing removed by members of the Household who had been out and about. The kitchen was the standard double-height room, with built-in ranges and ample natural light. It had an attached scullery with sinks, as well as a pantry, larders and a designated fruit store.

There was also, unlike at Osborne, a separate bakery with a brick beehive oven, and the upstairs bedroom provision included rooms for a baker, and an assistant baker, who shared with a pantry man. Other rooms were set aside for a roasting cook and two cooks of indeterminate status, again sharing two to a room. One master cook had his own room, and there was also a room set aside for one or more kitchen maids.[30] As with Osborne, this was a skeleton staff, producing relatively low-key meals without the full flourish of a state banquet. The Household still expected, and got, the full quota of dishes though; they were just a bit less complicated and tended to include more Scottish game, shot by the Household and transformed by the cooks.[31]

Balmoral was always intended to be a shooting estate, especially for the Prince, who was an enthusiastic, if not always accurate, shot. The Queen sometimes joined him on his expeditions, admiring his tweed suits, and lying in the wet heather at his side, sometimes sketching, sometimes just watching, much to the embarrassment of some of those involved. He particularly enjoyed deer stalking, writing that it was without doubt, 'one of the most fatiguing, but ... also one of the most interesting of pursuits'.[32] After his death, Victoria commissioned a posthumous portrait of him in his stalking gear, proudly staring out while in the background the ghillies bring home the results. The whole family joined in with inflicting death upon the local landscape: Victoria liked to fish, and encouraged her children to do the same, including salmon spearing. Sketches and official pictures all abound with pictures of royals enjoying the skill of the chase, including the much-praised *Evening at Balmoral*, in which the Queen and her ladies, all in evening dress, have emerged from the castle to admire a dead stag, proudly displayed by Albert. The painter, Carl Haag, had to endure several days of decaying deer smell as he worked on the details with the animal posed in a makeshift studio. Victoria popped in from time to time, and rapidly left as the stench worsened.[33] The Victorians had little of the modern distaste for blood sports, especially since everything shot was eaten. However, the British preferred to maintain the conceit that their prey might be able to escape and spawn next year's dinners. Albert came under fierce criticism when, on a trip to Coburg, he took part in a more efficient but decidedly less sporting German 'battue' in which the animals were simply herded into an enclosure and slaughtered. Worse still, in the eyes of the press, the Queen was there too. *Punch* published a ditty that summed up general opinion:

> Sing a song of Gotha, a pocket full of rye
> Eight and forty timid deer driven in to die;
> When the sport was over, all bleeding they were seen,
> Wasn't that a dainty dish to set before the Queen.[34]

It was a publicity nightmare, and Albert dropped the idea of putting in trenches at Balmoral so that he could sneak up on the deer more easily. A venison larder was built, however, (there was also one at Osborne). Most of the decorating was done with antlers, interspersed with the occasional unrealistic thistle and a great deal of tartan, which gave a much-needed and deliberate boost to the local textile industry, but rendered some of the more taste-conscious members of the Household almost apoplectic. Others were less critical, though even positive descriptions make the place sound

like a particularly surreal theme park: 'The wall-lights are
silver antlers, guns or game bags, and if one's pen needs
dipping, one must look for ink in the back of a hound or a
boar – who could describe all these little things, which if
they are well chosen enhance a castle so well?'[35]

Both of the couple's new homes brought new culinary
adventures, not only for the cooks, who gained valuable
experience, but also for the royals and all of their attendants.
In Scotland, the Queen discovered whisky, a taste that would
remain with her for the rest of her life. Whisky was everywhere: the ghillies all carried flasks with them, and the
annual ball was fuelled by it. It was not to everyone's taste.
Frieda Arnold, like so many of those who attended the
Queen, took as many opportunities as she could to venture
off and explore, embracing the walks as well as the food.
She tried whisky and Scottish bread, her reaction possibly
explaining the emphasis on baking facilities at Balmoral:
'The latter tasted like sawdust and chopped up straw, but I
ate a large piece of it because it was so curious, and, out of
politeness, while the wisket [sic] nearly burned a hole in my
throat, although I swallowed only a drop of it, as our host
was drinking our health. Nothing could persuade me to
empty my glass.' However, in the infamously eye-watering
cold of Balmoral, it grew on her, until she finally admitted
that, 'I drank a glass of it, and it rolled down my throat like
fire, but warmed me so agreeably from within that I shall
never think ill of the poor washerwomen who drink
schnapps on a winter night!'[36] In what would prove a canny
move, John Begg, who ran the Lochnagar Distillery, on the
edge of the estate, invited the Prince to come and see the
process. Albert enjoyed the science. Victoria enjoyed the

results. They later gained a royal warrant, and no visit to Balmoral was deemed complete, 'without a case or two of Begg's best'.[37] In later years, Victoria appalled her then prime minister, Gladstone, when she drank, 'her claret strengthened, I should have thought spoiled, with whisky'.[38] Some biographers have been equally outraged, but it's worth trying with an open mind, for it turns out to be dangerously good.

Both Victoria and Albert threw themselves into what they thought of as the unspoilt Scottish way of life. Victoria in particular developed a habit of dropping in on people, imagining herself to be unrecognised, enthusiastically sharing their meals. When they weren't needed, the upper servants went off on similar excursions, usually ending up at the Keeper's Cottage, being fed by his wife. She did quite well out of it, and would have been able to provide easily for 'surprise' visits, if this experience is typical: 'Our male companions never forget to obtain copious provisions from the royal kitchen. We gave the woman a roast chicken and all kinds of other things, with which she was highly delighted.'[39] All of the villagers for miles around recognised tourists from Balmoral easily, whether through their carriages or general demeanour, and were well prepared to offer apparently spontaneous hospitality to visitors who brought both publicity and prosperity to the area.[40] Picnics were also a way of life. Victoria rarely went out without someone with a hamper full of tea and cake somewhere around her. After Albert's death, according to John Brown, it was more likely to be biscuits and spirits, but the general gist remained the same, and the lucky Queen continued to 'find' tea wherever she ventured. The royals went on supposedly incognito longer excursions as well, staying at inns and hotels. The food varied, but Victoria relished the experience of eating what the gentry ate: it must have echoed some of the meals she'd had as a teenager being dragged on Progress. They didn't leave everything to the vagaries of roadside hostelries, and brought their own wine. Dinner was invariably served as one course. In September 1860 they ate, 'soup, "hodge-podge", mutton-broth with vegetables, which I did not much relish, fowl with white sauce, good roast lamb, very good potatoes, besides one or two other dishes, which I did not taste, ending with a good tart of cranberries'.[41] After dinner the cloth was removed, and the wine and glasses left on the table, which was an old-fashioned habit, remarked on as such by the Queen. Hodge-podge was also old-fashioned, derived from seventeenth-century British courtly cookery, but by the 1860s a predominantly Scottish stew or thick soup made from meat and potatoes or barley. By this point Victoria had become something of a potato aficionado, eating them in any form she could. On another trip out, in October 1861, she was outraged to find that, 'there was hardly anything to eat, and there was only tea, and two miserable starved Highland chickens, without any potatoes! No pudding, and no <u>fun</u>.'[42]

Victoria was willing to try everything offered to her, and delighted at least as much in the simple as, what were to her, quotidian examples of the exotic or complicated. In 1868 she published an edited selection of her journal entries, written while in Scotland (followed in 1883 with a second volume). They were exceedingly well received. She was praised for her innocence and freshness, as well as her interest in the lives of her servants, and the proceeds went towards educational bursaries for the children of the Balmoral residents: 'it is not the Queen, but the woman, who has written this journal,' declared the *Illustrated London News. The Northern British Review* called it, 'a homely book, made up of human nature's daily food'.[43] Food was woven into the text, from the excursions detailed above, to the steady, everyday consumption of tea boiled over a small fire up a mountain. Victoria especially noted the Scottish foods she tried, including oatmeal porridge – 'which I think very good', Finnan haddies, and, 'the celebrated "haggis", which I tried last night, and really liked very much. The Duchess [of Athole] was delighted at my taking it.' She revelled in the breakfasts, with, 'such splendid cream and butter!', and, as usual, visited dairies whenever she came across them. She also continued to be an avid kitchen garden tourist, and her journals are effusive on the subject of her much-loved fruit, including the 'fine peaches' at Inveraray Castle. She shared her love of the simple with guests, eating fresh trout (caught by John Brown and cooked with oatmeal) with Empress Eugénie, the widowed wife of the deposed Napoleon III, in 1879.[44]

Leaves from a Highland Journal was both a homage to Scotland, and an elegy to Albert. Victoria's love for Albert, and their (mainly) companionate relationship, comes across strongly (obviously the arguments have been edited out). But they spent relatively little time together at Balmoral, compared with the time she would spend there as a widow. By 1861 Albert was mournfully wandering around the proposed alterations to the landscape and muttering darkly about how he might not ever see them made; a self-fulfilling prophecy as he almost wilfully worked himself to death. His demise was unexpected and lends the photograph they had taken of themselves that year a poignancy it wouldn't otherwise have. After 21 years of disciplined eating and lots of exercise, she was still pretty trim, especially considering that she was now 42 and had had nine children. Albert, on the other hand, looked increasingly florid and podgy. He took less exercise than Victoria, despite his stalking expeditions, and was still beset with constant stomach problems. It seems very likely that they were caused by Crohn's disease, a debilitating illness that causes inflammation of the digestive system and for which there is still no known cure.[45] It was almost certainly complications relating to this, rather than the typhoid that was blamed at the time, which killed him, plunging Victoria into a deep depression from which she would emerge a less confident, though no less stubborn, monarch.

After Albert's death, Balmoral was effectively made into a museum. No changes were to be permitted, to the decor or the layout. Some were inevitable – electric light was installed in the 1890s, and rooms needed updating and renovating from time to time. The Queen took to dining in the library, which had, 'strips of crumb-cloth on the floor round the table', apparently indicating, 'a truly Scotch carefulness, and a desire to save the carpet from the wear of the footmen's tread'.[46] Victoria spent more and more time at Balmoral, a habit that her ministers loathed, and the house was almost universally despised for its distance, its cramped living conditions, and its unrelenting cold and drizzle. It wasn't a helpful move, for her almost total withdrawal from public life caused outrage among a public who wanted their money's worth from their Queen. While she continued to involve herself in politics from behind the scenes, and to keep up the practical, letter-writing, signing and advice-giving parts of her role, she failed to realise that a crucial responsibility of the monarch was to be seen, to provide a focal point for the public, as well as to host occasions, such as dinners and drawing rooms, upon which the great and good could come together and network. It was not enough to do the work: she needed to be seen to do the work: 'The mass of people expect a Queen to look and play the part. They want the gilding for their money. It is not wise to let them think ... that they could do without a sovereign.'[47] Instead, she hid, preferring to build herself a retreat from the retreat that was Balmoral, and get even further away from the pressures of state. In 1849 she and Albert had con-verted a hut on the Balmoral estate into a romantic getaway cottage, the Alt-na-Giuthasach. They would stay there with only nine servants and a lady-in-waiting, using it as a base for rowing on the lake, fishing and walking. She abandoned it after Albert's death as it was too painful for her to visit, and built instead the Glassalt Shiel, in which nineteen people sat down to dine in 1868. There was only one cook, Thomas Hollis, who was about halfway up his journey from appren-tice to chief cook at the time, and would have been preparing fairly basic food, the bulk of which was probably pre-prepared and transported over, ready to reheat as necessary. Ironically, the construction of her own building, not designed or thought of by Albert, marked the end of her deepest phase of mourning, and the start of the second part of her reign, alone, middle-aged, and at loggerheads with ministers who wanted her out and about, enlivening public life, not weeping at home.

Balmoral remains a private possession of the Crown, and is still in frequent use today, while Osborne, which is owned by the state, became a naval training school and a convalescent home. Queen Elizabeth II gave permission for it to be opened to the public in 1954, and it is now run by English Heritage. The royal dining room still glitters with gold, but in the 1960s the kitchens were converted into garages, and today the former hearth sits forlornly at the back of an oil-stained floor, with the words, 'Matron Only' written in black marker pen on the surrounding tiles.

7

Motherhood

Victoria and Albert had nine children, born between 1840 and 1857. In many respects they were fairly typical upper-class parents, busy with their own lives, and interacting with their children only for a few hours a day. The Queen, unlike her mother, did not breastfeed any of her offspring, employing instead a series of wet nurses. Most passed through the nursery with little comment, only staying for the six months necessary to wean each child, and didn't seem to make much of an impact. Edward's wet nurse later went on to murder her six children, which was a bit of a shock, but she'd been such a small part of his life that the Queen simply wrote her off as a bad lot. There's been debate about Victoria's parenting skills, largely based on her own descriptions of her feelings. She resented pregnancy, seeing it as curtailing the freedom of a woman. An unmarried woman of her class was chaperoned and guarded at all times, but with marriage came a degree of liberty, as married women were able to move about more freely, and to discuss subjects with one another in a way which, at the time, was deemed inappropriate for unmarried girls. By the 1850s, Victoria had come to look back on her whole marriage through rose-tinted spectacles, glossing over the ferocious rows of the early 1840s. She resented the fact that so many pregnancies so early in her marriage had stopped her spending time revelling in Albert, and wrote that pregnancies were, 'sufferings and miseries and plagues'. She admitted that she had felt, 'pinned down – one's wings clipped', and referred to the whole process as the 'shadow side' of marriage.[1] Albert backed this up, not terribly sympathetically, writing after Beatrice's birth in 1857 that, 'Victoria counts the hours and minutes like a prisoner'.[2] Sometimes fighting depression and physically weakened, Victoria looked forward to her 'churching', a formal ceremony of returning to church for the first time after the birth of a child, as a sign of her release. She also regarded it as a way of celebrating a safe delivery, and of revalidating her marriage each time, wearing her wedding veil and, until fashions changed, her wedding dress.

Childbirth in the nineteenth century was dangerous, and it remained the biggest cause of death in women throughout the period (fire was the second, and was one reason for a frequent ban on crinolines and large bustles in kitchens for women working below stairs). One of the few indisputable things that Victoria did for women during her reign was to embrace the use of chloroform in childbirth, using it for the births of her last two children and determinedly rejecting

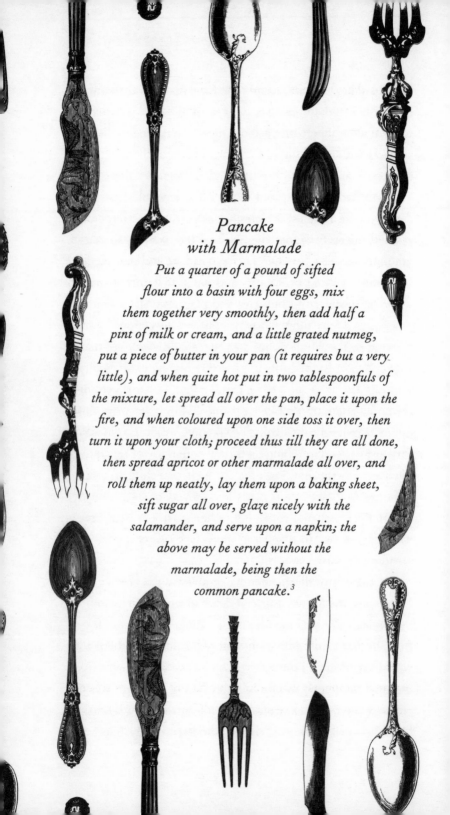

Pancake
with Marmalade

Put a quarter of a pound of sifted
flour into a basin with four eggs, mix
them together very smoothly, then add half a
pint of milk or cream, and a little grated nutmeg,
put a piece of butter in your pan (it requires but a very
little), and when quite hot put in two tablespoonfuls of
the mixture, let spread all over the pan, place it upon the
fire, and when coloured upon one side toss it over, then
turn it upon your cloth; proceed thus till they are all done,
then spread apricot or other marmalade all over, and
roll them up neatly, lay them upon a baking sheet,
sift sugar all over, glaze nicely with the
salamander, and serve upon a napkin; the
above may be served without the
marmalade, being then the
common pancake.[3]

claims that the pain was punishment for Eve's role in the expulsion from the Garden of Eden, or that suffering helped a mother to bond with her baby. It still took time to recover, and Victoria was usually absent from affairs of state for two weeks. She was also put onto invalid food, despite writing after the birth of Victoria (Vicky) that she 'had an excellent appetite'.[4] The standard fare of chicken broth, beef tea and boiled chicken characterises all of her post-birth meals, though she also ate endless rice pudding and macaroni in various forms. After Louise's birth in 1848 her progress can be clearly charted through four days of broths and chicken, to a further six days where roast beef was added, to the creeping in of a chocolate soufflé on day eleven, and on day twelve a gloriously garbled-sounding 'bouding von schwartz brod' with chocolate sauce. Two weeks after the birth, she took her place back at the main royal dinner table. In later years she recalled her ability to get up and get going again with pride, as ever glossing over her mixed feelings at the time. When her youngest daughter Beatrice dared to absent herself from dinner in the days preceding the birth of her own first child – and took three and a half weeks to recover afterwards, she dismissed her as moping, remarking that, 'in my case I came regularly to dinner (excepting when I was really unwell) up until the very last day, and the Prince never would have let me keep in my room unless I was very suffering'.[5]

She found the physicality of childbirth, and of young children, bestial: 'I think ... of our being like a cow or a dog at such moments; when our poor nature becomes so very animal and unecstatic,' though she also acknowledged that she was, 'particular to a degree', and that part of her unease with her first pregnancies lay with being singled out and pointed at, and treated as if she would break.[6] All of these declarations were written to her eldest daughter, Vicky (the Princess Royal, later Empress of Prussia), and the Queen was perhaps a little over-emphatic, desperate to dissuade her from the constant pregnancies that she had endured. When Vicky became pregnant almost immediately after her marriage, at only eighteen, he mother's response was that this was 'horrid news'. Given that the Queen had promoted her marriage into the Prussian royal family since Vicky was fourteen, there was probably an element of guilt. (She was also regrettably proven right, when Vicky nearly died in labour giving birth to her first son, later Kaiser Wilhelm II, who was born with a withered arm as a result of the appallingly long and painful process.) She admitted later that she had over-played her feelings: when Vicky accused her of 'hating babies', she defended herself, saying that, 'you know perfectly well that I do not hate babies (quite the contrary if they are pretty), but I do hate an inordinate worship of them and the disgusting details of their animal existence, which I try to ignore'.[7]

In fact, the Queen seems to have behaved much like any mother, alternating between wanting to throttle her increasing band of hoodlums, and absolutely adoring all of them. Lady Lyttelton, a lady-in-waiting, who was in her fifties and had seen it all, described the Queen with her first child as, 'like all very young mothers', worrying that her daughter wasn't progressing, and fussing over her constantly. Diet was a primary consideration, especially as they were weaned. The older children were undoubtedly worried over more than the later arrivals. Vicky struggled with digestive

issues from when she was a toddler, exacerbated by the
inability of her parents not to micro-manage the nursery: 'I
suspect [she] is over-watched and over-doctored, always
treated with what is most expensive, cheaper and common
food and ways being often wholesomer. She now lives on
asses' milk and arrowroot and chicken broth, and they
measure it out so carefully, for fear of overloading her
stomach, that I fancy she always leaves off hungry.' She was
the subject of a pivotal row between her parents, during
which Victoria screamed at Albert that she wished she'd
never married him, while Albert wrote one of his characteristic notes accusing his wife of starving her child and saying
that if she died, it would be on her conscience. In 1842 Lady
Lyttelton took over management of the nursery, and things
calmed down under her experienced guidance. Both parents
remained actively involved, seeing their children bathed (or
tearing round like naked maniacs, which vastly amused their
mother), and put into bed, as well as playing games with
them. Victoria's journals make quite clear her delight in her
growing family, and her pride in all of her children as they
grew up. She threw herself into making their childhood different to hers and Albert's, taking them on excursions which
were sometimes highbrow – the theatre and opera, plus
numerous recitals and plays performed at Windsor – but
were equally likely to be popularist. The pantomimes that,
as a seventeen-year-old trying to be seen as an adult ready
to rule, Victoria had declared to be, 'noisy and vulgar', were
now attended with gusto. They also visited Madame Tus-
sauds, the zoo and a Red Indian show.[8] They had magic
shows and regular children's parties. Of course, they were
nineteenth-century aristocrats, so they were also subject to

a rigorous education, intended to set them up to be the rulers, and wives of rulers, of large estates, if not small countries, and they were regularly whipped and beaten when they were naughty – which was relatively often.

Of all of the palaces, Osborne House was most associated with family life. As soon as the new house was finished, it was filled with children. They had a tent on the lawn in which to play, and, as each child turned three, he or she started to have breakfast with their parents. If there were no guests, as was often the case at Osborne, they would lunch with them too, gradually progressing off the standard nursery fare of chicken and mutton, broth, bread, rice and vermicelli and onto more interesting – but still fairly plain – dishes. At fourteen they would be allowed to dine with the adults, experiencing French cuisine, as a preliminary to the more elevated meals of Windsor and Buckingham Palace. At Osborne the children were allowed to be as noisy as they wished. Victoria frequently and indulgently referred to their being 'wild' in her journals, and they clearly egged each other on. It was a place associated with new experiences and a holiday atmosphere.[9] It was at Osborne that the six-year-old Prince of Wales, Edward (always known as Bertie), went out shooting with Albert for the first time, and they also got to grips with the technology behind their food: 'After luncheon, we went with the Children to see the Ice House fitted, which is quite a curious performance. The men were breaking it above & throwing it down through an opening & we went below to see it falling through, like rain.'[10] Ice houses were simple but absolutely brilliant facilities, consisting of a deep well (40 to 100 feet was not unusual), sometimes divided into vertical sections, which could be packed tight with ice. There was usually a drain at the bottom, and the top was covered with a low, brick, igloo-like structure, if it was not built into a hillside. Several thick doors kept warm air outside, and the ice could last several years without melting, ready for use for setting jellies and freezing ice creams as needed. There was one at every palace, and additional staff were taken on in the winter to help cut the ice out of ponds and rivers and cart it about. Kitchen apprentice Gabriel Tschumi described them as, 'muffled in thick coats and wearing heavy gloves, going round the estates with picks and shovels chipping out blocks of natural ice'.[11]

At Easter, the children hunted for painted hard-boiled eggs around the breakfast table, a custom Albert was used to in Germany, and popularised in the UK. Then they went off to watch the sheep shearing at the farm that was an intrinsic part of the estate.[12] In the winter they performed charades, cross-dressing merrily and pillaging each other's wardrobes for costumes:

At a little before 7 a charade was acted before Albert & very successful. The first part 'Break' represented by Vicky & Alice, who discussed the smelling of some flowers which Alice finally pulled down, I coming in as an angry grandmother. – 'Fast' the 2nd was 2 exhausted children (Vicky & Bertie lying on the ground) & a lady (I) & her 2 children (Alice & Alfred) giving them some food & restoring them to life; – The last 'Breakfast' represented the 5 children at breakfast. Vicky standing on a chair & writing some verses. Vicky & Alice & Lenchen were dressed as boys & Lenchen also looking

too funny in trousers of Alice's, a jacket & cap belonging to the boys – Bertie & Affie quite unrecognisable as
girls. – Lenchen was so delighted & too droll. I invented
the whole affair & wrote the dialogue of the two first
parts.[13]

In 1850 came a new departure. The children were used to
picking fruit with their mother from the kitchen garden, and
had sets of gardening tools among their toys, but now the
Queen recorded in her journal that, 'we showed the children
the plot of ground, which is to be their garden'.[14] They were
kitted out with gardening smocks and clogs, and given sets
of tools with their initials on, which were to be kept in a tool
shed built alongside the plots. Each child had his or her own
bed, the largest part of which was devoted to growing vegetables. They grew identical things, both soft fruit and
vegetables, all of which would be gravely examined by
Prince Albert, before he gave the children market price for
their produce. In later years Louise would recall how she
would rush to the garden to gorge on the strawberries,
gooseberries and peas, and they also grew radishes, potatoes, beetroot, parsley, currants and raspberries, as well as
carrots, turnips, beans, parsnips, asparagus, onions, artichokes and a couple of rows of flowers.[15] They grew maize
and gourds for drying as well, and in 1855 Vicky sent some
of each to Bertie, left in Windsor, so that he could make
them into lamps. In 1851 they gained a further source of joy
and snacks, when an orchard was added. Victoria commented that, 'their garden ... is a great source of happiness
to them all'.[16]

More joy was to come. In May 1853, the Queen recorded

in her journal that, 'we went with all 7 children to their garden, where they laid the first stone to a Swiss Cottage, built for them there'.[17] Present were Vicky, who was thirteen; Bertie, at twelve; Alice (known as Alee, who was ten); Alfred (Affie, nine); Helena (Lenchen, seven); Louise (Loo-Loo, six); and Arthur, who was four. Leopold would be born the following month, and Beatrice, always known as Baby, four years later (by which time Vicky would be engaged). Bertie, who also kept a (short-lived) journal, detailed the construction, during which the workmen were helped by the older boys: 'We worked altogether that day (that means to say only I and Affie), at the Swiss Cottage, 15 feet long, and 17 feet high.'[18] The cottage was a true Swiss chalet, copied from Alpine models, but made out of American wood, and constructed in Britain. The pieces were probably prefabricated off site, and erected, with the eager help of the junior royals, by local carpenters. There was a vogue at the time for chalets of this style, and they were springing up on English estates, although they were not generally intended as places in which upper-class children could behave like 'Swiss peasants'.[19] The inspiration in this case was probably a mixture of Albert's family getaway, the Rosenau, in the grounds of which Albert and Victoria had stayed in a Swiss Cottage in 1845, and a playhouse which Victoria's half-sister, Feodora, had built for her children, writing in 1851 that, 'I have had a little Swiss Cottage built in the garden which belongs to the children ... as their own; it contains one room and a kitchen.'[20] The Osborne incarnation was on a rather grander scale, consisting of a kitchen, a scullery, and a larder which probably doubled as a dairy on the ground floor, along with a four-room flat for the caretakers, and three rooms plus a WC on an upper floor, accessible via an exterior staircase which led to a surrounding balcony. Thomas Warne, one of the under-gardeners, took up residence in the flat, along with his wife Louisa, who acted as a housekeeper. Thomas oversaw the children's gardens, tending to their vegetables while they were away, and teaching them the techniques of gardening. Meanwhile it was almost certainly Louisa who took charge of the kitchen, where she taught the children to cook not just what they had grown, but a wider range of other dishes. The children became very close to the Warnes, calling Louisa 'Warnie'. When she died of a fit at Swiss Cottage in 1881, the Queen wrote that, 'all our children were so fond of her. One cannot think of the place without her.'[21] She and Beatrice visited Louisa's widower when he was dying, and the couple's headstone was paid for from the royal purse. It read, 'To the respected Memory of THOMAS WARNE Died December 27th 1881, Aged 69; and of LOUISA WARNE, his wife, died September 19th 1881, Aged 65, who during 27 years had charge of the Swiss Cottage, Osborne, where they died'. Their successors, George and Julia Stone, were appointed in January 1882, specifically to, 'take charge of the Swiss Cottage and Gardens and of any animals that may be there, and to make themselves generally useful to the Queen and Royal Family'.[22] There was indeed a succession of animals, including at least three gazelles, Beatrice's angora rabbits, a racoon, ducks, and, at least for a while, a Chihuahua, which the Queen described as, 'a curious tiny little dog brought me from Mexico – something like a very diminutive Italian greyhound. Mrs Warne is going to take charge of it.'[23] Bertie sent Lady Lyttelton a pair of bantams in 1842, almost certainly from the Swiss menagerie, indicating that the eggs the children cooked with would have been from their own hens.

The Swiss Cottage was officially declared open on the Queen's birthday in 1854, and the children immediately took possession. The downstairs kitchen and scullery were impeccably equipped: they had built-in sinks with water pumped from an exterior cistern, white-painted cupboards and dressers, hygienically tiled walls and floor, and a range which was of a style unusual in Britain at the time. It was made by J. Mathys, a Brussels-based ironmonger that held the Belgian equivalent of a Royal Warrant and had exhibited at the Great Exhibition in 1851, from where the British royal family either purchased or were given a not inconsiderable amount of stuff. It was about three-quarters of the size of a normal range, so ideal for children, and may have been a showpiece at the Exhibition – or it may have been a gift from Uncle Leopold. It had a double oven, a hot water boiler with a tap, and a roasting attachment with small clockwork spit. There was also a cast-iron set of charcoal chafing stoves in the kitchen, again scaled down for those of diminutive height, and in the scullery a fire with a hot plate and built-in boiler. For those children not quite tall enough or steady enough to be let loose with real fire, a toy range was also commissioned in wood, and joined the toy grocer's shop, with which the children played upstairs. The grocer's, which had the sign, 'Spratt, grocer to her Majesty', proudly emblazoned in gold across the front, was a stunningly intricate replica of a shop, complete with food displayed in boxes, drawers and baskets, and priced up. There were miniature tea caddies, jam jars and a tiny pair of weighing scales on the counter. It echoed the doll's house Queen Victoria had played with as a child, and was both a plaything and an educational device, teaching the children about food provenance, and life outside the palace, as well as building up basic maths skills.

The final downstairs room for the children was a larder, with drainage in the floor and tiled walls. Very little remains of this room now, so it's much more difficult to reconstruct than the kitchen and scullery, which were preserved after Swiss Cottage fell out of use. However, given the presence of dairying equipment in the collection of cooking materials, and the known interest of the Queen and the Prince in dairying, it's likely that the larder doubled as a dairy from time to time. Victoria was an avid dairy visitor at the houses in which she stayed, both as a Princess and as Queen, and Albert built the resplendent model dairy at Frogmore. Dairying was no longer particularly viewed as a fashionable activity for bored noblewomen, but in the eighteenth century there had been a real vogue for dressing up as a shepherdess and playing with butter. Dairies were safe, clean environments, and they remained key points on the visitor route for upper-class guests at any country house. They were often highly ornamented and isolated buildings, located away from other, muckier, service areas. Vicky certainly knew her way around the process, writing to her mother in 1863 that she had arranged a dairy for herself, as the milk was so bad that it ruined her tea and coffee. She'd bought two cows, and employed one of the gardener's wives to manage her new venture. Yet she was authoritatively sniffy about their technique, complaining that, 'they have deep earthenware dishes instead of milk pans; the consequence is that they have hardly any cream as it only rises in dishes that are moderately flat'.[24]

The Swiss Cottage batterie de cuisine erred on the side of cakes and pastries, rather than the drudgery of dinner. It had, for example, a veritable profusion of pastry cutters. Equipment came from many of the same suppliers as the royal kitchens themselves. William J. Burton of Oxford Street supplied a great deal, including tin moulds, enamel pans, a gridiron for grilling meat over the charcoal stoves (grilling here in the modern American sense – heat from below – as was the common usage in the nineteenth century), wafering irons, a chocolate pot and mill, egg whisks, pastry jaggers (tools for shaping and crimping the edges of pies), and baking sheets, but Benningtons was also used for pans, moulds and fire-tending tools. They presented a hefty bill for £34.0s.10d, which included a 'bright iron French omelette pan', several ornate culinary moulds for puddings and jellies, spice boxes, further gridirons, stewpans and a pancake pan. Silversmiths Garrard and Co. supplied a smattering of silver spoons; Richard Ordway, a wood-turner based near Buckingham Palace, made items such as sieves, a broom, brushes for cleaning the stoves, and a pair of lemon squeezers; while Faulding, Stratton and Brough, who, like all of the others, held a Royal Warrant, supplied lengths of cloth for the tables and curtains, along with napkins and dusters.[25] On 18 July 1854, the Queen recorded that, 'we sauntered about and went to the children's garden, where they were extremely happy unpacking all their things for Swiss Cottage'. By August they were cooking their own lunches, and showing the cottage off to visitors, and by the next year they had established the pattern of spending a part of every day at

Swiss Cottage, winter and summer. They harvested radishes and ate them with bread and butter in January 1855, and were sufficiently confident that they baked a cake for the German chemist and inventor of Marmite, Baron Liebig.

Birthdays were excuses to decorate the cottage with flags and bunting and spend all day cooking, though the standard may have been a tad dubious. Alice wrote to Prince Albert in May 1858, 'we are going to cook at the Swiss Cottage today: I wish you were there dear papa, to eat what we have made though – I am afraid you don't think our cooking very famous'.[26] Not necessarily surprising, when her own habits may not have been exemplary. Lenchen wrote primly a few days later to inform her father that 'Alice made a pancake yesterday afternoon at the Swiss Cottage. I had none of it as I was out driving with mama. Arthur told me that after she had finished it she touched it, with the dirty charcoal pinchers.'[27] Pancakes or fritters were popular, judging by the condition of the collection: the gridirons are pristine, while there's a cast-iron frying pan that seems to have been set on fire. The most used items all suggest that the bulk of the children's culinary experiments were concerned with the kind of dishes which made up a Victorian tea or light lunch or supper – pastries, cakes, omelettes, fritters, custards, puddings and biscuits. That same summer they also made wafers and Schneemilch, a German egg white and cream-based dish that they may have learnt from Feodora and her children when they visited in 1855. Feodora's children had been encouraged in similar practical activities, including gardening, and she wrote: 'You should have seen Eliza, how busy she was in the Vineyard cutting the grapes off; she had a little sickle and worked away, Charles tried to work too, but the grapes generally went into his mouth instead of the tub.'[28] They sometimes catered for their parents and other guests, in which case they would arrange a tea, either upstairs in the dining room, or outside on the lawn. A typical occasion was described by the Queen in 1861: 'Sitting out rather late and driving to Swiss Cottage, where I met Albert ... and all the children & where the results of the morning's cooking were displayed & relished. We all sat down to tea, including Beatrice and the little ones, & the Ladies who have also come, on purpose.'[29]

In the inventory of the kitchens taken shortly after Victoria's death, the drawer in front of the kitchen window contained a manuscript book of recipes, presumably the book from which the children cooked. It has long since disappeared, but the cookery writer Elizabeth Craig published a book of royal recipes in the 1950s in which she told the story of a friend of hers who had seen, and copied from, two books belonging to Queen Victoria, and bequeathed by her to a housekeeper. The tale is third-hand, but, if true, and it's entirely plausible, the books were a mixture of cuttings and copyings, and one had an inscription in the front stating, 'Given to Princess Victoria on her birthday – 1831', which would have been one year before she started her journal. According to Craig's informer, who sent her some recipes from the books, Victoria and her descendants added to it from 1831 to 1887. The dates fit, and the few recipes that Craig reprints with the annotations that accompanied them adhere to the general pattern of royal life. One recipe, 'to cook hare', was apparently 'given by my Uncle, the King, William IV', in January 1835, and certainly William's menus were replete with hare recipes, especially soup.[30] The same tendency to temper fun with education, which governed the decision to let the children loose at Swiss Cottage, comes through in other snippets of Victoria's handwriting: small crusts for cheese were, 'good for dyspeptics', and cheese-cakes were, 'as made for Queen Anne Boleyn', and 'copied from my ancient recipe book'. Especially in the tense years when she was ill or dieting in 1836 and 1837, she seems to have distracted her stomach by actively seeking out recipes, especially extraordinary ones, such as the animated pie (a hollow pastry case filled, when cooked, with live animals which then flew or ran out when the pie was cut), which was from, 'notes made out of an ancient book by myself', and in February 1836 she wrote down, 'a drink I like', which con-sisted of two pints of spring water, the yolk of an egg, the juice of one lemon, nine large spoonfuls of white wine, sugar and lemon syrup. It's impossible to know whether the books were fiction, but Craig clearly believed her friend, and it seems like a very elaborate hoax if they didn't exist. As to whether Victoria and her children really wrote them, unless the books re-emerge from the back of whichever drawer they are currently lurking in, it's impossible to say. However, a book did at one point exist, and the children undoubtedly wrote their recipes in it, and a book passed down through successive generations was exactly the norm in most families. It's entirely likely, therefore, that, while Victoria never seems to have joined her family in cooking, she did share with them the gathering of recipes from family, friends and printed cookery books.

Swiss Cottage provided a real outlet for the children's energies. In addition to the gardens and the kitchens, the older boys also helped construct a miniature fort as a surprise for their mother's birthday in 1856. Lenchen later laid the foundation stone for an adjoining barracks. All of the children played in it: division of play along gender lines seems to have been unknown. Prince Leopold's daughter Alice, who, like many of Victoria's grandchildren, also used Swiss Cottage, later remembered, 'Osborne also revives very happy memories for me. It, too, had its own wonderful smell which I can always bring to mind even now. It was a different smell from that of Windsor, but none the less a real part of the atmosphere of the place ... We used to play at the Swiss Cottage and at the dear little miniature fort.'[31] Upstairs at the cottage itself was a museum room, to which all of the children were encouraged to contribute. They collected shells and bones, and in 1855 added preserved examples of nutmeg and cloves growing, 'in all their stages'.[32] There was also an impressive collection of taxidermy, including one of Albert's pet bullfinches, and fossils. As the children grew up and started to travel, they sent back items for their younger siblings: Affie sent evidence that he was continuing in his father's footsteps when he was in Africa, in the form of exotic animal heads and two elephant feet from his shooting expeditions. In 1863 the collection outgrew the room it was in, and a separate museum was constructed in a similar style next door.

The cottage and its kitchens were a huge influence in the children's lives. Vicky married the heir to the Prussian throne in 1858. In December 1857 the Queen remarked sadly that it was, 'poor dear Vicky's last day at Osborne & she went to bid farewell to her dear Swiss Cottage, which quite upset her'.[33] Two months later, and now in Germany, the princess wrote to her mother:

> I must confess that I cried bitterly last night at the
> thought of your going to dear Osborne, and without
> me. My pretty rooms that I loved so much, the dear
> view out of the windows – the darling Swiss cottage,
> my garden, the tree I planted the day we left – and all
> those objects to which I am attached, you will see them
> all again the day after tomorrow and I can only dream
> and think of them, and look at the photographs and cry.
> Sometimes I cannot believe that I am so far away from
> you all, because I am so constantly thinking of you![34]

By 1860 she was receiving emergency parcels of Osborne
primroses, and the younger children also sent food parcels,
the fruits of their labours in the kitchens at Swiss Cottage.
In 1863 she arranged for her own version of her childhood
haunt, building a private garden for her children to play in,
'like wild beasts', along with a summerhouse. She continued
to be interested in gardening, writing to Victoria in 1867
that she has 'collected a basket of fruit, grown in our little
garden, as specimens of what it produces ... I sent it off last
week. I hope that it arrived safe and that you tried the fruit
as my gardener will be broken-hearted, I fear it is finer to
look at than to taste; it is grown on the French system of ...
dwarf trees.'[35] (The Queen replied, agreeing.) Vicky and
her mother wrote thousands of letters to each other, becoming much closer once Vicky had married than they had
managed to be before her departure.

Victoria herself recognised that she struggled with ado-
lescents, though she continued to adore toddlers and young
children. She wrote in 1856:

I find no especial pleasure or compensation in the company of the elder children ... only very occasionally do I find the rather intimate intercourse with them either agreeable or easy ... it is caused by various factors. Firstly, I only feel properly à mon aise and quite happy when Albert is with me; secondly I am used to carrying on my many affairs quite alone; and then I have grown up all alone, accustomed to the society of adult (and never with younger) people – lastly, I still cannot get used to the fact that Vicky is almost grown up. To me she still seems the same child, who had to be kept in order and therefore must not become too intimate.[36]

The letters between the two cover a vast range of topics, but in the initial flurry after Vicky first left, the most important things in the Queen's mind were her dress, her servants and her food. As ever, at times of stress, eating was a primary preoccupation, and she wrote anxiously, 'how do you like the houses and the diet?' Vicky sent her sets of menus and explained that she ate breakfast at nine or quarter past, 'just the same as at home'. The usual dinner hour was five, much earlier than she was used to, so she didn't eat lunch, causing a rush of worried advice: 'I think it hardly safe to go from $9\frac{1}{4}$ till 5 without anything? I would advise never to do it if you felt faint or hungry – but take a biscuit or a dry crust. You take, I suppose, a cup of tea at night?'[37] Later, they shared their weight worries, the Queen writing in 1859 that she meant, 'to be weighed, as I always thought I was light', after her favourite Highland servant, John Brown, who was, in her eyes, refreshingly blunt, commented that he thought she'd put on weight.[38] Vicky, meanwhile, called herself stout in some photographs that she sent in 1867, and then backtracked, saying she was actually quite slight.[39]

The children could not help but be influenced by their mother's love of food, and some, at least, learnt by example. Bertie grew up to be as much of a gourmand as his mother, and was nicknamed 'Tum-Tum'. Vicky stuffed herself as a child, 'cramming in eating', as her mother later put it, though as an adult she was not overweight.[40] Meanwhile Beatrice, who was indulged in a way that the older children hadn't been, misbehaved flagrantly around food. She was refused pudding on one occasion when she was three, with the words, 'Baby mustn't have that, it's not good for Baby'; 'But Baby likes it, my dear,' she replied, in a voice mimicking that of the Queen. On another occasion she wiped her fingers on a black dress, retorting when scolded that it would never be seen at night. For that one, her mother ordered her removed from the room, provoking her to declare as she was whisked out of the door, 'it was only for Her that I came downstairs. Such base ingratitude.'[41] Clearly a diet of chicken and mutton broth wasn't entirely to Baby's taste. Over in Prussia, meanwhile, Vicky missed the food of her childhood enough that she sent one of her cooks to Windsor to be trained up, specifying that he needed the opportunity to learn different things in all the departments: kitchen, pastry and confectionery.[42]

After Albert's death, the function of Swiss Cottage gradually changed. The children were growing up, getting married, and leaving, so there was less of a party atmosphere when those who remained went down to cook. They still used it, especially on birthdays: Leopold and Beatrice cooked there for the latter's ninth birthday in 1866, and for the same occasion in 1871 Beatrice cooked cakes with some of the Queen's ladies, serving them for a birthday tea. Later, they would bring their own children to cook there, but its role as a children's playhouse was increasingly superseded by its convenience as a place to take tea, and for the Queen to use as a writing retreat. She first recorded putting it to service as a place to work in 1855, using the table in what was known as the Queen's Room (now dining room), or setting up facilities outside on the lawn, but by the 1870s this had become its main function.

As with Osborne House itself, Swiss Cottage is now looked after by English Heritage. Open to the public for many decades as a static set of rooms, the copper chained down and all sense that children played there removed, it underwent a major conservation and reinterpretation project in 2012–14 and reopened as a child-friendly set of rooms in which the story of Victoria's children is told. The gardens are all still there, as is the museum, the exhibits still sporting the original handwritten labels. Upstairs the Swiss dining room is set for a Victorian tea: downstairs modern visitors have to make do with a cuppa and a cake from what is now a small café in the former gazelle house.

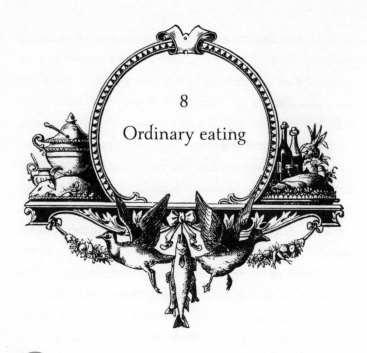

8
Ordinary eating

Queen Victoria was a woman who could eat. After 1861, freed from restraint, she gained weight rapidly. The foreign secretary in 1868 commented that she was 'well, but growing enormously fat',[1] and by the 1870s she was assuming the sturdy shape in which she would be immortalised in many portraits, photographs and statues. It's very hard to judge her exact proportions, for fashions changed a lot over the Victorian period, and the waistline on gowns moved down, while crinolines and bustles came and went, making cross-comparison of her surviving gowns, or portraits of her in them, rather pointless. She would have been able to comfortably take several inches off her waist with her corset, and full skirts were designed to emphasise nipped-in waists and carefully shaped busts.[2] There were limits on what corsets could do, though, especially in the face of determined eating. Whether served *à la Française*, *à la Russe*, or somewhere in the middle, diners at the Queen's table could choose from gargantuan amounts of food. In the 1880s, by which time dinner was served sequentially, the norm at the Queen's table was six courses, plus dessert and a laden side table. Her commitment to food was awe-inspiring, though it continued to cause her digestive problems. But what did she eat? Lots of people have come up with lists of apparent favourites, usually including chocolate cake, cranberry tarts, and the mythical Brown Windsor Soup (which didn't exist until well into the twentieth century, and was something of a culinary joke for a long time).[3] The notion of such favourites is invariably founded on one or two references, largely from books written in the 1890s of a somewhat flattering ilk. As is frequent in food history, however, this list has become law, and is widely quoted. Likewise, Victoria's much-declared love of plain food is disputable: she commented on plainer food much more frequently than on the complicated dishes which formed the bulk of her diet, it's true, but who comments on the everyday? While she certainly embraced the chance to try the foods of people she met, from sailors to farmers, and often wrote that she had enjoyed them, her daily menus don't indicate that particularly plain food was a concern. Inevitably what she ate, and what she liked, changed with age and experience, and any one menu or anecdote cannot be used to make generalisations about favourite foods throughout her whole reign. A lifelong love of fruit is the only thing that really stands out in the Queen's own journals and letters, as well as in the writings of others. She ate extremely well, with dishes to compete with any aristocratic

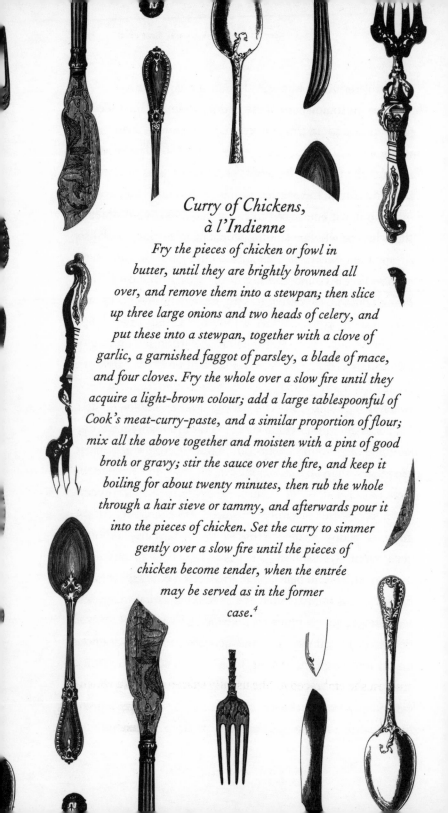

Curry of Chickens, à l'Indienne

Fry the pieces of chicken or fowl in butter, until they are brightly browned all over, and remove them into a stewpan; then slice up three large onions and two heads of celery, and put these into a stewpan, together with a clove of garlic, a garnished faggot of parsley, a blade of mace, and four cloves. Fry the whole over a slow fire until they acquire a light-brown colour; add a large tablespoonful of Cook's meat-curry-paste, and a similar proportion of flour; mix all the above together and moisten with a pint of good broth or gravy; stir the sauce over the fire, and keep it boiling for about twenty minutes, then rub the whole through a hair sieve or tammy, and afterwards pour it into the pieces of chicken. Set the curry to simmer gently over a slow fire until the pieces of chicken become tender, when the entrée may be served as in the former case.[4]

household, club or, by the end of the century, restaurant. In popular mythology Victorian food is stodgy and badly cooked, reliant on the seasons, and cooked with primitive equipment. Doubtless there were, then as now, poor cooks, and travellers' accounts show that there was very definitely bad food. But in the palaces, staffed by a team of able cooks, working in well-equipped, if at times malodorous, kitchens, and with the whole changing world of Victorian food supplies at their fingertips, this was definitely not the case. One of the reasons courtiers complained about the fast pace of eating was that they then missed out on the 'excellent fare handed so expeditiously'.

The Queen's everyday menus are listed in the dining ledgers in the Royal Archives, and they present a fairly clear picture of royal dining at the official palaces in the early years of the reign. However, the run is not complete after 1858, and does not include either Balmoral or Osborne (one ledger exists for the latter, at Osborne House itself, for 1897). As might be expected, certain dishes appear regularly, others come and go, and this is the case for all meals. Breakfasts were hefty: in September 1838 the Queen had 'a good breakfast ... of a mutton chop and mashed potatoes &c',[5] while 'Her Majesty's Breakfast' on 10 June 1848 was mutton cutlets and beefsteaks; elsewhere the ledgers record fish, eggs, bacon, roast meats, and the occasional vegetable. Despite the much-repeated myth that Victoria ate only a delicately boiled egg for breakfast in later years, she was nearly always offered a wide choice, and her journal entries suggest she embraced it. She usually shared this with whichever family members were around and for four people at a breakfast in 1875, sausages with potatoes, grilled whiting, poached eggs in stock, hot and cold roast fowl were on offer, while in May 1890 she was served bacon and eggs, fried sole, cold fowl, ham and tongue. There is no reason to suppose that food would be ordered that someone did not plan to eat: the palace wasn't a hotel and, while some left-overs were expected (and encouraged), food waste was generally frowned upon. In 1898, a year after the banned book *The Private Life of the Queen* lauded her tiny appetite, she was served asparagus omelette, grilled chicken, bacon, soles, fried whiting and cold meats. Not a boiled egg in sight.[6] Nor – another popular myth – was curry served at breakfast. The Victorian breakfast at an aristocratic level had evolved into a sort of hot buffet, with meats, eggs, toast and enriched breads all available for the taking. The House-hold had a separate breakfast room, in which they were supposed to eat punctually at 9.30 a.m. In 1847 the choice for the Queen's ladies was of roast beef, roast fowl, sau-sages and kidneys, and this was fairly typical.[7] There would also have been various breads, biscuits, spreads and por-ridge, which was introduced after Victoria discovered Scottish breakfasts. Those not needed for duties also had the option of taking breakfast and sometimes lunch, as well as afternoon tea, in their rooms.

Despite the change in service style, the dinner menus, and many of the dishes, show a lot of continuity. It's not surprising, given the long service of most of the cooks, that until at least the 1860s, the repertoire of the kitchens was, while broad, relatively repetitive. The ledger entries become more sporadic at this point in time, although some written menu cards survive, which continue to show a lot of simi-larities. Even by the 1880s, by which time Victoria had

almost certainly adopted *à la Russe*, and many of her original cooks had retired, the food had changed only slightly,
with more elaborate titles (all, as ever, in French), and more
reliance on sauces or garnishes to differentiate dishes, as
opposed to cooking methods or cuts. For example, where
1840s and 1850s menus refer to croquettes, fricassees and
braises, and vegetables are simply *'choux de Bruxelles'*
(Brussels sprouts) or *topinambours* (Jerusalem artichokes:
the prevalence of flatulent vegetables is impressive, considering the mild constriction imposed by the corsets), by the
1890s dishes are given additional descriptors, such as *'bordelaise'*, or *'maintenon'*. Examples of vegetable dishes include
'timbale de choux-fleur à la Polonaise' (puréed cauliflower,
set in a mould, covered with breadcrumbs), and *'fonds
d'artichauts printanières'* (globe artichoke bottoms with
spring vegetables). To some extent, this is simply a reflec-
tion of the codification of French cuisine at the end of the
nineteenth century, wherein menus became more elaborate,
and dishes which might previously have been called after
their principal ingredient gained a clarifying description,
which would have been recognisable to cooks, as well as
diners, and dictated what was in the sauce, and the garnish,
as well as, often, how exactly it was cooked. There would
also have been a change in presentation, for *à la Russe*
demanded that individual portions were easily served from
a large platter, to be held at the side of the diner, whereas in
à la Française it was more common for each diner to carve
out their own portion from the dishes placed on the table.
The food promoted in cookery books and, therefore, aspired
to by the middle classes, the main market for cookery books,
did become fussier at the end of the nineteenth century.

While many cookery books and the dishes in them enjoyed an extremely long life, remaining relevant from the 1840s to the 1890s (Francatelli's *Modern Cook* was in print from 1846 until at least 1911), the recipes being newly promoted in the last quarter of the nineteenth century were markedly different to those which came before, and the books in which they were published were much more detailed and, to a large extent, dictatorial. Victoria's cooks would not have been swayed by such aspirational fripperies as crossed golf club moulds in which to present their aspic-embellished chicken mousse,[8] but, even if the dishes themselves changed very little, the way in which they were expressed on the menus was, nevertheless, influenced by wider culinary trends.

Victoria ate predominantly French food, and her menus were always written in French, with nods to British and German traditions along the way. Her everyday meals were of the same type enjoyed by upper-class diners across Britain: rich, meat-heavy, time-consuming to prepare and with expensive ingredients. The menus were to a large extent defined by the pattern into which nineteenth-century dining had settled even before Victoria's accession, a pattern which successfully survived the service style change, and remained usual among the rich until the First World War. The meal always started with soup, with a choice provided between clear and thick. Thick soups, sometimes called purées, generally involved vegetables, simmered until they fell apart, and then passed through a tammy cloth, a process in which the mix was put in a cloth which was then twisted by two people, one on either end, until the purée oozed through the fine holes. It was messy, and an alternative was to use a tammy-sieve, which was a fine cloth sieve that one person could use, and which yielded – eventually – the same result. Francatelli, whose books positively buzz with royal references, despite his somewhat murky departure from royal service, published a recipe for potato soup à la Victoria, which is made in exactly this way, and garnished with potato quenelles, asparagus tips and French beans cut into diamond shapes. Other vegetables for which he gives purée recipes include turnips, chestnuts, peas, spring herbs, asparagus, carrot and lentils. A white carrot thick soup appeared on the royal table on 29 December 1847, and potato soup was a regular dish, giving credence to the idea that, 'Her Majesty confesses to a great weakness for potatoes, which are cooked for her in every conceivable way.'[9]

Clear soups were based on consommé, with garnishes, added just before serving, floating in a totally clear broth. One that occurs several times in the ledgers is *jarret de veau* (veal knuckle). This was a pale consommé, deceptively simple-looking, but which could take days to prepare. It was complicated enough that it was the responsibility of the first yeoman of the kitchen, six levels down from the chief cook, but by no means a junior position. The soups were usually the same on the Queen's table and the Household table, so he would have been making them for around eight to twenty people on an average day. Butcher's meat, which referred to any meat that was not game or poultry, was delivered on a daily basis, and in 1837 the main supplier was J. Armfield. In the first two weeks of Victoria's reign, he supplied nearly 4,000 lb of beef, over 2,500 lb of mutton, over 2,000 lb of veal and over 400 lb of lamb. In addition to this, his bill included over 200 lb of suet, 36 calves' livers, 3 calves' heads, 204 calves' feet, 28 sweetbreads, 12 lambs' feet, 7 quarters of house lamb (i.e. raised indoors), 10 lamb necks, 3 oxtails and 4 calves' brains.[10] This was for the whole Establishment: they ate well. This particular soup used a knuckle of veal, which would have been put in a vast copper boiling pot, along with beef and chicken for flavour, with the chicken breast meat removed and reserved for later. Once the stock was simmering, it would yield significant quantities of speckled froth or foam, which had to be carefully removed with a spoon, and when this was done, the cook would add vegetables: generally, carrots, celery and an onion. Some seasonings, including cloves and the obligatory salt and pepper, would also go in at this stage. Then the whole thing would be left on a low heat to simmer for three to four hours until the meat was tender. In houses with cast-iron ranges, the cook would just move the pan to the cooler back of the range, but in the royal kitchens, this probably took place in an auxiliary room. At this point, the soup was still only half done, for it would need to be strained, and then left to cool so that it could be clarified. Clarification then took at least an hour: a mixture of crushed eggshell, reserved breast meat, now minced, would be stirred into the cold soup, which would then slowly be brought up to a simmer. Control of the heat was crucial, so that the meaty-egg mixture would coagulate, sucking all of the impurities, which would make the soup cloudy, into its rubbery maw. In theory it all ended up as a thick, ugly, egg-white omelette on top of the soup, which could then be easily removed by being strained without pressure through a fine soup cloth, leaving the soup crystal clear. As with so much in the kitchens, this could take several hours, and required a great deal of patience. One of the Queen's apprentices, Gabriel

Tschumi, recalled one of the extra staff brought in for a big occasion being roundly sent off to reclarify a jelly, based on fish stock made using a similar technique, by the chief cook, with the words, 'a good jelly ... should be like a drop of whisky, quite clear, without the slightest cloud in it. Whisky. You know what that is, eh? Then <u>make</u> the claret jelly as clear as whisky.'[11] The soup was then garnished: rice was popular, as were vegetable shapes, or small morsels of the meat from which the soup was made, but alternatives included croutons which could be handed round with the soup, or small oval balls, in this case of puréed meat, which had been passed through a sieve, mixed with cream and egg, and boiled. Sometimes they were coloured, for an extra bit of visual stimulus: in February and March 1838 the kitchens took delivery of Spanish saffron, cochineal (a vibrant red, extracted from beetle shells), and 'French green colour'.[12]

There were also soups based on barley and rice, which were phenomenally popular on the royal table, and appeared with a certain monotony throughout the entire period. Some, like the crème d'orge, which crops up almost every week, were relatively plain: others, again, belie their simple titles. Francatelli included a recipe for a cream of rice soup in which a pure white rice purée was gently poured into a tureen in which stood twelve perfectly moulded steamed chicken custards.

As well as making soups from large quantities of slow-simmered meat, the kitchens relied on a range of stocks, made from different meats, bones and vegetables, and with different levels of finesse. A basic stock intended for making soup for the steward's room, or gravy for the servants' hall, probably used bones, scraps and general vegetable peelings, but for the Household, stocks of fish, chicken, beef, veal and game were required, depending on the menu. The lack of refrigeration didn't matter – the quantity of stock required on a daily basis was huge, and one of the basic tasks in any kitchen was to ensure that the stockpot was maintained, and the stock clarified and ready for use, at any given point. Such was the importance of stock in French-style cuisine in the eighteenth and nineteenth centuries, that recipes for 'portable' stock or soup were developed, in which meat, bones and especially feet were simmered and strained, and the result reduced to the point that it could be poured into moulds and set. Once dried out, it was as hard as plastic, virtually indestructible, and entirely suitable for travellers to take with them, ready to pop into water and dissolve. Another name for it was veal glue.

The next course was fish, where again diners could choose from two or sometimes more options. Fried white-bait was a perennial favourite, eaten consistently across the reign, and fried fish in general was a mainstay of this course, usually whitings or sole. More upmarket, and certainly more expensive, were the turbot dishes: in May 1899 turbot fillets were served with a red wine sauce (the '*bordelaise*' above), but the usual way of cooking and serving turbot was to cook it whole, and serve it with a sauce, and turbot bouilli (boiled turbot) was another dish which was extremely common. One early Edwardian recipe, for boiled turbot à la Victoria, explained succinctly: 'Wipe the fish with a damp cloth, place it in the fish-kettle, cover well with water, put in the onion and clove, also the parsley, vinegar and sufficient salt to taste: let it come quickly to the boil, and simmer until the fish is done.'[13] It included an illustration of a crucial piece of equipment, without which the dish could not be cooked, and which, along with the price of turbot, ensured that it remained a decidedly exclusive dish. The turbot kettle was a highly specialised pan, diamond shaped to fit the shape of the turbot itself, and often extremely large and very heavy, especially when full. It was fitting for a fish for which the kitchens paid 25 shillings each: most fish cost pennies, and the turbot kettles can still be seen sitting on their numbered racks at Windsor Castle today.[14] The poached fish would have been served with a sauce, although the earlier ledgers don't give details. That which goes with the recipe above is an egg-thickened sauce flavoured with chilli and tarragon: essentially a savoury custard made with stock. The garnish in this example is of lobster balls and parsley. Fish, like meat, was delivered on a daily basis, but in much smaller quantities, as it was only consumed by the Queen and her Household. One turbot would have been ample for each meal: in July 1837, in the same two-week period as above, 8 were delivered, part of a list of fish which includes 55 lb of salmon, 18 lb of red trout, 91 whitings, 36 lobsters, 7 dishes of whitebait and 1 crab.

In the menus up to the late 1870s, remove dishes are listed next. After May 1875, probably coinciding with the move to *à la Russe*, the entrées are next. The two were quite different: entrées were, in many ways, the peak of the savoury part of the meal, and were complicated, elaborate and always cooked (or at least thoroughly overseen) by the chief cook himself. Removes, on the other hand, were usually roasted, braised or baked butcher's meats, sometimes served with vegetables. Often they were larded, as was the case with the *poularde piqué financière*, served in

December 1837, which has an annotation regarding lardings. Larded meats were common before changing oven
technology meant that most people cooked their 'roast'
meats in an oven, rather than in front of an open fire. Pieces
of fat bacon (or sometimes vegetables, such as cucumbers)
were sewn through the flesh of a joint or piece of poultry.
They stuck out on either side of the hole through which
they had been sewn, creating a pimpled effect, which both
looked good, and added to the texture and taste of the item
in question. They also added much-needed fat to dryer
meats, such as pheasant. In some cases, quite long lengths of
bacon or vegetable were used, sewn in careful lines, and the
overall effect was not dissimilar to architectural brickwork,
or a geometrically patterned fabric. They could be safely
left to the ministrations of a lower yeoman or upper assistant cook, while the more senior staff prepared the entrées.
Ready-cut 'lardings' appear on butchers' orders throughout
the reign.

Victoria's entrées were many and varied, although lamb
cutlets appeared so frequently that it is remarkable to find a
menu without them, and her childhood love of mutton
clearly continued throughout her life. Entrée lists for the
1840s also include endless chicken fillets and fish fillets.
However, with a couple of changes of chief cook in the
1840s, the variety increased (while determinedly maintaining lamb or mutton cutlets). Now there were lobster patties,
sweetbreads, pasta with béchamel sauce, salmis of woodcock (salmis were puréed half-cooked meats, mixed with
sauces, rolled in caul fat and poached), bone marrow croustades, ragouts, quenelles, fricassees, macaroni cheese, and
the occasional gratin of larks. Other dishes might include

veal with cucumbers, pheasant, and other game or poultry
breast fillets, usually accompanied with a sauce that included
carefully cut and shaped vegetables. After 1880, marginally
more emphasis appears to have been put on moulded or
shaped preparations, such as croquettes, rissoles and timbales. This last term was pretty vague where French cuisine
was concerned. One version consisted of a purée of vegetables or meat, with a filling of truffles, cream, or a different
meat in the centre. It was made in a straight-sided, domed
mould, and the top and sides were usually garnished with
thin slices of vegetables or truffles, cut out with vegetable
cutters and put in the mould before the purée was pressed in
on top. The purée, incidentally, involved hours of pounding
meat in a giant pestle and mortar to ensure that its texture
was creamy and perfect, and in some cases it was pushed
through a sieve. Pushing meats through a wire sieve is not
easy, and the level of physical graft is hard to over-empha-
sise. (It's pretty hard on the sieve as well.) A hollow was left
in the centre, the timbale poached or steamed for a while,
and then the filling added so that it remained delicate and
was not overcooked. Another type of timbale consisted of a
garnished nest of deep-fried, pre-cooked pasta. Garnishes,
in Victorian cuisine, were not the equivalent of the forlorn,
unripe slice of tomato on the side of a plate of chips that is
so common in modern food, but were instead an integral
part of each dish. In the late Victorian repertoire of French
dishes, garnishes were especially essential to the whole, and
were often dictated by the name of the dish, and often
extremely fiddly and very delicate. In the case of the pasta
timbale, an example is two rabbit fillets, fried, cut into
medallions, and added, along with a third of their weight in

truffles, to an 'espagnol' sauce. Espagnol took a few days to prepare, and was an umami-rich reduction of beef, tomatoes and other vegetables – a staple of Victorian cookery and incredibly delicious. Yet another meaning of the word timbale was a pie. The French lacked a true equivalent of the British raised pie, with its thick hot-water crust and eye-wateringly meaty filling, crammed full of boned birds and game, or layers of meat and vegetables. French cookery did include various pâtés *en croute*, but the closest things to proper pies were referred to as pâtés *chauds* or – gloriously confusingly – timbales. These would have been made, not by the main cooks, but by the pastry cooks, including Alphonse Gouffé, whose brother's book, *Royal Cookery*, included pie-type timbales filled with a bewildering variety of ingredients, from macaroni to hare, and from sturgeon to chicken. Unlike with most British pies, Gouffé directed that the cook should cut the lid off, and garnish the top of the pie with additional ingredients. Truly, more was more. A chicken timbale of this type appeared on an undated, but probably 1880s, menu for 'Her Majesty's Dinner' at Balmoral.[15] The pastry cooks were also responsible for all of the various tarts and similar baked goods that appeared in later courses.

Curry was another entrée, either of veal or, more often, chicken, and curry powder appeared regularly on the spice supply lists throughout the reign. As in the recipe at the beginning of this chapter, many curries in the British repertoire relied on ready-made spice mixes, and curry powder had been available commercially since well before Victoria came to the throne. In 1854 the Queen's curry powder came from a specialist, B. Abrahams, who supplied one dozen bottles of it in May 1854. Dry ingredients all came under the purview of the spicery, and there are lengthy lists of spices, sugar, dried fruits and other delicacies, ordered from grocers such as L. Rushton and Charles Layton (later Layton Brothers and a supplier for the whole period). In the 1840s orders came in for almonds, currants, cloves, cinnamon, ginger, mace, raisins of several types, nutmeg, sugar of several types, semolina and sultanas. Other regular supplies were of arrowroot (for thickening sauces), allspice, almond butter, chocolate, figs and tapioca. Some of the same merchants were called upon for the oilery, under which heading came such things as lentils, rice and rice flour, pasta, soy sauce, anchovies, anchovy essence, barley, capers, gherkins, dried beans, isinglass (a setting agent for jelly, extracted from the gall bladder of a sturgeon), ketchups of various kinds, tomato paste, three different mustards, olive oil, salad oil, pepper, cayenne, salt, a huge range of flavoured and unflavoured vinegars and, by the 1840s, gallons of sauerkraut. There are also accounts for supplying wafer paper for the confectionery, and bladders, which were wetted and used for sealing jars. Britain traded with the entire world, and that was reflected in the variety of goods regularly ordered for the kitchens.

As the number of royal residences grew, and the edible requirements of the palaces settled into a rough pattern, Royal Warrants were issued to key suppliers, who were able to proudly proclaim that they were suppliers to Her Majesty. Most departments drew upon a large range of merchants, ensuring that royal largesse was well spread out, and that they could choose the best of any produce on offer. Some suppliers, especially those for fresh produce, were based near the various palaces, while others delivered mainly to Windsor, from where supplies were shipped off to the other residences. The Windsor payment books contain long lists of carting and shipping costs, with produce wending its way across the country in hampers, baskets, sacks and boxes. In the first half of 1854, nineteen different suppliers were used to provide butchers' meats, including the aptly named W. Giblett, and eight for poultry (where William Finch can't quite match up to Mr Giblett). Among them were several women: Ann Stubbing for meat; Anne Lutte for poultry at Osborne; and Harriet Townsend for poultry at Buckingham Palace. There were eleven fish merchants, including one oyster dealer and a specialist to provide the turtles. Six grocers overlapped with the twenty-four oilery creditors, among which were both Crosse and Blackwell, and Fortnum and Mason. Another familiar name is Twinings, who was one of two tea suppliers, providing five different varieties of tea. There were further suppliers for bread, fruit, vegetables, eggs, cream and milk, cheese and bacon, hams and tongues, wafers, and the vast quantity of beer, wine, sherry and whisky that was consumed. Finally, Gunter's and Bridgeman's, the leading confectioners of London, both regularly provided bottled and candied fruits, biscuits and the occasional cake.[16]

At this point in the meal, if it was served *à la Française*, the first course dishes would be removed, and the diners could have a breather while the second course was brought in. In service *à la Russe*, a sorbet was sometimes served as a palate cleanser, and then the most prestigious course would make its appearance: the roast. Roasting on a spit was inefficient, space-hungry, and yielded utterly delicious results.

The roast was invariably game, when in season, which meant a wide range of birds: woodcocks, snipe, partridge, pheasant, ptarmigan, plovers and larks all featured on the menu at various times. More exotic fare, probably from France or Scotland, included ortolans, dotterel, capercailzie and ruffs. Hare was also often served and, when game was not in season, duck, capon (a castrated chicken: illegal now in Britain, the process makes the flesh whiter and plumper), turkey and quail. They were served with heads and legs intact (except for the turkey, which was generally cut off at the ankle and neck), having been trussed in specific positions, sometimes with the liver or gizzard tucked under the wings. Carving them was an art, and had long been regarded as a mark of a gentleman, although in the royal Household, one of the senior footmen almost certainly carved the meats for the diners, especially if the regime was *à la Russe*. There were further, cold, roast meats on the sideboard which the Queen maintained throughout her reign, and on special occasions these were joined by pies and brawns, as well as cold tongue and other things suitable for a particularly peckish diner or, more realistically, a hungry staff member waiting eagerly for leftovers downstairs. Given the pace of dinner, it seems unlikely that any of the Household would have enjoyed the sideboard on a regular basis, at least by the 1880s. When they dined alone, as Victoria and Albert often did, they would combine the first removes and the entrées, before skipping straight to the entremets, and after Albert's death Victoria adopted this set-up until the 1870s, even at relatively large gatherings (although the roast would sometimes form part of the sideboard offering).

Much of the game served at the royal table was shot on the

royal estates, although extra was always ordered in. Albert's love of shooting and stalking must be seen in the wider context of both estate management and providing food for the table. A team of gamekeepers managed the land around all of the palaces, except Buckingham Palace, which only had a small garden. They were expected to be good shots, able to supplement the sometimes mangled efforts of royal guests, who were out for the sport and without the needs of the kitchens in mind. Cooks quickly came to recognise the birds that had been shot by particular people: if too far gone, they would barely even have been suitable for soup. Looks were paramount for the roasts – unbroken necks and legs, intact heads and unblemished breasts were required if the bird in question was to be presented whole. Care was also needed for deer and other four-footed prey, and one obituary of the head keeper at Windsor, John Cole, noted approvingly that, 'his greatest recorded feat ... was killing six [deer] before breakfast, all through the head and without blemish'. It went on, recounting merrily an occasion on which he, 'by accident killed two bucks by the same shot, but happily without spoiling a haunch'.[17] Game was also gifted to the Queen, from various courtiers and relations, as well as local hunts. When she was in brief residence at Brighton at the end of 1837, the game book recorded hares, partridges, rabbits, deer, snipe and blackcock from royal lands in the New Forest, Richmond, Windsor, Kew, Hampton Court, and from Brighton Hunt, as well as two haunches of wild deer from Lord Tavistock, ruffs and reeves from Lady Tavistock (small wading birds, illegal to kill now), and a host of others. The Duke of Norfolk gave her two cygnets: baby swans, and one of the most prestigious meats of the period.

The range of hunted game was, as with so many other types of food, far greater than today. (We have a more measured approach to extinction risks, as well as a more squeamish view about what is desirable to eat.) Swan eating was reserved for the wealthy, but was not reserved only for the Queen. Indeed, the widely held belief that the Queen owns all the swans in Britain doesn't seem to have a basis in law. Modern swans are protected by various pieces of legislation, but until the 1930s adverts for cygnets can still be found in newspapers. Norfolk swans were particularly favoured, eaten young, having first been fattened. Victoria didn't eat swan much – if at all – but she certainly kept them on the Thames, for they caused a flurry of problems in the 1850s: two escaped, were captured in error by a man who thought they were two of his, which had run away, and sent to a game merchant, from where they were recovered amid much excitement. On another occasion, a flock kept at Chertsey invaded the Earl of Lucan's land, provoking an apoplectic letter wherein he threatened to, 'shoot 6, leaving them on the ground and shall cause 6 to be shot every Friday until they are reduced to the number of 6. I have too patiently suffered this nuisance to be inflicted on me and I will be rid of it.'[18] Clearly, the royal swan-keeper earned his money. Recipes for roast swan appeared in cookery books until at least the 1870s, though even by the start of Victoria's reign they were dwindling in popularity.

Following the roast there was, in the early part of the reign, another remove course, usually a soufflé or a national dish such as mince pies or schwarzbrot pudding (black bread pudding). Later, again around the time that *à la Russe* was probably adopted in the 1870s, these were amalgamated into the next course, a second set of highly elaborate entremets. These fell into two categories: vegetable dishes and sweet dishes. The vegetable options showed off the whole range of the kitchen gardens, though home-grown produce was always supplemented by extra quantities bought in from grocers. Likewise, the sweet entremets often contained fruit, including pineapples, strawberries, pears, apples, raspberries, apricots and many others, again predominantly from the gardens, but supplemented with outside orders, especially in the 1830s and 1840s. The royal kitchen gardens were not in a good state when the Queen came to the throne. They were spread across eight sites: Kensington, Kew, Hampton Court, Richmond and Windsor. The last of these had four separate gardens that were so far apart that the head gardener had to spend half a day on horseback in order to inspect them all. Complaints had been circulating for decades, both in garden journals and directly, through the letters sent from the various gardeners to the holders of the purse strings, with changes made piecemeal, and normally only when a building was about to fall down. Immediately after Victoria's accession, a committee was formed to fully investigate the situation: their conclusions spoke of decay, depression and neglect. The reports reveal a lot about expectations in the 1840s, though, and show quite clearly how far seasonality did not apply at the Queen's table: even in February, when the gardens were inspected, they expected to find ripe fruit, fit for the table: 'The Crown possesses nearly 900 yards in length of forcing houses of all descriptions and yet they did not in the year 1837 furnish a strawberry or grape in the months of January and February, and scarcely even in March.' Instead, they found a travesty.

There were thousands of metres of walls up which to grow soft fruit, acres of greenhouses for vines, melons, pineapples and cucumbers, and virtually unlimited horse manure for heating hot beds in order to grow asparagus, leaf vegetables and herbs, and yet the kitchens regularly ordered all of the produce supposedly grown in the kitchen gardens from elsewhere, and then struggled when mismanagement produced enormous gluts, such as the 221 pineapples and 2,900 cucumbers in August 1837.[19] Such was the poor reputation of the gardens as a result that they struggled to recruit or retain decent staff, and the whole shambles just kept becoming worse.

A well-run Victorian kitchen garden was a very fine thing. It could be relied upon to produce any vegetable or fruit at any point in the year, drawing on a mixture of techniques to force (bring forward) or retard flowering and fruiting throughout the year. Many large gardens had coal-fired boiler houses, which fed hot air into the garden walls, and hot steam into greenhouses. Brick walls were vital, and gardening manuals advised on the best varieties of tree to plant on each wall, depending on which direction it faced, and the type of soil. Most also had mushroom sheds and brick-built cold frames, as well as pits for melons and cucumbers, and the variety of specialist greenhouses was bewildering. Even smaller gardens could do a good job: horse manure gives off tremendous amounts of heat as it rots down, and, in a country reliant on horses, there was no shortage of fuel to put around pots and pits to encourage plants to grow in the most inhospitable of climates. The range of fruit and vegetables commonly eaten was far broader than it is today, and included some delicacies, such as medlars and bullaces, skirret and sea kale, which are unheard of by many twenty-first-century consumers. (Medlars, also known as the dog's bottom fruit, are related to apples, and need to be 'bletted' — part rotted — before eating; bullaces are a type of plum; skirret is a fiddly root vegetable; and sea kale was a type of kale which was forced and blanched in pots like rhubarb: the long, slender white stalks were then tied in bunches, boiled and eaten with a sauce. It doesn't taste much like modern kale, and is more like thin celery in texture, lacking the sharp edges and tough stalks which characterise the familiar variety today.) Not only that, but the Victorians were ferocious plant breeders, constantly cultivating new varieties of fruit and vegetable, so that there was something suitable for every garden, and every possible taste. The Royal Horticultural Society recorded over 1,500 types of apple alone in 1883,[20] and the Victorians also introduced the distinction, unique to the UK, between cooking and eating apples. Most of the older varieties are suitable for both. There was little excuse for the state of desolation in the royal kitchen gardens, and the subsequent fact that the Queen's table was, 'not better supplied with fresh fruit than that of most private gentlemen'.[21]

Change, however, was afoot. The Kensington gardens were sold off, and are today buried under a street of exceedingly desirable houses (the rather literally named Kensington Palace Gardens — originally Queen's Road). At Kew, the kitchen garden was eventually given to the Botanic Garden, and is part of the expanse now open to the public. Hampton Court was given up entirely, while at Windsor ambitious work began on a new, amalgamated garden, totalling 27 acres and which, when finished, was 'the most perfect garden in Europe, of its kind … [supplying] the Royal tables with the finest fruits and vegetables which skill can produce'.[22] It was designed with royal visits in mind, and included, in the head gardener's house, reception rooms for the royal family, which looked out over rows of ordered produce arranged around a central fountain. The head gardener earned the same amount as the chief cook, and was entitled to the vails (tips) left by guests for distribution among the Establishment.[23] The kitchen garden books show the sheer quantity that was supplied to the kitchens, including, in 1869: 37 pecks (74 gallons) of Jerusalem artichokes, 138 bundles of asparagus (each bundle was of 100 stalks), 111 half dozen beetroot, 16,800 bunches of carrots from the main garden and 284 bunches from the forcing house, 1,080 brace of cucumbers, 603 dozen endives, 719 half dozen lettuces, 5,208 lb of old potatoes and 2,882 lb of new as well as another 254 ½ forced, 415 bunches of radishes along with another 254 forced, 132 bunches of rhubarb in the open ground and 110 bunches from the forcing house, 858 punnets of 'small salad' from the greenhouse, and 92 bunches of yet another forgotten delicacy, scorzonera, which was a type of root vegetable a bit like salsify (it bleeds white goo which turns brown when cut or peeled, and is most disconcerting to prepare). Additional produce was bought in when needed, and in 1854 – well after the new gardens reached full productivity – payments to creditors included bills for several hundred more asparagus spears, cauliflowers, carrots, potatoes and turnips, as well as more specialist vegetables and salad, including marjoram, tarragon, endives, asparagus peas, sorrel and phenomenal amounts of watercress, which was immensely popular for garnishing dishes.

Fruit production was evidently more up to scratch, for most of the outside supplies were citrus fruits, including blood oranges, mandarins, and lemons and oranges by the thousand. There were also regular extra orders for strawberries, including the aptly named 'British Queen'.[24]

The vegetable entremets themselves ranged from boiled or fried items, served with sauce, through to the inevitable moulded and layered gratins. Even the simple-sounding titles on the various menus belie the amount of work behind the final result. Anything that could be carefully turned into a fantastical shape was attacked with a knife. Even '*les epinards*', spinach, which appears on menus as a winter dish, was more involved than it seemed. Before it even got to a cook, a maid would have picked out all the stalks, washed it several times, drained it and boiled it in salted water before plunging it into cold water (to retain the colour), and squeezed it gently enough to dry it, but not so much as to obliterate it. The cook responsible, probably one of the assistant cooks, would then have pounded it in a mortar, rubbed it through the inevitable wire sieve, and set it aside. When it was needed, he would then warm it through in a pan with butter, nutmeg, a tiny amount of thick gravy, made glossy and stiff with plenty of calves' feet used in the initial stock, before presenting it neatly on a hot plate, garnished with croutons. Titles can be misleading: the immensely popular 'melted butter', with which many vegetables were served, and which was one of the only sauces with British origins, was actually a roux made of butter and flour, thinned to sauce consistency with water, with a generous glug of vinegar or lemon juice, and some more butter, along with seasonings, added at the end. It is gorgeous, but rather more than simply melted dairy fat.

1. Sketched in the wake of her illness, there is more than a whiff of the modern, slightly pouting selfie about this self-portrait (1835). Princess Victoria was now on a determined diet, skipping meals and comparing herself to the other women she met and she was very proud of her new, slender figure.

2. Held in the garish surroundings of the Buckingham Palace Picture Gallery, Prince Leopold's Christening Banquet took full advantage of all the spectacle that the royal plate room could provide. The gold on the table and displayed on the buffet is George IV's silver gilt service, complete with mirrored plateaux down the centre of the table serving as stands for the small trees. To the left is one of the serving stations, busy with footmen.

3. Seen here as a distant figure presiding over a mêlée of dignatories digging enthusiastically into their jellies, this was one of many lavish feasts Victoria attended in the early years of her reign. The menu for the Lord Mayor's Banquet, 9 November 1837, was strictly demarcated according to status: the royal table had seventeen first course dishes including boiled turbot with fried whiting, lamb feet casserole, woodcock pie and hare with tomato; twenty second course dishes, ranging from champagne jelly to buttered eel, and a further massive cold buffet to one side. The four tables immediately below her had a slightly different offering, and the four below that were different again. It was à la Française at its most exuberant — and everyone, inevitably, had turtle soup.

OSBORNE

Her Majesty's Dinner.

TUESDAY 25th DECEMBER, 1894.

Potages.

A la Tête de Veau claire   A la Cressy

Poissons,

Les Tranches de Saumon Sauce Hollandaise

Les Soles à la Colbert

Entrées.

Les Pains de faisans à la Milanaise

Relevé.

Roast Beef.   Yorkshire Pudding

Rôt.

Le Dinde à la Chipolata

Chine of Pork

Entremêts.

Les Asperges à la sauce

Mince Pies

Plum Pudding

La Geleé d' Oranges à l' Anglaise

Side Table.

Baron of Beef, Wild Boar's Head, Game Pie, Brawn,

Woodcock Pie, Terrine de Foies Gras.

4. The Queen was experimenting with different service styles for more informal meals from the 1850s, but did not properly adopt à la Russe until 1875. Written menus were introduced for every meal. Under an à la Française regime, the soup, fish, entrées and first relevés were all first course dishes, served simultaneously, while the rest were part of the second course. Now they were divided out and served sequentially from a platter to one side, and diners no longer helped themselves. In both service styles, dessert followed, generally composed of ices and fruit from the royal kitchen gardens.

5. *Commissioned by the Queen as a birthday present for Albert, this was one of several paintings showing industrious royals killing off the local wildlife. Both Osborne and Balmoral had game larders, and game featured widely on the menus.*

6. *The main kitchen at Windsor was described as chapel-like, with its high ceiling and light from above. The heated central table contains domes to keep food warm, and the octagonal table was occupied by a storekeeper, who kept track of the produce as it was transformed into finished dishes. The former open fireplaces of the medieval structure now contain charcoal stoves, and, hidden by a screen, is one of two roasting ranges.*

7. *This painting depicts a royal visit to the kitchens, which were a firm fixture on the internal tourist trail at Windsor. George IV's flamboyant taste encompassed the kitchens, and the battlemented roasting screens and huge canopies over the fires were all added during his renovations. The two chefs to the right are master cooks, working at their individual tables, lit, as can be seen, by gas, the fittings for which are as artful as the rest of the design.*

8. *The exterior of the kitchens at Osborne, with the service yard and various workers scattered around. The kitchens themselves are situated in the central block, under the large chimney, with the main kitchen wrapped around the earlier stable block. To the left was the knife room and the right wing of the former stables housed one of the servants' halls. Looming above is the main accommodation, which housed most of the various attendants and some of their personal servants, while under the clock tower at the back lies the royal pavilion.*

9. Gottlob Waetzig was the British-born son of one of a Swedish bandmaster. He joined the kitchens as an apprentice in 1838 and steadily rose up the hierarchy, making third master cook before his retirement in 1876.

10. George Dessaulles was the son of a man already in royal service. He joined the kitchens as an apprentice in 1853, several ranks below Gottlob Waetzig, and eventually became first master cook. He retired in 1881.

11. Taken nine months before Albert's death, this photograph shows a still trim Victoria with her increasingly florid-looking husband. Admittedly well-corseted, despite the crinoline and her taste for flounces on her clothing, Victoria's figure belies her nine children. At 5ft 10 Albert could carry extra weight rather more easily than Victoria, at 5ft 1, though there's a sharp contrast with the lithe young man she married twenty years before.

12. In 1853 work started on a replica Swiss chalet which Victoria and Albert's growing brood could use as a playhouse. To the front were the gardens which the children already looked after, while eventually its surroundings expanded to include a gazelle house, miniature fort and museum. It was a regular stopping-off point for both the Queen and the Prince and their visitors, and the children looked back on it with great affection in later life.

13. The three-quarter size kitchen at Swiss Cottage was provided with everything an aspiring cook could need. It looked out onto the individual plots which the royal children tended, linking plot to plate very graphically. Here they grew fruit and vegetables, prepared a range of simple dishes, and served their parents tea and cake.

PRINCE ALBERT THE BRITISH FARMER.

"Prince Albert has turned his attention to the promotion of agriculture ; and if you have seen, as most probably you have, an account of the sale of Prince Albert's stock, and the prices they fetched, I have not the slightest doubt you will give one cheer more to PRINCE ALBERT AS A BRITISH FARMER."—*Sir Robert Peel's Speech at Tamworth, October* 2, 1843.

14. Punch had a lot of fun with Albert's activities on behalf of British farming, here linking his active promotion of best practice with the domestic and private ideal he and Victoria were striving to create at Osborne and Balmoral. In some ways, given the children's vegetable gardens and the menagerie they kept at Swiss Cottage, which included bantams, it probably wasn't too far off.

15. Victoria, who was rarely vain, admired this portrait for its lack of flattery. Fourteen years after Albert's death she had gained weight, as she turned to food as comfort. Wearing the mourning dress which characterised the last forty years of her life, there's a hint of more than one chin. Her determined expression is equally characteristic: she became ever more pugnacious, not least if anyone dared hint she should curb her eating habits.

16. *Victoria, seated in carriage, is being handed tea by one of the Highland Attendants, while an Indian servant crouches by the fire preparing it. Tea-taking was a fixed part of the daily routine by the 1890s, and certainly not something to be disrupted by the mere fact of being out and about in the Riviera. The French still call afternoon tea 'le five o clock'.*

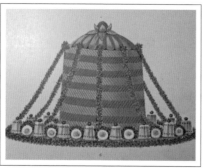

17. This selection of illustrations from contemporary cookbooks aimed at the middle and upper classes shows the wide range of presentation styles over the period. With the change from à la Française to à la Russe, dishes had to be served in a way which enabled them to be served directly onto a diner's plate. The royal batterie de cuisine included a huge range of moulds, intended for everything from jelly and ice cream, to meat purées. Roast meats were served heads and legs on, and aspic was used as a shiny, elegant garnish.

18. *In late 1839, just before her wedding, Victoria had determinedly dieted her way to 7 stone 2, with a BMI of 18.8. Her wedding gown reflects this petite figure. She wore her wedding gown for the successive christenings of many of her children, and her figure seems to have remained relatively trim until the death of the Prince in 1861.*

19. Never renowned for her dress sense, in later life the Queen was at times so beribboned and beruffled that she was only barely visible. This gown has two panels of crepe, associated with early mourning, on the front, as well as a handy pocket. Her gowns by this era were only lightly boned, but she still would have worn some form of body support: not a full corset, but still something which would have shaped her body and given her a visible waist.

20. *Victoria died on 22 January 1901, at Osborne House, with her funeral taking place ten days later. In the interim, her body lay in state in the dining room at Osborne, hastily fitted out as a chapel with drapes and flags. Behind the coffin, the sideboard, more usually laden with cold fowl and tongue, holds the flowers and a cross. The funeral colours, as seen on the coffin and its base, were purple and white, making this the first time she'd been dressed in anything but black for nearly forty years.*

Francatelli, well used to working with it, noted, 'though simple, it is nevertheless a very useful and agreeable sauce when properly made; so far from this being usually the case, it is too generally left to assistants to prepare as an insignificant matter; the result is generally unsatisfactory'.[25] He goes on to give a long list of sauces all based on the same principle, including a butter sauce for asparagus which was often used instead of hollandaise and is essentially melted butter sauce with added cream.

The vegetables were served at the same time as a range of other savoury entremets, such as chicken salad, cheese straws, plovers' eggs, chips and cooked oysters. But they were not alone, and would be surrounded by sweet entremets, which could be anything from chocolate profiteroles and meringues, to doughnuts, blancmange and pineapple pudding. Fruit was served in vol-au-vents, tarts, jellies, creams and puddings. None of these were the simple, domestic versions of the Mrs Beetons and Eliza Actons of the Victorian world. Instead, they were moulded, piped, garnished, spiced, shaped, sieved and pounded until the results bore little hint of the raw ingredients, and were elevated into edible art. Apparently simple lists of ingredients became glorious tributes to the chefs' skills, which ensured that a Yorkshire pudding would be the very epitome of Britishness, while the French dish next to it could compete with anything being cooked in Paris.[26] While the menus were in French, those dishes that were an established part of the British repertoire – essentially roast meats, puddings, raised pies and brawns – were always written in English. There were also German influences, and German sausage, as well as sauerkraut, appeared frequently in the supply ledgers.

Most of the sweet entremets were the province of the confectionery, which was in a bright, octagonal room away from the heat of the main kitchen. It was the main consumer of the four types of sugar that were supplied to the kitchens on a regular basis, as well as the vast quantities of nuts and spices. In May 1854, E. Clifford billed for 4 lb of allspice, 24 lb of Jordan almonds (the standard sweet type we are used to today), 4 lb of bitter almonds (for flavour, and to be used with some caution due to containing small amounts of cyanide), 2 lb of candy sugar, 2 lb of cloves, 150 lb of currants, 1 lb of caraways, 2 lb of cocoa, 1 lb each of mace and nutmeg, 96 lb of raisins, 936 ½ lb of single refined sugar, 66 lb of double, and 30 ¾ lb of triple refined sugar. Then there was another 186 lb of Lisbon sugar, 18 lb of sultanas and 4 lb of semolina. This wasn't all: G. R. & H. Whittingham added another 906 lb of the various types of sugar in total, along with another 46 lb of almonds, 96 lb of currants and 13 lb of muscatel raisins, 48 lb of standard raisins, several more pounds of spice, 6 lb of Fry's chocolate, and 2 lb of cocoa nibs. The vast quantities are not surprising: many of the entremets centred around sugar, from nougats to meringues, and from sugar baskets to the towering pastillage sculptures so popular for big events. On the Queen's first night at Buckingham Palace, in July 1837, she had nougats garnis, possibly a variation on the recipe for nougats à la reine (Queen nougat), published by Jules Gouffé in his *Livre de Pâtisserie* some years later. The nougat is fairly standard – almonds suspended in sugar, boiled to hard crack, and moulded into a shape while still warm. For anyone other than experts in sugar-work it's devilishly hard to make, not least as it sets so quickly: Gouffé advises that cooks should work in pairs. For the version à la reine, whole sugared almonds are used, half of which are coloured pink, the other half left white, along with white sugared pistachio nuts. He suggests that the nougat is moulded in a hexagonal mould, with alternating sides of pink-nut-based and white-nut-based nougat, garnished while still warm with the pistachios pressed into the cooling nougat along the joins. The sides can then be piped with icing, or have a moulded sugar sculpture applied to them. The confectionery was also shipping regular packages to the Queen on her travels: in September 1897 the list of delicacies packaged up for her included sixteen chocolate sponges, sixteen fondant biscuits, a box of wafers, a box of pralines, twelve plain sponges, a rice cake, a princess cake, a box of biscuits, a box of drop tablets and eighteen flat finger biscuits.[27]

As if working with hot sugar wasn't challenging enough, the confectionery was also responsible for the many set creams and jellies that were also part of the sweet entremets. Jellies at this time were either set with isinglass, or, more usually, with gelatine extracted from calves' feet – hence the many bills for calves' feet in the supply books. Rendering the gelatine took days, and was even more involved than making a stock, involving similar amounts of clarification and straining, plus a bit of flavouring with wine and sugar, and with the added pitfall of ensuring that the final thick liquid would set firmly – but with a perky wobble – when chilled. This basic wine jelly was used as the basis for some incredible dishes, often made in specialised moulds which enabled cooks to fill internal cavities with set creams, or, by the end of the century, to create elaborate, multicoloured, 3D designs. The jellies which featured on the everyday royal menus were probably more sensible than the fantastical creations of late Victorian cookery writers, however: fruit jellies made regular appearances, including orange jelly, as popular with the Queen in the 1890s as it had been when she was recovering from her mystery sickness at Tunbridge Wells in 1835. Jellies were also served individually in glasses, which would be presented on a stand if served à la Française: between August and September 1838, two gross (288 glasses) were ordered from the glass merchant. Meanwhile, in 1852, when the Buckingham Palace kitchens were being refitted, 48 plain moulds, large and small, were ordered from Benningtons, along with one 'temple top mould', and a 'copper Turk's cap mould with fluted centre'.[28]

To set, the jellies required ice, which was also a prerequisite for one of the standard dessert items: ices. These were also made by the confectionery, and, as moulded iced bombes or iced puddings, often appeared as sweet entremets as well. Those served as part of the dessert course were intended as palate cleansers, served in small quantities for replete diners, and would usually simply be presented in ice pails for diners to help themselves; the iced puddings were a tad more involved. Making the basic mixture was not, in itself, difficult: ice cream was simply a mixture of custard or sweetened cream mixed with the chosen flavour, while water ices were made with water, sugar syrup and flavourings. Sorbets were also served, and generally involved alcohol. The ice cream was made in a round-bottomed, heavy-lidded, pewter freezing pot, or sorbetière, which sat in a wooden bucket filled with ice and salt (the salt lowers the temperature of the ice, which can get to below −20°C extraordinarily rapidly). The chilled mix was put in the pail, which was spun round at intervals, interspersed with the lid being taken off so that the confectioner could scrape the freezing mixture away from the sides and ensure that the ice set smoothly and consistently. Victorian ice-cream flavours were wide-ranging and far more exotic than much of what is common today. One of the best books on ices from the period is Agnes Marshall's *Book of Ices*, which includes such flavours as cucumber, bergamot, banana, cedrat (citron), curaçao, filbert (a type of hazelnut), quince, tea, rose water, damson, chestnut and – possibly less appetisingly – curry. Her follow-up book, *Fancy Ices*, is a glorious romp through the never-ending possibilities that arise when skill, time and technology come together. It's not useful as a guide to what was on the royal table, for her market was not only aspirational and wanting to show off, but also those who were time-poor and lacking in traditional skills. They were, therefore, willing to embrace the terrifyingly long list of patent ingredients and ready-prepared concoctions required for many of her recipes (all of which were available via mail order through Marshall herself). However, it's another good reminder that simple titles didn't mean simple recipes: Marshall's easy-sounding ice-cream bombes were decorated to the extent that the central ice must have been, at times, almost invisible within the piped creams, sugar baskets, maidenhair ferns, and delicately moulded fruits made from coloured water ice. The royal kitchens made a lot of different ices, requiring a lot of sets of freezing equipment: in September 1838 four freezing pots with covers and the fabulously named spaddles, the specialist mixing tool for use with the pots, were ordered from John Roberts at a cost of £5.10s. The ice itself was harvested from the royal estates, though on occasion it was supplemented with bought ice, which was shipped to Britain from North America and Greenland and stored in huge commercial ice houses around King's Cross.

Throughout the meal, bread was on the table, which in the case of the Queen's table would have been individual French rolls. Although the kitchens included a bakehouse, and two bakers were employed, they clearly could not cater for all of the needs of the royal Establishment, and bread was always ordered in. Twenty-two separate bakers are listed as suppliers in the 1854 creditors' lists: some supplied only a few items, and others supplied predominantly yeast, both brewer's yeast and the new, compressed type known as German yeast (which is roughly what is sold as 'fresh' yeast today). Others made rusks, cakes, muffins or biscuits, including Albert biscuits, for which Francatelli gave a recipe in his *Modern Cook*, and some supplied mainly flour. The bulk of the bills, however, were for bread: plain loaves, cottage loaves, twists, rolls, fancy breads (for breakfast), and the intriguingly named 'tops and bottoms'. To be fair to the in-house bakers, bread was the staple food item in Victorian England, and a vast quantity was required to fulfil the expectations of those who lived and worked at the palaces, especially the lower servants who would have been consuming the plain and cottage loaves.

Those same servants were almost certainly the main consumers of the beer and ale, which came from sixteen different suppliers in 1854, including Whitbread and Bass. They would also have been consuming the cheapest of the tea varieties – mixed tea – as well as the standard drink of the poor, water. The more senior servants, especially those in personal contact with the Queen, expected – and received – wine. Wine came in by the hogshead, and included sparkling Moselle, red Bordeaux (including claret, Château Lafitte and Margaux), champagne, and many, many others. Sherry was also phenomenally popular among the members of the Household, along with port, Madeira, brandy, and various liqueurs including curaçao, noyau, Danzig Gold Water and cherry brandy. Whisky was also ordered by the hogshead, along with soda water and seltzer water, which were regarded both as mixers and health drinks. Different grades of wine, port and sherry were ordered: good stuff for the Queen's table, and slightly less so for those of lower standing, who consequently drank the quality of product which could have been found in most middle-class homes. The cellars were kept very well stocked: nearly 112,000 bottles were counted in an inventory of 1841. Consumption levels were high as well, and while Victoria did not have the reputation of a heavy drinker for most of her reign, she was no fan of temperance. In the early days of her marriage, Albert's chief advisor Baron Stockmar insisted to him that he should curb his wife's drinking for 'a Queen does not drink a bottle of wine at a meal'. By the 1850s, the court had become (relatively) sober: a half bottle of wine per meal per person on average (so, a bottle per day),[29] as, amid much grumbling from the Household, Albert tried to showcase the royal family as sober and financially responsible. The whiff of the bourgeois was undermined by the actual cost of many of the wines, though, and, indeed, no one with any understanding of everyday fare at the royal table would ever have considered their monarch to be anything other than at the very pinnacle of British society.

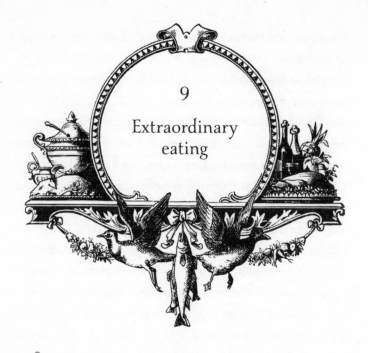

9

Extraordinary
eating

As an aristocrat, Victoria would always have eaten well; as a Queen, however, there was a great deal more to dinner. Entertaining went with the job, and meals were opportunities to impress, to forge friendships and to conduct international diplomacy in ways that were far more intricate and personally involved than the official policies and treaties signed by politicians and elected representatives. Everyday dinners with three or thirty court members were one thing, but whether she liked it or, as became the case in later life, loathed it, as the focal point of British politics, Victoria was also the focal point of most state visits. Dinner with the Queen was what people wanted, both at home and abroad. As she grew older she did her best to travel incognito, as a mere Duchess, avoiding the palaver of hosting and being hosted, but as Queen and, later, Empress, she ultimately had to accept that putting on a show was part of the point.

The endless parade of heads of foreign states got going early: even in July 1837, when guest lists, included in the dining ledgers, are first available for Victoria's reign, various princes, dukes and the occasional king make frequent appearances. Naturally, Uncle Leopold hastened across the Channel to see his protégée now that she had become Queen, staying for three weeks in September 1837. Victoria was ecstatic, revelling in the ability to show off in her new role, not just as Queen, but as hostess, finally in charge and installed in her own home: 'At 7 o'clock arrived my dearest most beloved Uncle Leopold and my dearest most beloved Aunt Louise. They are both, and look both, very well; dearest Aunt Louise is looking so well and is grown quite fat. I and Mamma as well as my whole court were all at the door to receive them. It is an inexpressible happiness and joy to me, to have these dearest beloved relations with me and in my own house. I took them to their rooms, and then hastened to dress for dinner. At 8 we dined.'[1] The visit was as much a family get-together as it was an official state visit, and Victoria, her uncle, his wife Louise and the Duchess of Kent all breakfasted together every day. There were no grand balls or receptions held in Leopold's honour, but large dinner parties took place every night, though no particular effort was made beyond the already lavish provision of the everyday royal dining experience. Indeed, on the majority of occasions when heads of state dined, the dinner was a normal one, and the food no different to usual. Victoria hosted so many people, of different ranks and persuasions, that every dinner at the main

Boar's Head with Aspic Jelly

Procure the head of a bacon hog which must be cut off deep into the shoulders; bone it carefully, beginning under the throat, then spread the head out upon a large earthenware dish, and rub it with the following ingredients ... When the head has been well rubbed with these, pour about a quart of port-wine lees over it, and keep in a cool place for a fortnight; observing that it must be turned over in its brine every day ... When about to dress the head, take it out of the brine, and wash it thoroughly in cold water; then absorb all the exterior moisture from it with a clean cloth, and spread it out upon the table. Next, pare off all the uneven pieces from the cheeks, &c., cut these into long narrow fillets, and put them with the tongue, fat bacon, and truffles, prepared as directed for the galantine; then, line the inside of the head with a layer of force-meat (the same kind as used for galantines), about an inch thick, and lay thereon the fillets of tongue, bacon, truffles, and here and there some pistachio kernels (the skin of which must be removed by scalding); cover these with a layer of force-meat, and then repeat the rows of tongue, &c., and when the head is sufficiently garnished to fill it out in its shape, it should be sewn up with a small trussing-needle and twine, so as thoroughly to secure the stuffing. The head must then be wrapped up in a strong cloth, previously well spread with butter, and sewn up in this, so as to preserve its original form: it should next be put into a large oval braising-pan ... Set the brazier on the stove-fire; as soon as it boils up, skim it thoroughly, then remove it to a slow fire (covered with the lid containing live embers), that the head may continue to simmer or boil very gently, for about five hours.[2]

palaces of Windsor and Buckingham Palace was an important one, and every dish was expected to reflect her royal
status. The number of people who sat down at the royal
table in any given year could be astonishing – over 113,000
in 1841 alone.[3] Some were, however, afforded special status.

The Tsar of Russia was the first really significant guest,
in June 1844, and hosting him occasioned a huge amount of
agonising. Victoria's journals record daily trips around the
apartments that were being prepared for him and his entourage, with lists of what pictures were being hung where, and
details of the drapery. His visit coincided with that of the
King of Saxony, with whom Victoria felt much more at ease,
and her slightly nervous summary of the first evening of the
visit makes clear the stresses of entertaining strangers:

> The Emperor who was in civilian evening dress, led me
> in, & I sat between him & the King of Saxony. There is
> a strange expression in the Emperor's eyes, one might
> almost say wild, which is not prepossessing. But his
> manners are excellent, dignified & simple. However, he
> gives me the impression of not being a happy man, &
> not being quite at his ease. He seldom smiles, & when
> he does, it is hardly an amiable expression. Altogether,
> to me, he is not fascinating & Albert agrees with me.
> The Emperor's health was drunk, & he then proposed
> mine, saying 'la sante de Sa Majesté la Reine', which he
> did extremely well, kissing my hand afterwards.[4]

He grew on her, and, as with Leopold and her other important state visitors, she shared more meals than just dinner
with him, although at times it must have been awkward,

given the fairly set routine of court life: 'The Emperor's punctuality is quite embarrassing, for already before 8 he was in the Corridor, & yesterday he came over before the dinner hour. We breakfasted at 9, with him & the King of Saxony.'[5] The older children usually joined such breakfast parties, or appeared as if by magic shortly thereafter, adding to the informal atmosphere in which all topics could be discussed, and the illusion of love and friendliness maintained. Politics were not avoided: 'The Emperor came upstairs, to Albert's room, just before luncheon, & then led me down to the small Drawing-room, where we lunched with him & the King. The Emperor began to talk about politics & did so very frankly & fairly … when we got up from luncheon, he kissed my hand, begging my pardon for having said all he had, but that he had been anxious to lose no opportunity of being well understood', although, in true dinner party fashion, as soon as the Tsar had disappeared safely out of the country, the royal couple and the King of Saxony immediately started lamenting the way he ruled and the political beliefs he'd professed.[6] The Tsar, as with most visitors, was treated to a full tour of Windsor, including the aviary, farms, kennels and gardens, kitchens and plate room. He was able to get to grips with their output too, as on 7 June he shared not only the family breakfast, but also had lunch with the King of Saxony, dinner for 39 people, and attended a state ball with 259 invitees and refreshments served in the throne room at Buckingham Palace at 10.45 p.m.[7] The Queen at the time was six months into her fourth pregnancy, and remarked that she was very tired by the end of it. All of the efforts seemed to be worth it though, and the way in which such visits were conducted, with all and sundry sharing every meal, and living as closely as was possible within the confines of royal decorum, was picked up on by Albert in a characteristically perspicacious moment: 'Albert talked of the great advantage of my having, not only seen the Emperor, & other great people who have visited us, but got to know them by living in a familiar way with them, thus getting over mere formal reception & entertainment. It is that which has pleased them so much & makes them look upon us, as more than mere acquaintances.'[8] Essentially, Victoria had treated the Tsar as a friend: not unusual in Europe at the time, but far more work than the simple dinner invites and firm departure afterwards which characterised the later part of her reign.

Having established that large state visits could be not only handled, but also enjoyed, Victoria was in her element when Louis-Philippe, King of the French, came across four months later. The British royal family had been to France the year before, the first time an English monarch had paid a state visit to France since 1520, and Victoria adored the entire trip. This was a chance to return the hospitality she'd enjoyed in Normandy, and over the six days that Louis-Philippe was resident at Windsor, the kitchens catered for 435 mouths at the royal table.[9] On 9 October, Victoria and Albert conducted the French party around the grounds of Windsor, including, once more, the kitchens, 'where Moroy (the Chef) was named to him, being a Parisian, & the King very kindly talked to him'.[10] (Moroy was Pierre Moret, chief cook since 1842, but presumably Victoria wrote it down phonetically.) Later that night they sampled Moret's best, with a large dinner in St George's Hall. Among the more elaborate dishes were turtle soup, turbot, larded venison fillets, calf's head, truffled capons, lamb's feet vol-au-vents, grouse, stuffed lettuces, cardoons, champagne jelly, pineapple jelly and poached apricots with a pudding rice border. The previous day they'd also had turtle soup, turbot and venison, along with larded hare kidneys (fiddly), and a parmesan cheese fondue. This latter was more of a cheese custard in a pastry case than a 1970s après-ski filler, and formed a savoury element in among a wealth of patisserie, which included cream-filled doughnuts and delicate orange-flower-flavoured biscuits. The most time-consuming element was the turtle soup, a classic dish for lavish entertaining, as it relied on the chefs knowing how to kill, eviscerate and make delicious a whole, live turtle. Sometimes the fins were used for another dish, as was the case here, where they were one of the first course removes. It was a little bit nouveau riche, popular at corporate banquets for it was extremely expensive and showed the reach of British commerce, and had reputedly been one of George IV's favourite dishes. Turtle soup wasn't reserved entirely for entertaining high-status visitors at the palaces, but it was hardly a late-night spontaneous snack. In 1840 four were delivered, including one which weighed 140 lb.[11] The dinner was served *à la Française*, as usual, but, as was often the case for very large dinners, the various dishes were repeated at intervals down the table. As ever, a menu alone does not give an indication of how much each diner ate, and the dangers of royal eating were highlighted in a series of worried letters sent by Queen Louise of Belgium, Louis-Philippe's daughter (and Uncle Leopold's wife), in advance of the visit. In them she implored Victoria not to allow Louis-Philippe to join them for breakfast (even though he would want to), and to provide only chicken broth for his first meal nor any snacks, although she added, 'you must not tell him that I wrote you this'. She went on, 'We are quite sure ... that you and Albert will take care of him, and that he is with you in safe hands ... what makes my mother uneasy is the fear that, being at liberty and without control, he will make too much, as she says, le jeune homme, ride, go about and do everything as if he were still twenty years old. If I must tell you all the truth, she is afraid also he will eat too much.'[12] The reputation of the English court preceded it.

Planning for state visits was always fraught, but some caused more worry than others. The last really big state visit in which Victoria participated fully before Albert's death was that of Emperor Napoleon III in 1855 – by which time Louis-Philippe had been deposed, fled to England, been lent Claremont by the Queen (where he promptly suffered lead poisoning due to faulty cisterns), and eventually died. His family stayed as refugees in England. In the run-up to Napoleon III's visit the Queen again fussed over the rooms and worried about the preparations, though the awkward-ness of the situation was not lost on her when Louis-Philippe's widow, who had remained a friend, visited:

> She was most kind & most discreet, saying she felt my kindness most deeply. I feel so much for her. It made us both so sad to see her drive away in a plain coach with 4 miserable post horses, & to think that that was once the Queen of the French, who but 6 years ago was sur-rounded by the same pomp & grandeur, which now belongs to others, – & that in 3 more days we shall be

receiving with all possible respect, pomp &'éclát the Empr of the French, – just the same reception, as was given here to her late Husband! Now swept away – another dynasty reigns in that fickle country! The contrast is painful in the extreme.[13]

The visit went off very well, with large events at both Buckingham Palace and Windsor (where the Waterloo Gallery was hastily – though temporarily – renamed). Victoria was overjoyed, writing that, 'this visit, this great event, has passed, like everything does alas! in this world. It is a brilliant, successful & pleasant dream, the recollection of which will always be firmly fixed in my mind. Over all it has left a pleasant, satisfactory impression. Everything went off so beautifully, – not a hitch or 'contretemps', – fine weather, & all, smiling. The nation, enthusiastic & happy in the firm & intimate alliance & union of 2 great Countries, whose enmity would prevent peace between us.'[14] Again, for the large dinners which characterised the visit, dishes were generally repeated along the table, but on 17 April these included a couple of one-off and truly spectacular roasts, in the shape of a bustard and a peahen. Bustards, which can be up to a metre tall and are extremely impressive both alive and roasted, were extinct in Britain by this time, while peacocks were very rarely eaten, despite the potential for breathtaking feather-based displays around the crispy roast carcass. The second course featured garnished sugar baskets and moulded sugar trophies, though along with all this glorious extravagance, some dishes were familiar from the 1844 French state visit, including calf's head, turbot, larded sweetbreads, biscuits and an apricot entremets, this time a vol au vent. Other menus from the visit included turtle soup, truffled capons and pineapple pudding.

There was also a buffet supper served for 600 people after a concert on 20 April. This was in addition to dinner, and was similar to the ball suppers that were held for vast numbers of people throughout Victoria's reign. Ball suppers were not only a standard part of state entertaining, but also held more generally, for example for Victoria's birthday each year. Most suppers were by now eaten standing up, though tables could be provided, and the food was largely served cold. Supper menus varied very little across the reign, always starting with a couple of soups, and then progressing onto a variety of dishes which were, as with large dinners, repeated at intervals around long tables. Whether for Victoria's nineteenth birthday in 1838 (500 people), or Napoleon III's concert supper in 1855 (600 people), or the ball supper for 1,800 people in June 1871, the list of food was remarkably consistent: chicken fricassee, cold roast meats, veal and beef galantines, lobster salads, plovers' eggs, cold hams and tongues (sometimes set in aspic), potted game, sandwiches, raised pies, fruit tarts, meringues, biscuits, jellies and set creams, cakes, nougats and vol-au-vents.[15] There were also large display dishes of sugarcraft or of elaborately presented meat. Similar fare – albeit on a rather reduced scale – went in hampers to the theatre, or Epsom racecourse, or to Aldershot Military Camp when foreign powers were treated to an unsubtle display of British military might – providing ample lunches and suppers for royal guests as they worked their way around the sights of London.

After Albert's death, the pattern of entertaining changed.

Visitors were no longer lodged at Windsor, access to which Victoria guarded jealously, when she wasn't referring to it as a dungeon and fleeing to Balmoral. Instead, the Establishment split when necessary, catering to both the Queen, and her guests, who were put up at Buckingham Palace with a small team of cooks seconded from the main body of staff to look after their culinary needs. Increasingly, the duty of state entertaining fell to the Prince of Wales, who, with his reputation for affability and fun, rose to the occasions magnificently, and the palace, by now largely avoided by the Queen, became a sort of glorified hotel and party venue. Many left without seeing her, but she gradually emerged from the deepest phase of her mourning, hosting official courts from 1864, and opening Parliament in 1866, admittedly under duress. There's no doubt that she suffered some form of breakdown after Albert's death, and for several years she remained mentally very fragile. She struggled with the routine of being Queen, writing in 1863 (in the third person and with characteristic underlinings) that: 'she feels it <u>almost a duty</u> to do something for her <u>wretched health</u> & nerves, to prevent further increase of depression and exhaustion. God knows her <u>own</u> inclination would be to do <u>nothing</u> for her health, as <u>her</u> only wish is to see her <u>life end soon</u>, but she feels that <u>if</u> she is to go on, she <u>must</u> change the <u>scene</u> completely sometimes.' Her ministers and children were sympathetic and frustrated in turn, for she was as physically robust as ever, and her mental turmoil was not always understood. Princess Alice, admittedly not the most sympathetic listener to her mother's woes, said that, 'the Queen owned to her she was afraid of getting too well – as if it was a crime & that she <u>feared</u> to begin to like riding on her Scotch poney &c&c'.[16] Pressure from her family, ministers and the press grew, and in 1867 she was finally persuaded to receive the Sultan of Turkey at a luncheon at Windsor. It marked the beginning of a new phase of entertaining, more muted than before, but still an obligatory part of every significant state visit. Although she admitted to feeling 'very wretched and unwell' after the luncheon, having been nervous and missing Albert desperately in the run-up to it, the visit did revive her, and she noted the details in her journal with her characteristic eye for detail:

> Sat down 17, the table covered with gold plate I at the head of the table with the Sultan to my right. He ate of most things, but (which I was glad to see) never touched wine. He seemed to me to cut his meat with difficulty this generally being done for him. He is not tall, & broad & stout, has a fine, dignified, pleasing countenance, with a pleasant smile. He has good features & his hair is grey. He & all the others wore the dark blue coats & trousers, now the fashion in Turkey & fezzes on their heads … The Band played during luncheon & the 6 Pipers … The Sultan expressed himself as delighted with his reception & his accommodation at Buckingham Palace. He also said he longed to thank me for all England had done for Turkey.[17]

The band played at every such occasion, situated on a balcony just outside the dining room. This was only accessible from inside, so they had to be in position well before guests arrived. Usually it was seamless, and visitors frequently remarked on both the band and the Highland Pipers.

Occasionally it went wrong, and there was at least one instance where the palace fire brigade had to be called in with their ladders so that the players, presumably laden with instruments, could climb up from the outside. They missed the national anthem, but slid into place and struck up the overture as the Queen started her soup.[18]

Heads of state travelled with significant entourages, and the kitchens had to cater not just for the official receptions, but also for the many servants and security staff who came with each group. They usually ate separately to the British contingent, and required separate dining rooms, as well as living accommodation. On occasion even Buckingham Palace wasn't big enough, and entries in the wage books which cover the state visit in 1873 of Naser al-Din, the Shah of Persia, show that several of the cooks, including Charles Jungbleeth and John Mountford, both master cooks, were displaced to make room for his servants, and had to go and stay in lodgings for the duration of the visit. The visit was fraught with issues, although more in the planning than the reality. Official communication was lacking, and instead the planners relied on a whole host of unofficial rumours and letters from witnesses to dinners at earlier points in the progress of the Shah, making his visit a hotly anticipated and somewhat dreaded one. He was described as 'savage', and one rather overcooked report delightedly remarked that 'he is a true Eastern potentate in his consideration for himself and himself only: is most unconcernedly late whenever he chooses: utterly ignores every one he does not want to speak to: amuses himself with monkeyish and often dirty tricks: sacrifices a cock to the rising sun, and wipes his wet hands on the coat-tails of the gentleman next him without compunction'.[19] He was further rumoured to be oversexed, partly because his harem had been sent home after they had been mobbed by curious crowds in Russia. Reports came in from Germany that 'the free and easy manners of the Shah, who is not yet accustomed to the society of European ladies, have given offence to the Royal family, the disastrous effects of the Persian encampment in the magnificent apartments of the Palace have irritated the Imperial Household, and the habit of His Majesty's followers not to pay for what they order in the shops has exasperated the tradespeople of Berlin', and that at dinner it was hard to persuade him not to 'raise his voice so as to startle the company, or put his fingers into dishes, or take food out of his mouth again to look at it, after it has been chewed – or fling it under the table if it does not suit him'. There were further fears about what he would be doing with the ten live fowls and occasional live lamb which were delivered to his suite every day (would he really be sacrificing them?) and which probably weren't helped by a Foreign Office report instructing that 'His Majesty generally dines alone, and when so, prefers to have his meals on the carpet. For that purposes a moveable carpet should be kept ready whereupon his servants will put the dishes etc. brought to the door by the English servants. About four yards square nice coloured leather upon which a tablecloth is spread, and all put upon the carpet of the room. The Shah does not like to have to cut up his meats. Rice, lambs, mutton, fowls are favourite dishes. The cuisine should be somewhat relevée.'[20] It was possibly a little disappointing to some that the Shah behaved impeccably. He met the Queen at a luncheon at Windsor on 20 June, before which they invested each other with various orders while vying with each other as to how many jewels they could reasonably wear. Victoria, who had been over to the hothouses in the kitchen gardens the day before to look over the fruit for the luncheon ('it is a very bad year for peaches and cherries'), was won over when he declared that he had had *Leaves from a Highland Journal* translated into Persian for him to read. Her only comment on his table manners was that he 'ate fruit all through luncheon, helping himself to the dish in front on him, and drank iced water'.[21] He, meanwhile, commented favourably on the 'fine fruits', while being somewhat taken aback by Prince Leopold's bare knees in his Highland kilt.[22]

Behind the scenes, things were more tense. Extra wages were paid to some of the cooks at Buckingham Palace who found that, just because the kitchens were staffed only by a small crew seconded from the main body of cooks, there was no reduction in the expected quantity or quality of the food. During this visit the Shah did, as predicted, dine alone in his room when he was not being hosted by various corporations or aristocrats, and his menu resembled a standard royal dinner: soups, fish, removes, entrées, roasts and entremets. He was treated to some English classics as well, including plum pudding, which seems to have become a habit when hosting overseas visitors – the King of Siam was given roast beef and Yorkshire pudding in the 1890s – and the juggling of suitably recherché and regal dishes with dietary requirements and the desire to showcase the edible glories of the country must have been challenging. There were other issues as well: the Shah was lodged, as was usual, at the Lord Warden Hotel in Dover on his arrival in the country, and there was a protracted row over the costs incurred. The landlord at the Lord Warden had form, having submitted bills for flowers and flags which had not been ordered for the Emperor in 1855, and this time he claimed that he'd misunderstood a garbled direction about the Shah's lunches and incurred costs he now had to charge on. The lunches were lavish: two top-class luncheons for the Shah and Prince of Wales at £4 a head, then twenty first class at £2 a head, eighty second class at £1 a head, and thirty servants' luncheons. Fruit and flowers on were on the table throughout the meal, and the wines for all apart from the servants included champagne, Bordeaux, liqueurs, maraschino and curaçao.[23] Eventually the dust settled, but when the Treasury was totting up what the visit had cost in preparation for a second round in 1889, they waspishly noted that they had not only paid for food, lodgings and extra servants, but also 'for loss of plate which somehow disappeared'.[24]

Stealing the tableware was one way to remember a foreign adventure, but exposure to the different tastes and habits of a country could also make a permanent impression. The Queen's first state visit was to France in 1843, when she and Albert stayed with Louis-Philippe and his family at the château d'Eu, his family estate, and she enjoyed it so much that it influenced the purchase of Osborne as a family home of her own. It was relatively low-key, being in the countryside of Normandy, and Charlotte Canning, one of Victoria's ladies-in-waiting, found the whole thing deliciously ramshackle, describing the coaches as, 'the most wonderful carriages, a mixture between one of Louis XIV's time and a marketing cart from Hampton Court'.[25] Meals were perplexing, with the whole royal family arriving en masse to escort the Queen and her ladies – already dressed and in attendance having had a snack in their rooms – to a huge breakfast: 'All walked arm-in-arm upstairs, as if to dinner, to long tables in 3 or 4 rooms … Breakfast began with soup, & hot meat of all kinds & wine then came eggs; then sweet things & then tea, coffee & chocolate, & bread & butter. All of the meals of the day in one.'[26] The process was repeated for lunch and dinner, which was held at 7 p.m. – very early for the English contingent – and 'handsomely done', although there was a bread issue: 'Why does Louis-Philippe have a pile of bread & rusks of all sorts at his side? Our Queen did not know what to do with her great French loaf. The table was not tidy & every body's bread & crumbs & dirt stay all thro' dessert.'[27] Victoria also noticed the differences: 'The "Service", was very splendid, but everything differently served to with us. The King & Queen carve themselves',[28] but she thoroughly approved of the fact that the gentlemen and ladies all left the table together, without a lengthy gap while the men got drunk, the women got bored, and everyone seized upon the chance to have a wee. Back in England, she tried to implement a similar policy, but she was advised that it would cause an uproar and had to settle for simply cutting down the time that the parties were separate. The after-dinner gathering in France proved to be as tedious for everyone who wasn't royal as its counterpart back in England: 'In the evening … the Royals went into a room by themselves. We were sent for to sit with them in time … The pretty little Princess de Joinville amuses us very much; she gets dreadfully bored & now and then jumps up as if quite unable to stand it. She goes and whispers to somebody or to help herself to a glass of water & then back to her place.'[29] Victoria was oblivious, revelling in having company of her own status with whom she could happily and easily converse with utter freedom, commenting on her return that, 'I had never before lived in a family circle of persons of my own rank, with whom I could be on terms of equality & familiarity, & I miss this pleasant intercourse very much.'[30] One of the highlights were the trips out into the estate, where they visited the church and the park, stopping to eat peaches and assembling for a bucolic picnic, which the Queen described as 'so pretty, so gay, so champêtre'.[31] It was not quite as spontaneous and rustic as she decided to believe, being organised with utter precision, as Charlotte Canning pointed out: 'I believe Louis Philippe has a great fondness for these expeditions; the apparatus is complete; camp stools for everybody, one or two tents, & a great table – the whole packs up, & it is curious in how short a time it is put together', and it was reported in the *Illustrated London News* in typically breathy prose: 'Forty decanters of wine, alternated with carafes of water were set on the table in the English style; whilst down the middle was placed the collation, composed of meats, pâtés, confectionery of the most recherché description, in fact everything that the most exquisite taste could suggest and wealth provide.'[32]

Emboldened by a successful trip across the Channel, the next excursions were to Germany and Belgium, both countries Victoria would visit regularly. She was particularly keen on the refreshment breaks: 'We went down to what is called the Painted Room & had tea, quite in the German way. We Princesses sat down to a table, on which there was no cloth, & excellent cakes of all kinds were served, whilst the Queen's Ladies made the tea',[33] and tea and cake became an important part of her daily ritual, especially in later life

— exactly the same era when afternoon tea was becoming a
solid social ritual among her subjects.[34] She also fell for the
coffee, commenting repeatedly that it was 'excellent', as
were the cakes and 'fancy bread', and she enthusiastically
drank chocolate with Albert's brother Ernest.[35] Again, she
enjoyed herself greatly, not least because she was with her
family and able to let down her guard somewhat. Charlotte
Canning, wearily commenting that, 'royal legs are surely of
other stuff than ours', was an onlooker on this trip too: 'I
heard great approbation expressed at the Queen's hearty
dancing, & I suppose she enjoyed it exceedingly as she
allows herself to gallop, valse & polk with her cousins, she
went on incessantly till the ball ended.'[36] Occasions such as
this were interspersed with more tedious affairs though, for
every town the Queen passed through vied to show their
hospitality, including naming a vineyard after her in Hoch-
heim (it still exists, along with the typically monumental
gothic edifice erected in commemoration). Often dismissing
the frequent stops as 'a stuffy luncheon with the Authori-
ties', sometimes even Canning was impressed. At Ghent,
'the déjeuner was well done; great pains were taken to
procure rareties [sic] & there was a dish of roasted gold
pheasants with their heads & tail feathers put on again, &
quantities of disgustingly fat ortolans'.[37] She was similarly
approving in Hohenlohe in 1845, when the Queen paid a
visit to Feodora, and they, 'bethought themselves to have a
luncheon of the hot sausages out of the street. Lady G & I
left in an outer room & half dead with fatigue were delighted
to get a sort of beggar's share of this meal which was really
very good.' Indeed, Victoria took every opportunity to
sample new foods, and her summary of the same occasion is

glowing: 'had some refreshments there, sending for "Brat-würst" from the Market, which are the "spécialité" of Coburg, & so good & drinking some excellent Coburg beer.'[38] Again, the hours were different to those in England, with breakfast at 9 a.m. and dinner at 4 p.m., and the local customs could be alarming, as Charlotte Canning found out to her cost in Brühl when the group had an evening supper on board a steamer as they looked at the illuminations on the river: 'below, the cabin was decorated with plants & brilliantly lighted, & tables covered with eatables. Eight young ladies with blue gowns & white dahlias handed about tea & coffee & a sort of pickle. I thought they were orange flowers, or bonbons, & that it was ungracious to refuse, so I took a pinch of something & to my horror I found I had got a little fish.'[39]

Foreign visits could prove problematic for the unwary, as cultural differences combined with the sheer pressure of being constantly on show. Frieda Arnold's letters home are, at times, as full of fatigue as the memoirs of Charlotte Canning, and there is no doubt that Victoria's attendants and servants worked extremely hard. When the royal family returned Napoleon III's visit in 1855, they stayed at St Cloud, just outside Paris proper, but visited the Emperor in the Palais Elysée (now the official residence of the French President), went to the theatre, opera and an enormous state ball at the Hôtel de Ville. Arnold fell asleep in the carriage on the way back to St Cloud at one stage, and was reduced to fortifying herself with seltzer water and champagne between hasty dressing sessions and snatched meals. She commented that champagne 'flows like water in the Emperor's household', and, while she was exhausted by the pace, explaining that, 'days at St Cloud seemed to go on for ever, one saw and heard so much; and yet it was all over so quickly. We rarely got to bed before two or three in the morning: at midnight there was often as much going on as at midday at home', the Queen seemed to have endless supplies of energy: 'I have <u>never</u> seen her tired; she is always alert and ready.'[40]

The ladies-in-waiting had their own troubles. They were, at least, fed regularly, but found the footmen to be disagreeable and selfish. Mary Buteel complained that the footmen were badly trained and that at dinner, 'they did not seem to know their business as ours do, for instance you constantly heard behind your chair a great scuffle of five or six over something, and an authoritative "imbecile!", which seemed to denote that all was not going on precisely as smoothly as could be wished … Every now and then also one saw a large white glove on the table, gathering up the crumbs in a primitive manner.' One man served out truffles with his fingers when they proved 'rebellious in the spoon'. Lady Churchill, another of the Queen's attendants, recounted similar traumas when asked what the meals were like: 'She described her horror at finding herself seated at breakfast with three wine glasses by her plate. Wine she declined and was resigning herself to the idea of cold water when near the end, tea or coffee were offered! She added that the French wondered how they could eat at luncheon again. She tried to explain that our breakfasts were not composed of hot and cold meat and vegetables, etc. etc. like theirs and that our luncheons were not dinners.'[41] Even the Queen suffered slightly, though in her case it was through the overbearing heat of Paris in August. She escaped – or

didn't notice – awkward footmen, instead saying, 'everything magnificent, & the serving very quiet, so different to
the time of poor King Louis Philippe, – much more royal &
dignified'. She enjoyed the streets of Paris as she drove
around, envious of the grandeur and the laid-back attitude
of its citizens, 'there were people sitting & drinking in front
of their houses, & outside the Cafés, to my eyes so foreign
looking, & gay', and she was utterly bowled over by the ball
and accompanying supper, held in her honour at Versailles
– the first ball to take place there since the Revolution of
1789:

> After all the Company had gone into the Supper Room,
> our procession started, the Grands Officiers, &c,
> walking before us, & we went through a number of fine
> rooms & a long gallery, to the theatre, where supper
> was served. The sight was truly magnificent. The whole
> stage was covered in & 400 people sat down at 40 small
> tables, 10 persons at each, presided over by a Lady &
> nicely selected, all by the Empress's own direction &
> arrangement. The whole was beautifully lit up with
> endless Chandeliers, & there were many garlands of
> flowers. The boxes were full of spectators & a band
> (not visible) was playing. We sat at a small table, in the
> centre box, only ourselves, with the Empr & Empress,
> the 3 Children, Prince Napoleon, Princess Matilde &
> Prince Adalbert. It was quite one of the finest & most
> brilliant sights we ever witnessed.[42]

Victoria loved travel, embraced new experiences, especially
the culinary ones, and thrived on meeting new people.

Unlike Albert, who found that the food in France played havoc with his sensitive stomach, and seized upon a visit alone to Coburg in 1858 to go on a fasting cure, she took every opportunity to broaden her palate, and, just as she 'dropped in' on local denizens of Balmoral and Osborne, so too did she pop in on farmers and producers on her travels around Europe.[43] Even the travelling itself carried opportunities for adventure. The European trips inevitably involved travel on the royal yacht, which was also used for more general travel, both around the Solent when at Osborne, and, in the 1840s, trips up to Scotland. The chefs loathed working in a cramped galley, and there were supply issues, not helped by the Queen's love of animals coming to the fore: 'Our dinners grow very bad for wherever we go the shops are shut, and nothing can be had. We have milk from the cow on board, and a sheep was given to the Queen at Portland, but she has taken an affection for it & it is not to be killed as long as she is on board.'[44] It was often unrelentingly hot, and on one occasion, having taken shelter in the lee of the cow shed, the Queen inadvertently caused a problem when she was found, to the consternation of the sailors, to be sitting on the grog tub: '"Please my Lord, the grog tub's jammed." "What?" "The grog tub's jammed" – "what do you mean?" – "please my lord, Her Majesty's right afore it."' Noticing the commotion, she moved, requesting that she be sent some grog to try, just as she had when sailing around the Solent as a teenager. This time she dryly commented that 'it would be better if it were stronger'.[45] Victoria was an excellent sailor, rarely sick, and although even she couldn't withstand some of the trips, in general she was one of the last people left standing, or rather sitting: 'The Queen was stoutly breakfasting in her pavilion. She made me sit by her for at least three hours in one of the sheltered paddle-box seats & was in high spirits all the time, except for five minutes under the influence of an overpowering smell of roast goose – even then a little O de Cologne set her right, & she laughed heartily at the sight first of Prince Albert dreadfully overcome, then Ld Liverpool, & then Ld Aberdeen, all vanishing in haste.'[46]

As the railway network expanded, and stations were opened to serve Windsor, Osborne and Balmoral, the royals and their entourage increasingly travelled around the country by train. While most of her domestic trips were to and from Balmoral, Victoria, and Albert while alive, did occasionally descend upon various noble houses, and they visited Ireland in 1861. The journals record endless corporate luncheons in towns across Britain, interspersed with grand dinners at country estates and days spent wandering the gardens, visiting dairies and the occasional kitchen. They were a mixed bag. At Stratfield Saye, the elderly Duke of Wellington 'helped us himself, – rather family, giving such large portions, & mixing up tarts & pudding together, but he is so kind & attentive about it', while at Chatsworth the highlight was Joseph's Paxton's conservatory, 'the most stupendous and extraordinary creation imaginable'.[47] The railways made possible lengthy journeys in much more comfort than the carriages in which Victoria had crossed the country in the 1830s. Although she imposed a theoretical speed limit of 40 mph (her actual journey times belie this), and regular stops were made for refreshments, she could nevertheless travel more quickly than before, and with everyone in the same vehicle. There were no dining cars until the 1870s, and even then they were slow to catch on, and in general the royal train, as with all trains, would stop at a station so that passengers could either disembark and eat or have provisions handed to them. York became a favourite stopping place on the frequent Balmoral trips, and the royal party were invited for a lunch in the station refreshment rooms in 1849 (there was a subsequent fuss over who would foot the bill, to which the Queen put a stop by declaring that in future she would pay for her own food), and ate in the station hotel from 1854 until 1861. It was always rather rushed, for they had half an hour in which to eat eight courses (plus sideboard contents), but despite this, the proprietors of the hotel ensured that the food was of a suitably regal nature: consommé de volaille à la royale, crème d'orge à la reine and 'pouden' à la Victoria all featured on her 1854 menu. This was printed in the local press, so it was very good advertising, although Eleanor Stanley's commentary showed that, once again, the royal attendants were left on the sidelines:

> At York, we had lunch, the first day, with the Royal party the consequence of which was that we got very little to eat, as the Royalty did not seem much to approve of the York cookery, and kept changing their minds and sending away their plates to try one thing after another, in a way that was very tantalising to us, who had breakfasted at seven; the only thing that kept our spirits up was the recollection that the Royal servants, who don't like either to starve themselves or see others starve, had put an elaborate luncheon-box into our carriage, in which we had seen two large packets of grouse and

partridges, besides biscuits and grapes, so that we could always fall back upon that; but we did at last ... get some mutton broth, and cold beef, though I am not sure the grouse would not have been better.[48]

Exactly the same pattern was followed when the Queen travelled on the continent, with the royal kitchens providing hampers of stew and huge luncheon baskets in case of starvation, but most meals, as well as tea and endless coffee, being taken at stops en route.

Continental train journeys formed part of a travelling habit that Victoria adopted after Albert's death. Although she went to Coburg and Brussels in 1862, this was more in the nature of a valedictory tour than anything else, and she struggled with the crowds and lack of privacy. By 1863 she had decided that a proper holiday would do her good, something devoted to fresh air and isolation. She fired off letter after letter, negotiating her way through all obstacles, until arrangements were made for her to stay in Switzerland in summer 1868. She travelled incognito, as the Duchess of Kent, and, while she both expected to be recognised and duly was, the illusion was largely maintained, and she escaped attendance at any large events. She sought to create a cosy, familial atmosphere, taking only a small entourage: 'The Queen can and would put up with the homeliest food and provisions. She would take her meals (excepting perhaps breakfast and luncheon) with her very small suite; she would take only 1 gentleman and 1 lady & a Dr. besides her children – & very few servants. In short to live quite on a reduced scale and taking only those servants who would be really useful.'[49] The eventual party was not quite as small as this rather optimistic letter from Victoria would suggest: Joseph Kanné, the Queen's courier who accompanied the royals on most of their trips, kept a list of travellers, which in this case consisted of the Queen and three of her children, seven attendants including a doctor, the children's governess, and seventeen servants, among whom was Charles Jungbleeth, one of the master cooks.[50] More were taken on in Lucerne, and provisions and equipment were sent on ahead, along with instructions for the various places the party planned to visit, and one newspaper reported breathlessly that, 'for weeks purveyors of victuals have been learning to prepare these after the manner of the English Court, for example making sandwiches in perfect cube form with butter and ham, to be enjoyed for breakfast and which are really very tasty'.[51] However, for a royal visit it was a very small group: when Victoria and Albert had taken over Blair Castle in 1844 they had brought with them two clerks of the kitchen, seven cooks including a pastry cook, roasting cook and confectioner, and a baker, and there had been 114 people in total.[52] They stayed in Lucerne at the Pension Wallis, taking over the whole hotel, but when it proved too hot, retreated further up into the mountains in search of colder air. There were a few minor upsets, mainly with those not used to travelling, especially the Queen's doctor: 'Jenner who has never seen foreign [Lavatories] before runs about to each in a state of high disgust and says they must be entirely altered – Jenner is right of course – but he rather over estimates the idea of bad smells, because perched up here there are not except in one or two places.'[53] Large quantities of toilet cleaner were subsequently ordered, but frankly, to anyone used to Buckingham Palace in the 1840s it must have been rather a moot point.

It was on this Swiss trip that Victoria established the daily routine which would characterise her later continental holidays. Mornings were spent in the gardens, breakfasting outdoors and attending to business, before excursing out into the surrounding countryside or local towns. A paddle steamer was laid on for her to wander around in on Lac Lucerne, and carriages were hired for long-distance road travel. There was a great deal of tea-taking, for example on 9 August, 'got out and took our tea, which was most refreshing, under a tree', and on the 12th, 'stopped to take tea in our carriage', and on the 17th when they found 'everywhere quantities of blackberries (of which we have excellent tarts)'. They also saw blueberries and cranberries growing wild. As was her habit in Scotland, these teas had an impromptu appearance, despite the undoubted organisation necessary to make them appear so: 'I walked slowly back to where Hoffmann has kindled a fire, & we sat on the grass under a small bank, watching the water boil in a casserole, a kettle being unknown in these parts. Had some delicious tea, then hurried off to our carriage.' She said she'd never had a better appetite, and felt wholeheartedly revived, buying holiday souvenirs including two goats for the children, and was determined to plan another holiday forthwith.[54]

In the decades which followed, Victoria holidayed a few times in Hohenlohe, where she stayed in Feodora's villa, left to her in her half-sister's will, but she found that she was constantly disturbed by the requirement to be seen and to be on show. She enjoyed several stays in Italy, in Baveno and Florence, and learnt Italian in preparation, proudly writing that she had 'talked to the under gardener, & was proud at getting on so well with my Italian. Was able to ask questions about all the plants & trees, & understood him perfectly.'[55] She took the opportunity to see the food of the country people, commenting on 'minestra', a dish of rice and chestnuts which a group of children were eating outside Feriolo. She also stayed in Biarritz in 1889, emerging from holiday mode to become the first British monarch to cross the border into Spain, where she met the Spanish Queen Regent. They attended a dance in the main square in San Sebastián, and were served tea, 'but it was quite undrinkable, & I only touched it'.[56] Although Victoria loved Italy, she is best known for the series of holidays which she took in Aix-les-Bains in 1885, 1887 and 1890, and on the French Riviera: Menton in 1882, and Grasse, Hyères and Nice from 1891 to 1899. Aix was chosen on the basis that it was a health spa, though the Queen largely avoided the massage and bathing possibilities and concentrated on day trips with tea and cake. In 1887 she went round the monastery at La Grande Chartreuse where refreshments were served. The monastery was famous for its eponymous liqueur, still made today, although no longer on site, and so when Victoria was offered wine, she was prompt in asking to try some Chartreuse instead. For once she found it rather strong, and then, 'I took some Chocolate Cream, & in doing so put my sleeve into it, & made a dreadful mess, which caused a deal of rubbing, washing & wiping. The poor "Procureur" stood opposite with clasped hands & kept saying: "Mon Dieu, que je suis desolé!"'[57] Embarrassing, but hardly fatal, though as usual Victoria's dressers were kept busy. Her souvenir from Aix was a donkey called Jacquot, who was shipped back and forth between England and France and used to pull her cart when she became lame and found it difficult to walk in later years.

The holidays in the south of France were significant for the Queen, who adored the area and missed it when she wasn't there, and also for the Riviera itself, which developed under British influence to a very large degree, and was renowned for being full of mosquitos in the summer, and foreign royalty in the winter.[58] In Nice, the enormous Hotel Victoria Regina was built in anticipation of Victoria's visits, and had lifts, hot and cold running water, private bathrooms, and a staff prepared to cater to every whim. Guides to the towns of the Riviera which were produced for British visitors show that a wide range of amenities were available for those who preferred not to patronise too many French establishments. The discerning traveller could eat out, or order in, and, for those such as the Queen, who travelled with a skeleton staff, there were both confectioners who would cater to parties, and bakers supplying English and German bread. As with the Swiss trip, Victoria brought a relatively small staff with her.[59] The French detective assigned to shadow the visits of foreign monarchs, and assure their security, Xavier Paoli, was bowled over by the number of attendants, but he was not one of the inner circle, and his impressions were often false. He happily asserted in his memoirs of Victoria that she brought with her a 'French chef, M. Ferry, with three or four lieutenants and a whole regiment of scullions'. Oscar Ferry was born in London in 1855, to a French father and English mother and was the fourth master cook in 1891. Lady Lytton is rather more reliable: 'The cooking, a mixture of one of the Queen's cooks and one of the hotel, was really excellent.'[60]

As with previous holidays, Victoria usually dined with one or two family members and her Household ate separately. She refused to adopt the Riviera custom of a light snack for breakfast and early lunches and dinners, but stuck resolutely to a full English, before driving out or writing letters in the garden. She then 'did full honour' to her luncheon before going on an excursion during the afternoon.[61] She proved an indefatigable tourist, going out in all weathers, and all conditions, returning covered in dust with a smile on her face. Dinner for 16 March 1895, served to three people at the Queen's table, was recorded by the local newspaper: creamed rice soup; gratin of soles and fried whiting; truffled chicken croquettes and lamb noisettes with asparagus tips; braised beef with macaroni; roast duck; fresh peas, chocolate soufflé, strawberry ice cream, and the usual selection of cold meats plus dessert.[62] It wasn't remarkably different from the food at Windsor, but she did, as ever, find some new experiences to whet her appetite, including sampling bouillabaisse courtesy of an old lady she happened upon on a beach. The fisherman who recounted the story many years later recalled her wonderful bearing, bright blue eyes and stupendous purple bonnet, all of which sounds entirely in character.[63]

She took part enthusiastically in the local festivals, throwing flowers at floats at the fête des fleurs, and buying decorated gourds at the fêtes de cougourdons: 'Went up to the Château, which I admired more than ever, & then back to the Monastery, where the "fête de Gourdes" was in progress. The crowds were very great. It was a beautiful evening & everything looked very bright & gay. The people were in great good humour.' (Cougourdons are a locally grown oddly shaped gourd, generally hollowed out and either decorated or made into musical instruments: the festival is still going, revived as part of Nice's many carnivals.) Paoli was also there, fending off potential vegetable-shaped dangers: 'On her second visit she was not a little surprised to find that a large number of gourds or cougourdes were adorned with her coat of arms or covered with inscriptions in her honour … the Queen laughed merrily to see me grappling with the salesmen and especially the saleswomen.'[64] By now, afternoon tea-taking was an established routine, as reported in the *Illustrated London News* in 1897, 'five o clock tea at some pleasant spot by the roadside … has become something of an institution',[65] and Victoria had clearly gained something of a reputation as a keen cake-eater, as a fairly tongue-in-cheek letter from Edward Lear, who had taught the Queen drawing in 1846 and hoped she might visit him near Menton, testified: 'It is known that the Queen of England eats macaroon cakes continually, and she also insists on her suite doing the same.' She brought back from one of the trips a pair of salt cellars in the shape of paniered donkeys, continuing the souvenir animal theme but with the advantage that they didn't need actual stabling.[66]

The Italian and French trips formed a spring break for the Queen, who loathed the heat and preferred to avoid anywhere warm if she could, travelling with ice blocks liberally festooning the carriage if it was hot when she went by train. After 1861 she spent most of late spring and early autumn at Balmoral, and the summer and Christmas at Osborne. Christmas was a period she always looked forward to, maintaining the festivities even in mourning, lamenting in 1862 that it was 'xmas eve & all the joy I used to take in it gone'.[67] Nevertheless, there were duties to be carried out, not just in the giving and receiving of family gifts, but the distribution of cake, toys and fabric to the local schoolchildren, which happened every year, along with another gathering for the estate workers: 'went ... down to the Servants' Hall where there was a tree for the labourers & their wives. The women all got pieces of woollen stuff for dresses, & the men each had a piece of meat, & some pudding & cake.'[68] The whole royal Establishment feasted, with roast beef, plum pudding and turkey provided for all. Although the location moved from Windsor to Osborne, the general gist of Christmas remained similar. Christmas Eve was present-giving day, which started with breakfast, during which the younger children were allowed one gift from the selection awaiting them on tables in the 'present room', and was followed by church, distribution of presents to the personal servants, lunch, distribution of the estate presents, and then at 6 p.m. the lighting of the Christmas trees, present-giving for the immediate family, and finally dinner. The main Christmas dinner took place on the 25th, which was more family-focused, with the trees lit again at 6 p.m., as they were on New Year's Day and Twelfth Night. Victoria proudly took credit for the popularisation of Christmas trees in Britain, although they had been known before – George III's Queen, Charlotte, used to hang sweets, dried fruit and nuts from the branches of a candlelit yew tree for the local children – but were usually seen only in the houses of German immigrants. In 1848 the *Illustrated London News* published a picture of the Queen and Prince, surrounded by their family, gathered around their laden tree, with a border of suitably Christmassy items, such as dead hares, deer, game birds, fish, fruit and, in the spirit of the new, reinvented Victorian Christmas, some moralising sketches of charitable

giving and children having fun. The pre-Victorian Christmas had tended rather more towards raucous drinking and
partying than family-friendly celebration, although there
had still been cake. One of the fatalities of the new Christmas was the old tradition of the Twelfth Cake, which had
survived from the medieval period into the nineteenth
century and was now emasculated and renamed as Christmas Cake, where it promptly got lost in the plethora of
other Christmas foods. Twelfth Cake was a rich fruit cake,
eaten on 6 January and used as a way of celebrating the end
of the festive season with a proper bang. Originally it had
contained a dried pea and a bean, used as a means of select-
ing a Twelfth Night King and Queen. By the Victorian era,
this role play had developed into an annual ritual, wherein
printers competed with each other to devise the most topical
and deliciously pointed sets of characters possible. They
came printed on sheets of paper, to be cut up and put in a hat
and chosen at random by the partygoers. The royal supply
books carry orders of characters, along with enormous
amounts of cake: 21 cakes from C. Layton in 1838, with
three dozen characters, and another 6 cakes and 12 sets of
characters from Gunter's, and 7 cakes with sets of characters
from Bridgemans. In 1844, 212 lb of cakes came from C.
Layton, with 12 sets of characters, and in 1853, 3 cakes and
6 character sets. These were probably for distribution
around the Household and Establishment and to be sent to
friends, for the royal confectioner was charged with making
and decorating the Queen's own cake. The *Illustrated
London News* published a picture of John Mawditt's effort
for 1849, which had a bucolic summer picnic in (not very)
miniature on top. Twelfth Cakes were wildly popular, and

came in forms to suit almost any budget or fantasy, being 'decorated with all imaginable images of things animate and inanimate. Stars, castles, kings, cottages, dragons, trees, fish, palaces, cats, dogs, churches, lions, milk-maids, knights, serpents, and innumerable other forms in snow-white confectionery, painted with variegated colours',[69] and yet, from an early nineteenth-century peak, by the 1870s they were in terminal decline. The Queen held on grimly in the face of the encroaching, countrywide, conversion to Christmas Cake, commenting in 1880 that, 'The Twelfth night cake, was, as usual, exhibited; a very pretty one, all snow and figures, made by my confectioner', and in 1892, 'The Twelfth Night cake with a hunting scene was exhibited in the Drawing-room.'[70]

Twelfth Cake wasn't the only food that made its appearance exclusively at Christmas. Although the royal menus for 25 December included a lot of dishes that appeared on other days, they did have a certain bias. In 1855, with 30 for dinner, in addition to the usual soups and fish (turbot and fried sole, so not unusual), there was a remove of stuffed turkey with chipolatas, and an entrée of carp, fished from the Windsor Great Park. Carp was a Germanic Christmas favourite, and remains popular in Austria, Poland and parts of Eastern Europe today. Other entrées were the inevitable lamb chops (with chicory), a foie gras pie, grouse, venison, and chicken with asparagus. Mince pies always appeared as one of the entremets or sweet removes at Christmas (though were not exclusive to Christmas day). On this occasion there was no plum pudding, but later menus always included it. Other dishes changed, but in 1900 the turbot, turkey with chipolatas, and mince pies were still there, joined by roast beef and plum pudding, asparagus and chocolate eclairs, among others. The most consistent element was the sideboard, which Victoria described in the reminiscences of Christmas with Albert which she wrote down in the 1860s: 'at dinner there were all the Christmas dishes, of which we generally had to eat a little. First the cold baron of beef which stood on the large sideboard all decked out – brawn – game pies from Ireland and others – stuffed turkey – wild boar's head – which Albert was so fond of with a particular German sauce which the Coburg cook ... invented – mince pies etc. etc. – and then all sorts of Bonbons and figures and toys were brought at dessert, many of which were given to the children; and there used to be such great excitement and delight.'[71] The sideboard contents barely changed, and in 1897 Marie Mallet noted, 'baron of beef, woodcock pie from the Lord Lieut. of Ireland, boar's head displayed on sideboard'.[72] A photograph taken in 1888 shows the whole thing laid out, with the date marked out in flowers on the baron of beef, the tail curling round above what is, in essence, the entire back end of a cow (it usually weighed in at 350–400 lb) and the boar's head looking mildly comedic to one side. Most people who wanted to display a boar's head in the Victorian period had to decorate up a pig's head with piped lard and lurid pastry patterns; the Queen's cooks had the real thing, so barely dressed it up at all. The kitchens were, of course, in full swing during Christmas, and before 1861 a visit to the Windsor Great Kitchen to see the beef roasting was an obligatory part of the season for many people. Affie went down with his tutor in 1851, recording that, 'I saw the baron of beef and boar's head, and I went down to the larder where I saw hares, pheasants, grouse and a great quantity of fat meat: and we saw the pastry room and a model of Windsor Castle in sugar. In the evening Bertie and I supped with our sisters in the Oak Room and played with some of the presents. When I had finished playing I went to the great dinner and had a very happy evening.'[73]

Christmas was one of the few occasions when those outside the palaces got a glimpse of the food within, for the newspapers continued to write up the sights and smells of the Windsor kitchens cooking up the beef and boar's head even after Victoria started to spend the season at Osborne. Her daily fare was not exactly influential on the populace at large, the vast majority of whom could barely aspire to tripe and bacon, let alone roast joints crackling merrily in front of an open fire. The closest most people got to a royal dish was one of the many food items named after her, including the still ubiquitous sponge sandwich, various biscuits, soups, sauces and sweets, along with a lot of fruit and vegetable varieties.

10

The wider world of food

On 22 June 1897, Victoria awoke to a 'never to be forgotten day'.[1] She breakfasted with her eldest daughter Vicky, visiting from Prussia, along with Helena and Beatrice. They had a choice of omelettes and fried soles, beef fillets and cold fowls, while surrounded by the madcap grandeur of the Chinese room at Buckingham Palace, its furnishings recycled from Brighton Pavilion and shoe-horned into their new home in the 1850s. Victoria then went off for a two-and-a-half-hour carriage ride, along streets filled to bursting with cheering people, before returning for lunch with Beatrice and her children. They ate some of her favourite dishes, including lamb cutlets, asparagus, cold fowl, cinnamon rice pudding and a (German) fruit compote. She rested, had tea in the garden and then attended a large dinner, with 108 people seated at eight round tables. The

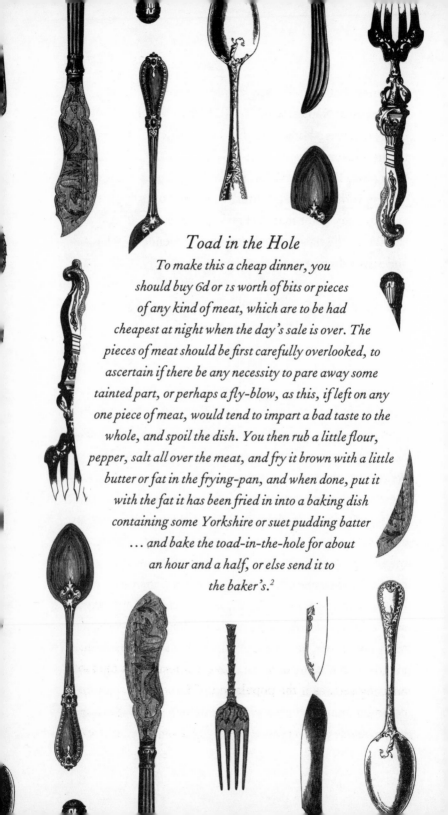

Toad in the Hole

To make this a cheap dinner, you
should buy 6d or 1s worth of bits or pieces
of any kind of meat, which are to be had
cheapest at night when the day's sale is over. The
pieces of meat should be first carefully overlooked, to
ascertain if there be any necessity to pare away some
tainted part, or perhaps a fly-blow, as this, if left on any
one piece of meat, would tend to impart a bad taste to the
whole, and spoil the dish. You then rub a little flour,
pepper, salt all over the meat, and fry it brown with a little
butter or fat in the frying-pan, and when done, put it
with the fat it has been fried in into a baking dish
containing some Yorkshire or suet pudding batter
… and bake the toad-in-the-hole for about
an hour and a half, or else send it to
the baker's.[2]

Queen sat between the Archduke Ferdinand of Austria and the Prince of Naples, with Vicky nearby. The menu, served *à la Russe*, was a homage to the skills of the cooks, as well as to the Queen herself, featuring the impressively named 'bernoise à l'imperatrice' as one of the soups (chicken consommé with a nod to her title as Empress of India), as well as roast beef. After that, feeling very tired, but determined, she sat on the dais in the ballroom, resplendent in a black and silver dress and tried to speak personally to all of the notables who thronged around her. She was 78 years old, and this was her Diamond Jubilee.

Queen Victoria's jubilees directly affected a large proportion of her population. In 1897, people from all over the country flocked to see the procession, spending all day either in the streets or on balconies rented at inflated prices from those lucky enough to own a house along the route. Opportunistic street-sellers supplied those below with fruit and other snacks ('penny ices, currant buns and "pennywinkles", which, like death, seem to have all seasons for their own'), while upstairs the wealthier onlookers, once they'd found their numbered seats, also discovered that 'all sorts of eatables and drinkables had been provided as a matter of course, tea, coffee, claret and champagne, cold meats, salads, cake and sandwiches'. People were in place by 8.30 a.m., waiting for a lengthy procession which didn't start until 10.30 a.m., and went on for hours. Throughout the whole thing, according to an American visitor, 'eating and drinking were going on in every direction, at the most amazing rate, as if the population of London, moved by a common impulse, for some unexplained reason had turned out en masse to breakfast al fresco; up and down the streets, in doorways and windows and on the uppermost roofs were parties eating and drinking and passing up their cups and plates to have them refilled. It was not only a remarkably decorous crowd, but it was in that complacent good humour when everything amuses.'[3] They were also excuses for large-scale parties, organised by villages, towns and cities across the country, part of a long tradition of street festivals held to celebrate royal doings, from coronations, to the birth of heirs, to jubilees. Some were pleasant outings for middle-class families, such as the fête held on the Isle of Wight in August 1897 where the Queen dropped in and watched games, including climbing the 'tall pole well-daubed with grease from which dangled a tempting leg of mutton' (won by a sailor from the royal yacht), and which carried on despite the rain.[4] Others were charitable feasts, paid for by subscription or by the council budget, and designed to feed the poor, often specifically the elderly or schoolchildren. Victoria saw one in progress at Windsor: 'drove at ¼ past 5 … into the first field, under the Castle, near the S. W. station in which 6,000 children from different schools, in the neighbourhood were assembled, & were being feasted in Celebration of my Jubilee'.[5] They were run by committee, planned months in advance, and subject to involved wrangling, as local bigwigs jostled for position and grew outraged in the face of independently minded shop-keepers putting up their own decorations in non-approved colour schemes. They were often huge affairs, and nearly every baker, brewer (or publican), caterer, butcher and cook benefitted, supplying a universal diet of beef, plum pudding and copious amounts of beer and tea to the deserving poor (those deemed to be undeserving weren't invited). Beef and

plum pudding were the edible symbols of Britishness to foreigners and satirists, and there was a large grain of truth in
the image of John Bull sitting down to a steaming roast and
cannon-ball-shaped pudding. Frieda Arnold commented
that the British had 'well-organised stomachs', and ate 'huge
quantities' of beef and plum pudding, while Alfred Suzanne,
writer of a book aimed at French chefs seeking work in
England and America, stated simply that, 'of all their
national dishes, that of which the English are most proud,
and boast – rightly – that they know how to prepare, serve
and eat better than any other people on the Earth is without
doubt roast beef'.[6] Puddings, meanwhile, were 'peculiarly
English … a national dish'.[7] Yet this ideal masked a much
more brutal reality. A huge gap between rich and poor was
nothing new, and nor was both urban and rural poverty, but
for the first time surveys were carried out which revealed
the extent of the problems. For those parts of Victoria's
reign for which data exists, three-quarters of the population
were working class, and around two-thirds of the British
people lived near or below the poverty line. The physical
effects of poverty were stark, and undernourishment
affected growth, stamina and health, as well as contributing
to high infant mortality rates and susceptibility to disease
and infection.[8] The infamous Manchester returns for the
Boer War in 1899 showed that around a third of eligible men
were too undernourished, or ill due to malnourishment, to
sign up for military service, shocking the ruling classes into
attempts to tackle the issue lest they run out of cannon
fodder in the future.

Although the Queen's food, and the technology used to
cook it, did not change much across her reign, the pace of

culinary development more generally in the Victorian period was enormous, and the diet of many people altered almost beyond recognition from the 1830s to 1900. In 1837, Britain had a largely agrarian population, around 80 per cent rural, centred on a network of small villages and towns, eating food produced in a fairly local area and generally cooked at home. There were regional differences, and already the south of England showed a marked tendency towards buying staples such as bread and beer, while further north these were still made at home. Obviously significant amounts of everyday items such as tea, spices and sugar were imported, and unseasonal produce was available – at a price – to those with access to market gardens, which sported the same technology as the gardens at Windsor, though on a smaller scale. The upper classes had productive gardens of their own, and even the middle classes usually found room for a fruit tree or two, especially in the suburbs. Towns were swelling, and with them came restaurants and taverns, as well as street hawkers selling ready-made hot and cold food. For many people, though, their everyday food was little changed from that of their parents and even grandparents.

The upper classes had their three-course *à la Française* extravaganzas, but they were a very small proportion of the population, although disproportionately represented in food writing at the time. Below them came the middle classes, whose income levels varied hugely and who aspired to staff, but who in the vast majority of cases could afford only one or two maids who did everything between them, often with the active help of their mistress. The majority of domestic servants – and service accounted for about 13 per

cent of women's employment by the 1871 census – were
employed in small establishments of this nature, and not in
the large country houses we tend to associate with the
mention of service today.[9] They may have aspired to grand
set-piece dinners, but their reality was more likely to be a
one- or two-course meal of somewhat smaller proportions.
Meals such as these could only have been eaten by a small
number of people, but were nonetheless more representa-
tive of the norm than were the huge dinners at the palace.
Maria Rundell, whose *New System of Domestic Cookery*, first
published in 1806, remained in print until at least the 1870s,
provided ideal menus for family dinners: in one example a
scrag of veal smothered with onions, replaced by a fruit pie
remove, sat on the table with mashed potatoes trimmed with
small slices of bacon, peas soup, hashed hare and broccoli
(the hashed hare would be made from previously roasted
meat). Another has pig's souse (feet and ears) fried in batter
removed with Yorkshire pudding, with potatoes, peas soup,
salads and roast veal.[10] The vast majority of people ate only
one course for dinner, of many dishes, with sweets, mains
and starters all on the table at once. They did not habitually
refer to their food with French names, and, although ragouts
and fricassees, and curries and sauces appeared regularly on
ideal menus and in books aimed at the middle classes, much
of the food eaten at this level was solidly British, and consisted of the classic British repertoire developed in the late
eighteenth century: pies, puddings, roast meats with gravy
and simply (and arguably over-) boiled vegetables with a
butter sauce. Breakfasts were of breads and buns, lunches,
where taken, of leftovers and simple dishes served without
fuss. Most middle-class men worked, and lunched at clubs,

chop houses or taverns, and among the middle classes lunch was viewed as a rather feminine experience.

Mealtimes were in a state of flux. At the palaces the routine of breakfast – luncheon – dinner was well-established, but at a lower social level a lot of people still ate dinner around midday, where it had been since the seventeenth century. For the working classes, the pattern was breakfast – dinner – supper, but whoever you were, dinner was the main meal of the day. The confusion continued throughout the nineteenth century, and the disparity between urban and rural, upper middle class and lower, was illustrated brilliantly by Elizabeth Gaskell in the opening of *North and South* (1855). Margaret Hale, the heroine, is at home with her family in Hampshire when her would-be suitor, Henry Lennox, descends from London. Margaret's mother is completely thrown: 'It is most unfortunate! We are dining early today, and have nothing but cold meat, in order that the servants may get on with their ironing; and yet, of course, we must ask him to dinner.' Margaret replies, 'Never mind the dinner, dear mamma. Cold meat will do capitally for a lunch, which is the light in which Mr Lennox will most likely look upon a two-o-clock dinner.'[11] By the 1870s the working-class supper was often called tea, as the afternoon tea of the upper classes met the eating habits of the lower, and in some contexts, especially northern English, Scottish and rural, tea further mutated into high tea, which was, in essence, a slightly more elevated form of supper.[12]

Downstairs, kitchens were often unchanged from the century before. Spit roasting technology had been a major technological development in the seventeenth century, and was widely adopted in the eighteenth. Depending on status,

the kitchen might have a smoke-jack, as per the royal kitchens, but it might also have a spit turned by clockwork or
weights. Experiments with dog-driven spits had been
restricted to the West Country and petered out despite the
breeding of a special turnspit dog (dogs tended to run away
when faced with turning a giant hamster wheel for several
hours, or ate the dinner when the cook's back was turned).
The simplest expedient was a length of string or wire suspended from a hook and twisted round on itself so that the
meat would turn as the string untwisted and re-twisted. It
only worked for small joints. The majority of kitchens,
apart from at an upper-class level, did most of their cooking
on the same open fire that the meat was cooked in front of,
with pots suspended on iron supports which could be swung
into place as required. Some fires incorporated a water
boiler, and a very few also had a built-in side oven. Ranges
had been introduced at the end of the eighteenth century,
and closed ranges roughly of the type which survive in
museums today were slowly spreading, but they used more
fuel than the older open fires, and were expensive to install.
Most went into new-build urban houses, as the suburbs of
towns and cities started to sprawl beyond the original town
boundaries and into the countryside beyond. These new
ranges had ovens, fire and hobs all in one, although many
cooks complained that mastering the range was the most
challenging part of the job, and they were often scapegoated
and blamed for whatever burnt offering was served up in
lieu of a tasty dinner. Ovens, when not part of a range, were
of the brick-built beehive type, fired with wood or sometimes coal, and, while they were usual in substantial rural
and older urban dwellings, they were rare in the houses of

the poor, who either cooked everything on the fire, or took their food to the baker to be put in his (or her) oven. This practice continued until at least the 1960s in some areas of Britain, especially at Christmas, when small domestic ovens were least likely to cope. The very poor adopted a one-pot cooking method in which all the foods that made up a meal were suspended in bags in a large, bubbling cauldron on the fire. The cooking liquid could then be thickened with bread-crumbs or oatmeal and used as a basic pottage to bulk out the meal. Again, there are records of this continuing until the mid-twentieth century.

On the first of her Progresses in 1832, Victoria passed through the West Midlands, commenting on the grime-smeared populace that 'the men, women and children are all black'. Never the most socially aware of people, she fell romantically in love with the idea of a family of travelling coopers at Claremont in 1837, reading up on the subject of itinerant workers, and visiting them regularly. She made sure they were supplied with soup and blankets, and worried about doing 'something for their spiritual benefit', person-ally giving them New Year's gifts and declaring that they were 'a superior set of gypsies, & very nice to each other'.[13] Her direct dealings with the poor continued along similar lines for the rest of her reign, as she glimpsed them from carriage windows, read about their plight, and occasionally met them, when they were conveniently near a palace or stopping place, sometimes tasting their food. She veered between successful ignorance, and empathy – or at least sympathy – for their problems, writing to Vicky in Prussia in 1866 that 'the lower classes are becoming so well-informed – are so intelligent & earn their bread & riches so deservedly that they cannot & ought not to be kept back – to be abused by the wretched ignorant Highborn beings, who live only to fill time'.[14]

Diet depended entirely on income. Staples for the very poor were as they had been since the eighteenth century: bread, bread, tea, potatoes, and bread, eked out with cheese, milk, butter, treacle, and the occasional bit of bacon if affordable. Some people kept a pig or maintained an allotment, but even those in rural areas struggled to find time to grow their own vegetables, as their working hours were long and many houses were without land. As income increased, items such as fish, sausages, cheaper cuts of meat, cream, beer, more cheese, sugar, fats, flour and fruit were added, but the diet of the majority remained monotonous, even at a relatively affluent level. Meat was the big prize, especially fresh meat ('butcher's meat'), and in families where it was scarce, it was prioritised for the male head of the household, then the children. Animal husbandry had been a subject of concern since the early Industrial Revolution, when the results of breeding techniques were lavishly celebrated in hundreds of pictures of sturdy cows with tiny legs (and all those pubs called after them, especially the hugely famous Durham Ox), and cereal and vegetable crops were also the subject of a great deal of study aimed at better, bigger yields. One of Prince Albert's most uncontroversial achievements was his championing of British farming, and his dedicated efforts to lead by example. He rebuilt many of the farms on the royal estates according to the latest principles and brought them all back into profit – no mean feat, as they were as lackadaisically run as the rest of the palaces at the time – won awards for his improved cattle, and was cheered at agricultural societies as 'a British Farmer'.[15] He threw himself into his role as an improving landlord in the late eighteenth-century model, writing that, although expensive, it was vital because, 'agriculture stands very high in this country, and is a very powerful interest as the latest elections have shown, and it needs encouragement from the Crown, which V naturally cannot give'.[16] He brought in chemical fertilisers, steam-driven machinery including ploughs, and designed and built workers' housing which included continental-style cottage ranges similar to that on which the children learnt to cook at Swiss Cottage. As a result, he was both elected president of the Royal Agricultural Society, and lampooned in *Punch* (which showed him proudly presiding over a farmyard in which the Queen milked a cow, and the children collected eggs and ate turnips). Meanwhile, at Frogmore the model dairy which he helped design was a fairy-tale palace of carved wood, marble and Minton tiles. It was too expensive to be copied directly, but its underlying principles of good ventilation and attention to hygiene were nevertheless influential.

Albert's reforms hardly alleviated rural poverty, although they did encourage British agriculture and helped to focus attention on increasing productivity. In the 1840s things got particularly bad, to the extent that the decade later became known as the 'hungry forties'. This was also the decade in which potato blight struck for the first time, in 1845, killing off the vegetable crop upon which the poor most relied, and leading to the Irish Potato Famine, in which around a million people died, while another million emigrated. Victoria read the reports avidly, aghast at the suffering. She blamed rapacious landlords for part of the problem, but wasn't all sympathy, adhering to the general English line that the 'heedless and improvident way in which the poor Irish have lived' had contributed to their present misery.[17] The urban poor suffered too, and the plight of the Spitalfields silk workers, in terminal decline due to the opening up of the market to global competition, and their refusal or inability to mechanise, became a particularly notorious cause. Victoria's response to these specific crises was to host a series of fundraising balls and other events, which raised several thousand pounds as well as giving vital publicity to the causes she supported. An 1842 ball, in aid of Spitalfields, was held at the Italian Opera House, which the royal party went to after an early dinner, armed with a light supper of rice soup, ham, tongue, lobster salad, cold chicken, sandwiches and plovers' eggs, along with the usual patisserie, jellies and creams.[18] The Queen donated to charities providing poor relief, including £2,000 for the main fundraising group helping in Ireland, and £500 to a Ladies' Clothing Fund, and stood as a very public figurehead for charitable endeavours. In a general effort at boosting the wool, silk and lace-making trades, ladies at court were required to wear only British clothes. In May 1847 the Queen even briefly rationed bread at court to a mere pound a day per person, and insisted that the Establishment eat, 'no fine flour – only seconds'.[19] (Flour at this point was bolted (sieved) to remove the bran, and the finer the cloth, the finer the flour. Seconds was the standard grade for most people, and included a higher proportion of bran than the fine flour that was sometimes called firsts.)

At the height of the Potato Famine, meanwhile, in 1847, she endorsed a public fast day, although she was uncomfortable with the idea. Fast days rarely involved actual fasting but instead were treated as serious holy days, with shops and businesses shut, and the nation theoretically at prayer.[20] The Queen certainly didn't give up her meals, although both the royal and the Household dinners that day were fish-based and meat-free (mainly – there was still a sideboard with some beef and chicken). This was vaguely in keeping with the pre-Reformation Catholic rules about eating on fast days, although it ignored the restrictions on eggs and cream. Victoria's issue was less about the eating and more about the concept. She was uneasy at the way in which the church co-opted the crisis to scare people into suddenly remembering their religious duties by putting about the idea that starvation in Ireland was somehow punishment for sin, writing, 'I think it almost wrong & presumptuous to say that the present troubles are judgement for our sins. We all recognise that we are sinful, but I cannot see that we are more so now, than we were some 60 years ago!'[21] She had ambivalent feelings in general towards public fasts, which were an established tradition, but one which she found old-fashioned: 'I spoke to Ld John Russell for a little while in the garden, chiefly about the proclamation of a Fast Day, which the people desire immediately, in hopes of abating the Cholera! It is curious how this superstitious belief still prevails, & to my mind it seems to me as if it misleads people. We ought always to be praying to God to avert & mitigate such diseases, & use the faculties & the understanding He has given us to take the necessary precautions, in cleansing streets & houses & in watching premonitory symptoms.'[22] The issue rumbled on, with the Queen increasingly impatient at the self-abnegation, which she found reeked of medieval Catholicism and served no actual purpose, but denied working people a day of pay while stopping traders making money: 'This "Day of Humiliation & Prayer", which from being neither a Fast or a Thanksgiving is not legally a holiday & this produces a very serious effect on the Bank & all money transactions. As Parliament is not sitting, it is impossible to pass a Bill making "Humiliation & Prayer" equally a holiday. Consequently there must be a Council for another proclamation, which is to be precisely the same, – leaving the denomination of the day, – the same, but inserting the word Fast in support of it. This seems very absurd.'[23] Although deeply religious, Victoria was never a fan of abstinence, especially when it was imposed upon people, and she was furious at the rise of the Sabbatarian movement in the 1850s, which sought to make Sunday a day of total rest. For her, Sundays were for enjoying oneself, and she saw it as an attack, not just on her own way of life, but on the one day that the working classes had for enjoyment (and tending their rather crucial vegetable plots – which counted as work and would, therefore, have been forbidden): 'They should legislate for themselves & leave the poor people alone, who work all the week round & who require innocent recreation on a Sunday!'[24] By the 1860s she had managed to make official public fasts a thing of the past, and Sundays were established as days of leisure.

By 1851, just over half of the population lived in towns; the country was rapidly becoming the first urbanised nation in the world, further fuelled by a second phase of industrialisation in the 1870s. The population was ever more reliant on shops for provisions, by now increasingly supplied by railway links to ports, and the outlying areas which both grew the crops and bred the animals that fed the towns. Such was the demand for certain products that special services were laid on, including the nightly Rhubarb Express, which ran from the 1870s to the 1960s, taking Yorkshire forced rhubarb from Wakefield to London. The same train network that enabled Victoria to sally forth to Osborne, Balmoral and various country houses also brought migrant workers from country areas to the capital, seeking work. Country house employment records for the Victorian period show that cooks, maids, footmen and personal servants were recruited from across Britain (and France, for cooks and lady's maids), though the stereotype at the bottom end was that of the poor Irish girl, reflecting the desperation of the Irish to find work at any cost. Indoor staff were often found through the informal servants' network, but could also be recruited via an agency, and many employers preferred to take on people without local connections for it was feared that a family down the road would encourage pilfering and absenteeism. In Mary Elizabeth Braddon's contemporary drama, *Hostages to Fortune*, a great deal of the plot is taken up with the heroine's problems with her cooks – one is useless, one steals all of the leftovers (and quite a lot that isn't left) to feed her relatives – which drive her husband almost into the arms of the evil villainess of the piece.[25] Drastic times.

The railways also enabled foodstuffs to be brought to cities quickly and in large quantities. It's not accurate to say that they revolutionised the diet of town dwellers overnight – they took time to get going, and the food they brought was often expensive – but they were part of a process of change that eventually affected almost everyone.

Producers, too, benefitted, and some foods, such as Finnan haddie (smoked Scottish haddock), or Grasmere ginger-bread, found a whole new audience. Meanwhile, the immense flocks of turkeys (clad in shoes or with their feet tarred to harden them on the roads) that used to leave Norfolk in time to be fattened up in London for Christmas, and the cattle that once tramped the roads to markets, became a much rarer sight.

The trains benefitted those with enough money to spend it on leisure as well. The biggest event of the mid-century, and one with far-reaching effects for many of those involved, was the Great Exhibition. Prince Albert, who championed it in the face of often severe cynicism, went on a tour around the country to drum up support. In York in 1850 he was hosted in the Guildhall, adjacent to the mayor's residence at the Mansion House. As was often the case, the in-house cook was deemed not good enough, and instead the leading chef of the day, Alexis Soyer, was hired to mas-termind a spectacular banquet. Soyer was indisputably one of the great characters of the age: a showman, an entrepre-neur, a brilliant chef and, eventually, lauded as a military hero (he invented the Soyer stove and revolutionised army feeding during the Crimean War). He was French, but had come to England in the 1830s amid the turmoil of yet another revolution, working briefly for Victoria's uncle, the Duke of Cambridge, before climbing up the culinary ladder to become head chef at the Reform Club and London's greatest gastronomic star. In 1847 he had been employed by the government to set up large-scale feeding initiatives in Ireland, as charitable efforts to alleviate the Famine peaked. He also set up soup kitchens in Spitalfields, and published a book promising tasty and nutritious recipes for very little outlay. In this, as with his other books, and indeed career, he was competing with Charles Francatelli, whose *Plain Cookery Book for the Working Classes* came out in 1852 (Soyer's somewhat more patronising version, with its section on the 'general ignorance of the poor in cooking', was first published in 1854).[26] At the 1850 York banquet, he produced a typically flamboyant menu (at a cost of £600 excluding wines). The dessert fruits, including two pineapples sent from Chatsworth, glittered on the table, and the meal was served *à la Française* around it, named with typical Soyer flair – there was a soup 'à la Victoria' (though she wasn't there), chicken fillets 'à la York Minster', fruit baskets 'à la Lady Mayoress' and, just on the royal table, two creams 'de la Grand Bretagne', one 'à la Victoria' and the other, 'à la Albert'. The most bizarre dish was 'the Hundred Guinea dish', which was a terrifying-looking concoction complete with turtle heads vomiting skewers of sweetbreads, truffles and cockscombs. It was so-named because, as Soyer put it, 'if an epicure were to order this dish only, he would be obliged to provide the whole of the above-mentioned items', and if he (or she) did, it would cost them a hundred guineas. The dish was a total construct, made of the choicest morsels from a range of (meaty) raw ingredients, which included the oysters from 100 snipe, 40 woodcocks and 45 partridges, the heads and part of the fins and green fat from 5 turtles, and a few whole birds including Belgian ortolans, six dozen larks and 6 plovers. It was garnished with mushrooms, crawfish, American asparagus, carved bread croustades, quenelles and mangoes, amid all of which it's hardly credible that anyone noticed the accompanying 'new sauce'.[27]

Inevitably, the Prince found that it disagreed with his stomach.

Soyer also found a role at the Great Exhibition itself, presiding over the (loss-making) Symposium of All Nations, a restaurant at which he hoped to showcase the (mainly French) food of the world, with the capacity to seat 1,500 people, and tours of the kitchens for interested parties. Most of the six million visitors to the Exhibition either brought a picnic or fell prey to the catering inside however, for tickets wouldn't allow for re-entry, and there was a lot to see. The organising committee put the catering out to tender, stressing that it should be of the highest standard in terms of service and value for money. Visitors came from all over Britain on excursion trains, by coach and on foot, many taking advantage of the single shilling day tickets which enabled the working classes to feast their eyes on the manufactured wonders of the whole world. Schweppes, who won the contract, supplied over 2 million Bath buns, 1.1 million bottles of carbonated water and 1,000 gallons of pickles via a central tea room. Two further outlets provided bread, cheese and ginger beer (no alcohol was served), but, despite their best efforts, complaints abounded, and letters were published in the *Morning Chronicle* regarding 'the worst and smallest sandwiches I have ever tasted', and 'little, dry, sixpenny dollops of pork pie'.[28] Clearly mass catering never changes.

The technological changes that were showcased at the Great Exhibition were also making their mark on kitchens. Soyer was one of the first to adopt gas cooking, installing gas ovens at the Reform Club in 1841 and experimenting with steam ovens for bread baking in the 1850s. In a domestic context, including at the palaces, gas was much slower to catch on, despite being given a boost by all sorts of gas apparatus being displayed at the Great Exhibition, and it took until the 1880s for gas ovens to be installed in any great number in middle-class homes. Windsor was by no means alone in being entirely fuelled by coal until the twentieth century, and the vast majority of country houses maintained a coal-fired range with spit mechanism for the all-important roast, even if – and it was rare – they experimented with gas as well. Cooking equipment was large and expensive, and people were used to cooking on coal. There were fears that gas would taint the food, or leak into the house. There was also a skill involved in working a coal-fired range, and a resistance to changes that might be seen to devalue a job, in this case cooking. By the 1860s a number of products were newly available which seemed to be a great boon to the hard-working cook, but which were remarkably slow to catch on, at least in professional contexts.

The list of foods which were commercialised in the middle of the nineteenth century is significant, and contains many things deemed vital in cookery today: baking powder, custard powder, ready-to-use gelatine, vanilla extract, processed yeast (the stuff sold as 'fresh' yeast now, which was known as 'German' yeast then, and replaced brewer's yeast), cornflour, condensed milk, and Liebig's extract, which was the forerunner of Marmite, Bovril and a whole range of flavour enhancers, and which was launched with aplomb at a dinner cooked by Francatelli. Tinned foods were also making headway, especially tinned sardines, which had first been sold in the 1830s, and tinned meats, which were taking off by the end of the 1860s. A lot of these foods were cheap fillers, regarded with suspicion, and others were seen as deskilling cookery. Isabella Beeton's somewhat ramshackle *Book of Household Management*, without doubt the best known of any British Victorian cookery book, illustrates well the confused state of mid-century middle-class cuisine. The book is totally unoriginal, and Beeton flagrantly plagiarised other writers for both the recipes and much of the philosophical prose on eating, which fills the book. Yet it was a bestseller, for her tone was empowering and refreshingly direct, and it delivered what it promised: a way through the minefield of social convention and expectation to the overall goal of successful budget management and even more successful dinner parties. She took recipes from books written over the last half-century, and old methods sat side by side with new ones: sponge cakes risen by the power of egg alone, and measured out by weighing all of the ingredients in proportion to the weight of eggs and, for the next recipe, another sponge cake using baking powder, and reliant on pounds and ounces. She provided ideal menus, mainly served in a variation on *à la Française*, with four courses plus dessert (she called them first course, entrées, second course, third course), but acknowledged the rise of *à la Russe*, pointing out that it was 'scarcely suitable for small establishments; a large number of servants being required to carve, and help the guests', but that there was, if handled properly, 'no mode of serving a dinner so enjoyable as this'.[29] Her primary market was the lower middle class, women whose parents had probably been working class, and who found themselves needing to hire and fire servants, furnish houses, plan parties, and impress the neighbours, all while doing a great deal of the actual work themselves, including the cooking. Predominantly urban (or suburban, as she was), they would have no problem obtaining the fancy culinary moulds which she recommended for jellies, creams, pies, tarts and puddings, for they were now mass-manufactured, and available in ceramic, copper or cheap tin. They would not have dreamt of making their own mushroom ketchup (although there was a recipe if they did), and probably favoured instead the Harvey's sauce or Worcester sauce that was used in the more modern versions of the recipes. Their dinners, when not dinner parties, were simple and often centred on a roast on Sunday, reused during the week: 'cold meat cookery' formed a significant part of many books, not just Beeton's, and the concept of 'leftovers', with its somewhat inferior connotations, was still in the future. A typical small family dinner according to Beeton was jugged hare (from the remains of a roast hare the day before), boiled knuckle of veal and rice, boiled bacon cheek and apple pudding – not hugely different to those of Maria Rundell a half-century before. Even the more impressive menus she helpfully provided for dinner parties were designed to be manageable in small kitchens with limited staff: mock-turtle soup, brill and lobster sauce with fried whitings; then fowl à la béchamel and oyster patties; roast sucking pig, stewed beef à la jardinière, and vegetables; and finally charlotte aux pommes, coffee cream, cheesecakes, apricot tart and iced pudding; all followed with dessert of fruit and ices.[30]

For those with a bit of money and access to shops, industrialisation brought new culinary possibilities, as things previously out of reach due to the time and effort required to make them became feasible with the help of new technology, and the standard of living slowly improved. In towns, the range of hot and cold food sellers was immense, and by the 1870s it was possible to buy (among other things) muffins, hot cakes, eels, pies, soup, baked potatoes (also helpful as hand warmers inside a fur muff), fritters, roast chestnuts, sandwiches, oysters, trotters and, an increasingly important part of the working-class diet, fried fish and chips.[31] The rural poor were still living through dire times, though, and on Victoria's visit to Ireland in 1861, she commented on the 'many ragged people'.[32] The effects of undernutrition were compounded by the lack of regulation in the food industry at the time, which, with manufacturers under commercial pressure, and customers unwilling or unable to pay more, led to the habitual adulteration of many basic foods. Some additives were well established: alum in bread, for example, was known as an 'improver' for it made lower grades of flour seem whiter, and white bread was what customers wanted – it was seen as more digestible, more refined and better for you. When it wasn't added, there were complaints. Yet it also enabled the baker to add a significant amount more water to the bread, which was free, and increased his or her profits. Consumers got the white bread they wanted, but there was less nutritional content in the loaf and in some cases the levels of alum, which is highly astringent, would have been high enough to cause digestive upset. The bakers didn't add enough to cause (much) of an issue, but they bought the flour from a miller, who also didn't add enough to cause (much) of a problem. Put together, not much of a problem had the potential to become quite a large problem, especially for young children, whose diet revolved around the inevitable bread and milk (which was usually watered down, and probably skim in the first place). Bread adulteration was truly pernicious, as the population at every level relied upon their daily loaf, and very few people in towns still made their own.

In this context, the discovery that not a single loaf analysed by Arthur Hill Hassell in London in the 1850s, including the ones guaranteed to be pure, was free of adulterants was a huge shock. Indeed, given that the palaces regularly ordered in bread, it's entirely possible, if not probable, that the royal Household was enjoying alum and plaster of Paris in their breakfast buns along with the rest of the population. Tea was also very commonly adulterated, and a widespread cook's perk was the right to sell used tea leaves, which were 'upcycled' in one of the tea 'factories' which specialised in adding a tiny bit of real tea, some dried random leaves and anything else they found handy to produce fake tea for the poor.[33] Hassell's analyses covered a wide range of goods and showed how hard it was to obtain pure foods: coffee contained chicory and acorn, with brick dust for colour, sweets were coloured with lead and copper, sugar had added lime dust. The 1850s surveys, which were given a great deal of publicity, proved to be a turning point, however, and a mixture of voluntary reform under public pressure, and governmental legislation when that eventually proved not to be enough, did change things. By the 1880s the worst of the abuses had been stopped, and the rise of branded goods marketed on purity and healthfulness had become commonplace.

Another factor that influenced the diet of the nation for the better was the importation of goods from abroad. Meat was particularly important, enabling the poor to get much-needed protein into their diets, and from the 1870s cookery books aimed at the lower end of the market tackled the problem of tinned meats head-on. The author of *Buckmaster's Cookery*, in 1874, in a section called 'Australian meats', admits that the meat is overcooked and overpriced for what it is, but denies that it started as poor quality, or that there are 'kangaroos and elephants and horses' in it.[34] The book mentioned experiments with freezing meats, but admitted that to date they had failed. It was a year out: the first successful shipment of Argentinian meat, kept almost frozen, at −1°c on a voyage of 90 days, reached London in 1875. The shipping company, Eastmans, was canny enough to send a baron of beef from the consignment to the Queen at Windsor, who pronounced it 'very good'. Properly frozen meat was introduced in 1877, and in 1880 Victoria received a lamb carcass from an Australian shipment (they also sent one to the Prince of Wales).[35] The frozen meat trade not only benefitted the British populace, but it had a significant impact on Australia and New Zealand, which were now able to profitably sell surplus meat (and they had a lot of it). Foreign grain imports, too, benefitted Britain, and as the American west was opened out to large-scale farming in the 1870s and 1880s, good-quality, white flour poured into ports, to be milled in the new roller mills, which produced whiter, finer flour than ever before. The process also allowed the wheatgerm to be removed for the first time, which stopped the flour going rancid after six months (and incidentally removed much of the nutritional value with it). Bread consumption was, for the first time, declining as living standards gradually rose, even for the poor, whose diet had now expanded to include margarine and condensed milk (often spread on the bread), cheap jam and some of the canned goods on the market. It still wasn't healthy or nutritious, and it remained monotonous, but it was almost certainly better than it had been when Victoria came to the throne.

The pace of industrialisation, the availability of overseas goods, and the reliability of preservation methods all contributed to a surge in manufactured foods in the last quarter of the century. Even the royal supply books included branded items by the 1880s. The spicery ordered Worcester sauce, Harvey sauce, ready-made chutney, bloater paste (bloaters are cured herrings), curry paste and polenta in 1888 and in February 1891, in a shock move, an entry for baking powder finally crept in.[36] Boiled sweets were also ordered in huge quantities from the 1850s onwards, presumably not tainted with lead or arsenic, which had killed twenty people at a sweet-maker's in Bradford in 1858 (in the maker's defence, he meant to adulterate his lozenges with plaster of Paris, but got the wrong bottle).[37] The enterprising Crosse & Blackwell, who were suppliers to the royal kitchens, published a guide to 'preserved meats, fruits, condiments, vegetables &c' in 1889 which revealed the range of foods now available ready-made; not just fruits in syrups and large quantities of sardines, but almost-complete dishes such as 'financière ragout': 'This delicious preserved mixture consists of cocks combs, cocks kernels, small button mushrooms, truffles, scallops of sweetbread, etc.' The author recommended it be served with meat extract or used to garnish other dishes. There were baby foods, pies, herb and fruit essences, mayonnaises, soups, fish and meat whole or as pastes, and exotica such as tamarinds, larks and reindeer tongues. Jellies and creams were available in bottles, and the range of patent sauces was bewildering. Many had royal names, including Payne's Royal Osborne Sauce, apparently made by 'Her Majesty's Chemist on the establishment at Osborne', and particularly excellent in a Welsh rarebit.[38]

The mid-1880s revision of *Beeton's Book of Household Management* also showed how much more reliant the average middle-class consumer had become on manufactured goods, with jolly line drawings of common jars and bottles, although the recipes largely remained those of the 1861 edition. It now included sections on vegetarianism (featuring fried bananas, lentil rissoles and the entirely grim-sounding vegetable goose, made of breadcrumbs, onion and a few herbs), and the cookery of America, Germany, France, Australia, India and Italy. The book had become a staple item, so presumably it was deemed useful to have a few recipes from other countries in case the reader emigrated (and so that relatives could see what they might be eating). The results were a tad bizarre, with, in the Australian section, the standard British pigeon pie reworked as a parrot pie sprouting bright feathers, and roast hare reborn as roast wallaby, complete with tail, head and perky ears. The casual plagiarism continued to make some of the recipes hard to follow, with a picture of Jules Gouffé's biscuit-and-sort-of-soufflé Punch Cake cropping up as an illustration of a much easier set of instructions for Tennis Cake, itself a typical example of the late Victorian need to codify everything, even down to the snacks. Those who emigrated to New Zealand and Australia probably didn't find the Beeton compendium terribly useful, although the British in both countries were renowned for maintaining a British style of cookery in the face of all obstacles, especially at Christmas, where joints of beef and poultry were served despite the baking heat in December.[39]

Emigration was a global phenomenon at the time, with Europeans seeking better lives in other European countries as well as in America and Australasia. It didn't always go well. At Osborne back in 1851, the royal family became directly involved when a boatload of German emigrants landed unceremoniously on the Isle of Wight, as their boat collapsed under them. Most were agricultural labourers, and Victoria sent down a coterie of servants to see what condition they were in, and set up an impromptu soup and coffee kitchen to feed them. She took the children down to see them:

> Went again to New Barn, where, after waiting a little, we saw the poor people, as they were waiting outside & coming out from the Kitchen, each having a tin can, or vessel in their hand. They looked miserable, but not ragged, or in extreme poverty. One young man, well dressed, & evidently of a better class, we spoke to, & he expressed their gratitude. They were 219 in number, of which I hear 90 are men, 38 married women, 33 single, 48 children & 10 little infants! ...They were much in need of soap, which we sent them.[40]

The children were encouraged to donate their old toys, and they also sent clothes to them, and they remained stranded for several weeks. It happened again in 1854: both boats had been bound for America, but plenty of Germans also stayed in the UK. The *St James's Gazette* in 1887 complained that the number of foreigners in Britain had increased from 113,000 to 135,000 between 1871 and 1881, and that about a third of them were German (mainly working as bakers). Meanwhile the British, especially the Irish and Scottish, continued to leave despite the perils – Victoria's journals detail her horror at disasters, including an outbreak of smallpox on board one ship, a fire on another, while yet another was run down by a steamer while at anchor in 1873, with the loss of more than 300 would-be Australians.[41]

By the end of the century, the very poor still ate a diet based predominantly on bread, cheese, potatoes and tea, as they had in 1837, but it was now likely to include some tinned meat or fish, condensed milk, and sugar or jam. In general, the working-class diet had improved, but it remained the case that the more money a family had, the more likely they were to afford fresh meat, vegetables and whole-milk products, and that for many people malnutrition was still a problem. The upper-working-class diet was, however, significantly better and more varied than it had been 70 years before, and much of that was due to the new wave of industrialisation that was also likely to provide their employment in the last decades of the century. The middle classes had without a doubt benefitted the most from Victorian technological development in culinary terms, and the class had expanded and encompassed a much wider range of incomes and lifestyles than the term can easily cover. They were the buyers of cookery books, and the users of gas ranges, they employed the cook-maids emerging from the new cookery schools (where cooking had been rebranded domestic science, and was increasingly reliant on weights and measures, and no longer on instinct); they ate the tinned pineapples and fresh bananas, and the mass-produced goods, in mass-produced packaging, and they worried, terribly, about what people thought. The upper middle classes were the first to really embrace service *à la Russe*, which was easy to manage, simple to understand, but could be rendered delightfully difficult in practice. A few judicious customs around the 'correct' way to handle your fruit fork could be invented which were unique to each family or group, and enabled people to make those all-important judgements about others which litter Victorian literature and filled the pages of magazines. They also increasingly adopted the aristocratic habit of naming all of their dishes in French, and cookery book writers obliged them, finding a suitable 'à la', no matter what the dish. Above them the landed aristocracy cared rather less, and retained old service styles and old cooking methods because it suited them, and they could afford the staff and had the space. Of course, there were exceptions; some of the new country houses of the period such as Cragside and Tyntesfield led domestic technological development, for example with the installation of electricity, and their owners – usually industrialists rather than nobles of long-standing title – embraced modernity wholeheartedly. Electric lighting was gradually installed at the royal palaces in the 1890s, although it was characteristically badly done, at least at Balmoral, where Lady Lytton complained that 'there is a huge burner at the top which makes such a glare on the ceiling'.[42]

Yet, despite the changes, there was also a great deal of continuity in cookery and food. Rich fruit cakes raised by yeast hung on until the 1870s, egg-raised sponges a while longer. Calves' feet continued to be the base of upper-class jellies, and debate over whether meat could be called roasted only if it had been cooked in front of a fire, on a spit, raged on until the end of the century. Chocolate was still understood to be a drink, albeit made of cocoa powder rather than cocoa mass, until after Victoria's death (although eating chocolate was commonplace by the 1880s), and the edible symbols of Britishness remained tea, pudding and roast beef. They were consumed in 1837, 1887 and 1897, and they would be again in 1902.

11

The ageing Queen

By 1897 very few of Victoria's subjects would have been able to remember a time when she was not their Queen. Her granddaughter Marie, looking back on her childhood, summed it up succinctly: 'Queen Victoria! Even then she was becoming an almost legendary figure; how much more so, therefore, today when looking back on her! She had lasted so long that one could hardly imagine the world continuing to turn without her.'[1] In her old age, she had become iconic, and stories about her grew up so quickly that they became part of the mythology that surrounded her, regardless of whether or not they were true. After her death, it became obligatory for anyone who had even vaguely passed through the court to write down their reminiscences, no matter how garbled, and, as a result, the last twenty years of her life are in sharp contrast to the first twenty, about which comparatively little is known. Fact and fiction merged, even within her lifetime, and it is from the late nineteenth century that many of the most pervasive food myths about the Queen derive, mainly due to exactly the phenomenon that Edward (later Edward VIII), one of her great-grandchildren, admitted: 'So deeply had the power of Queen Victoria's personality pervaded the existence of her family that I can no longer differentiate with certainty between what I actually saw of her with my own eyes and what I later learnt from my parents or the courtiers who had served her, or what I learnt from books.'[2] She was a woman to be approached with awe and respect, and it was almost unthinkable that, less than four years after the Diamond Jubilee brought cheering crowds to the streets, a new monarch would be on the throne, and Victoria in her grave.

The Queen was very rarely ill. There were the usual colds and occasional bouts of flu but apart from the 1835 illness at Tunbridge Wells, she sailed through most of her life, nine pregnancies and all, without a serious physical problem (she went through the menopause in around 1865, later remarking that she'd suffered from hot flushes).[3] Her mental state was more fragile, and, while she resolutely ignored physical discomfort or exhaustion, frequently putting her ladies-in-waiting to shame, after 1861 she was quite happy to use her nerves as an excuse for avoiding public performances, or for going on holiday at inopportune moments. She became something of a hypochondriac, and travelled with a succession of doctors in constant attendance, bombarding them with notes about minor symptoms, and diagnosing herself with all sorts of things. The last of these, James Reid, came to be one of her closest confidants,

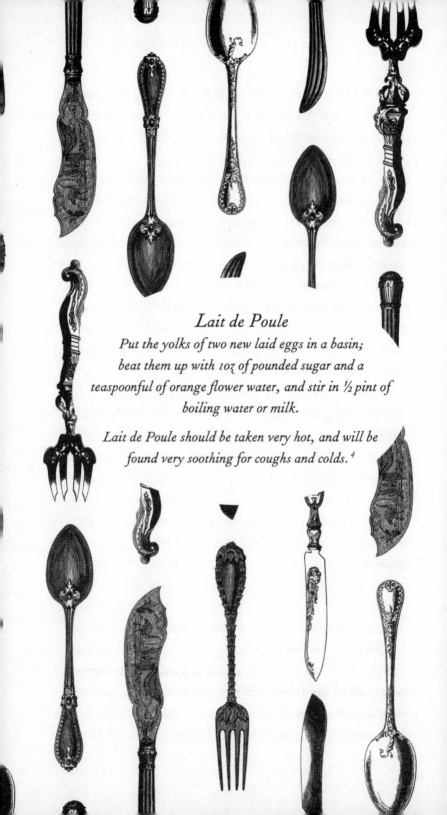

Lait de Poule

Put the yolks of two new laid eggs in a basin;
beat them up with 1oz of pounded sugar and a
teaspoonful of orange flower water, and stir in ½ pint of
boiling water or milk.

Lait de Poule should be taken very hot, and will be
found very soothing for coughs and colds. [4]

and after John Brown's death was the dominant male figure in her life, one whose role encompassed far more than just medicine. He found himself in the position of unofficial chief go-between for the Household and the Queen, as he saw her up to five times a day, and she trusted him enormously. He started work for her in 1881, and found a woman who had accepted the contradiction inherent in her role, and learnt to use it to her advantage. Randall Davidson, the Dean of Windsor, writing at around the same time, said that she had an 'irresistible charm', based on a 'combination of absolute truthfulness and simplicity with the instinctive recognition and quiet assertion of her position as Queen'. He was not alone in seeing her both as a woman, in this case 'shy and humble', and as a monarch who 'asserted her position unhesitatingly'. She was someone who insisted in the face of ministerial resistance that she would wear a bonnet for her 1887 Jubilee, but then carried it off as if it was the crown that they would have preferred. She trod the line between being head of state and a Victorian mother and widow with panache, and, at 68, she was becoming ageless. There's a modern tendency to regard Victoria as old from surprisingly early on, which is deeply unfair – even at the time life expectancy was well into the seventies, provided you survived childhood, and her immediate predecessors had lived until 68 and 72.

The Queen did have a couple of long-running ailments. In 1871, the only time she had been incapacitated through illness, she'd had a vicious attack of gout, which affected nearly all of her joints and was incredibly painful. It followed hot on the heels of a very badly infected arm (she'd been stung by something while at Osborne in August 1871), which eventually had to be lanced. She was pained and ill throughout much of August, September, October and November, complaining at one point that she hadn't felt as bad since Tunbridge Wells in 1835, and noting in displeasure that she had 'little appetite, & difficulty in swallowing very distressing, as I feel as if I would choke. Remained in my room the remainder of the day & did not go down to lunch or dinner.'[5] The gout came on in October, at Balmoral, and affected her hands and ankles. Despite this, as usual, she soldiered on: 'Made an effort to go to the Ball Room, where I was giving a dance to the people, & was carried down at ½ past 9. It made me very nervous, but still I was glad to please the people. The Ball was very animated, but I suffered all the time from my hand, & could not remain long.'[6] By mid-October she was depressed and irritated by her growing incapacity, which meant that she had to have meals in private: 'Beatrice helped to cut up my meat for me at my solitary little dinner.'[7] It got worse, and soon she faced a new low, being fed with a spoon like an infant: 'Had my feet & hands bandaged. My utter helplessness is a bitter trial, not even being able to feed myself!'[8] She continued to lament her sorry state, especially the 'hateful' inability to hold a knife and fork, and rejoiced when she could finally 'move the fingers again and even help myself'. On 22 October she noted with palpable relief that she 'could feed myself with my left hand – a great improvement', and the next day her appetite started to return. By the 27th she was happily dining with others again, and wrote with relief on the 29th that 'I actually dined downstairs, for the first time since I came here.' She'd lost two stone and loathed every second of the experience – which was soon to be eclipsed by Bertie getting typhoid and nearly dying at Sandringham. In her annual summary of the year in December she wrote rather feelingly that it had been 'a most trying one'.[9]

The other recurring problem was with her knee. Even in 1838 Thomas Sully, painting her full-length portrait, commented that she had a week knee which caused her pain when climbing stairs, and in 1883 she tripped on the stairs at Windsor and twisted her knee so badly that she couldn't walk on it.[10] After this point she was prone to rheumatism and flare-ups of pain that caused her to need a stick. She fell over a loose bit of carpet in 1892 and further aggravated the problem, and from that point on never fully recovered proper use of her knee. The image of the old lady, walking with a stick or being pulled in a donkey carriage, owes a lot to this one injury, which annoyed her, and which, in characteristically pugnacious fashion, she ignored as much as she could. In the wake of John Brown's death in 1883, while she was recovering from the first knee injury, she temporarily lost the use of both legs (as she had after Prince Albert's death in 1861). Although devastated by Brown's death, she was also annoyed at the incapacity it had caused, waspishly complaining that it was cramping her style: 'How can I see people at dinner in the evening? I can't go walking about all night holding onto the back of a chair.'[11]

The ageing process was in fact considerably more gradual than the traditional image of the black-clad 'widow of Windsor' would suggest. With the exception of the knee injury, she showed no outward sign of infirmity, and even her occasional lameness didn't stop her when she put her mind to it. Henry Ponsonby, her private secretary and a determined hater of the annual Balmoral ghillies' ball, watched in awe and mild chagrin as she turned up every year without fail and danced at them. In 1891 he noted that she danced with 'light airy steps in the old courtly fashion; no limp or stick but every figure carefully and prettily danced'.[12] As late as 1900, only a few months before her death, she turned out on foot to review the troops at Windsor. The only aspect of her health which age did affect was her eyesight, and she developed cataracts that eventually almost blinded her, although she resolutely blamed the deficiencies of her vision on bad light or poor handwriting. Her own already fairly illegible scrawl got steadily worse, creeping like a bad-tempered spider across the black-edged paper which she used for every letter after Albert's death. It was very different from the beautiful handwriting she'd had as a well-watched teenager, when she wrote to her half-sister on delicate, lace-edged pink paper that she'd been given at one of the paper factories she'd visited when touring the country. (Feodora expressed delight in it and asked Victoria to send her some – and a few weeks later used it to write and thank her.[13]) Her ladies-in-waiting were reduced to trying out new pens, in ever thicker black writing, until by the 1890s the Queen was forced to give up even trying to read or write, and became reliant on her youngest daughter, Beatrice, to read out the political dispatches she still diligently went through, commented on, and signed where necessary. It caused issues, both with security and the Queen's ability to truly grasp what was going on. Frederick Ponsonby, one of the secretaries (and son of ball-hating Henry), crushingly identified the cause: '[We] may write a long precis of things, but they are often not read to Her Majesty as Beatrice is in a hurry to develop a photograph or wants to paint a flower.'

He went on: 'Her memory is still wonderful, her shrewd-
ness, her power of discrimination as strong as ever, her long
experience of European politics alone makes her opinion
valuable, but when her sole means of reading dispatches,
precis, etc., lie in Beatrice, it is simply hopeless.'[14]

Lameness and sight problems aside, Victoria continued
to live life as she wanted. Although she'd admitted to
wanting to die in the immediate aftermath of Albert's death,
by the late 1870s she'd recovered much of her verve. She had
by now re-emerged into public life, though very much on
her terms, and without interfering with her continental
jaunts or sojourns on the Isle of Wight and in Scotland. Her
ladies-in-waiting were constantly awed by her as she
approached her seventies, and Marie Mallet's letters are full
of comments such as this in 1889 after a long and bitterly
cold drive: 'the Queen was wonderful, not a bit tired and as
brisk as a bee all the evening. I wish I might think I shall be
like her at 70.' Mallet was far more aware of Victoria's age
than the Queen was herself – '[the Queen] to my intense
astonishment ascended a huge ladder in order to mount a
horse twenty six years old which pranced along quite gaily,
only conceive what energy at seventy one!' – and her determination to enjoy life seemed only to increase as she got
older.[15] She did transfer some of her more arduous duties
onto Bertie, who, despite a reputation for philandering, glut-
tony and occasional stupidity, was shaping up to be an
excellent host and king-in-waiting. He and his wife, Alexandra, hosted drawing rooms and levees (formal court
presentations for women and men, respectively), and some
state visits. Others were entertained by Victoria herself,
with those all-important lunches at Windsor taking centre

stage for many visitors. Marie Mallet's comment on Leopold II of Belgium made clear that this wasn't always purely out of interest or desire for status: 'He is an unctuous old monster, very wicked I believe, we imagine he thinks a visit to the Queen gives him a fresh coat of whitewash, otherwise why does he travel five hundred miles in order to partake of lunch!'[16] The Aga Khan had an audience with Victoria in 1898, commenting that, 'she received me with the utmost courtesy and affability ... The Queen, enfolded in voluminous black wraps and shawls, was seated on a big sofa. Was she tall or short, was she stout or not? I could not tell: her posture and her wraps made assessments of that kind quite impossible. I kissed the hand which she held out to me.' By this stage, she'd given up on full corsets, and adopted a softer form of shaped body support, although it was virtually invisible under all of the ruffles and ribbons on her elaborate gowns.[17] He was impressed by her vigour, especially in eating: 'The dinner was long and elaborate – course after course, three or four choices of meat, a hot pudding and an iced pudding, a savoury and all kinds of hothouse fruit – slow and stately in its serving. We sat down at a quarter past nine, and it must have been a quarter to eleven before it was all over. The Queen, in spite of her age, ate and drank heartily – every kind of wine that was offered, and every course, including both the hot and the iced pudding.'[18]

There were also occasional state visits hosted more directly by the Queen, although she regarded these as something more like family get-togethers. The main one was the visit of the Tsar of Russia to Balmoral in 1896. Edith Lytton, another of the Queen's ladies, was invited on board their yacht, where she had lunch, noting that, 'the gentlemen had

their salt bits and liqueurs in the Russian fashion at the sideboard, and I longed to taste all but was rather too giddy to
run risks ... There were several Russian dishes and the
more foreign style of luncheon so superior to our heavy
English ones.'[19] Inevitably the castle, where by now over-
crowding was so bad that the laundry-maids slept four to a
bed, was too small to accommodate the massive Russian
party, and *The Times* commented on the measures taken to
host them: 'To overcome the difficulty to some extent, the
servants' apartments within the house have been appropriated, and accommodation had been provided for them by
the erection, in two parallel lines behind the Castle, of a
number of temporary rooms. These have been brought
from Windsor, and are so constructed of timber and iron as
to be rendered portable. They have also taken over
Abergeldie Castle, and the Balmoral Ballroom has been
fitted out as a dining room for the household, draped liberally with the Russian colours.'[20] Victoria took advantage to
have 'a few words' with the Tsar on the topic of troubling
foreign affairs, while his wife, who was yet another of Victoria's granddaughters, trotted around the neighbourhood
buying souvenirs and revisiting childhood haunts – including the shop where a Mrs Symonds had taught them all to
bake scones.[21]

Food was as important as ever, possibly even more so,
and, when there were no eminent guests to entertain, she
could now eat extremely fast: her table, her rules. Marie
Mallet, who ate with her regularly, complained that 'the
Queen's dinner was timed to last exactly half an hour. The
service was so rapid that a slow eater such as myself ... never
had time to finish even a moderate helping. Pecking like a

bird I could usually satisfy my hunger, but could not enjoy [it].' This was in sharp contrast to the Household dinners, which Lady Lytton found exhaustingly long.[22] Courtiers' experiences of dining with the Queen differed hugely depending on her mood, and on who was present. At ladies' dinners, which were frequent at Balmoral in particular, she opened out more than she did in mixed company, often roaring with laughter and delighting everyone around her, but she could also be moody and shy, especially with politicians present, one of whom made the acerbic observation that, 'I personally never heard her say anything at dinner which I remembered the next day. Her manners were not affable; she spoke very little at meals, and she ate fast and very seldom laughed. To the dishes she rejected she made a peevish moue, with crumpled brow more eloquent than words.' The pace could be problematic, as everyone's plates were cleared away as soon as the Queen had finished each course, and the same politician, Lord Ribblesdale, recounted a dramatic incident over the roast mutton. Victoria had opted for peas, which she could dispose of 'with marvellous skill and celerity, and had got into conversation with Lord Hartington, thus delaying his own operations ... anyhow, in the full current of their conversation, the four-year-old mutton was taken away from him. He stopped in the middle of a sentence in time to arrest the scarlet-clad marauder: "here bring that back!". We courtiers present held our breath – we were mostly of a deferential breed.' Fortunately, she was able to see the funny side: 'I knew this by one of the rare smiles, as different as possible to the civil variety which, overtired, uninterested, or thinking about something else, she contributed to the conventional observations of her visitors.'[23]

Fun was often rather lacking, and when Dr Reid – not
officially a member of the Household but a sort of senior
servant rather than full attendant – started hosting small
dinners in his rooms, they became very popular. He was
entitled to breakfast and lunch with the proper Household
but not to dine with them, so he was well known to everyone, and was a popular figure. Inevitably Victoria got wind
of the jolly gatherings, exclaiming, 'I hear Dr Reid has
dinner parties!' Whether it was intended (or taken) as promotion or punishment, he was invited to join the Household
after this and, eventually, occasionally joined the royal table
as well, where he took delight in getting away with small
breaches of etiquette, just to relieve the tedium.[24] Life at
court had never been riveting, but it did seem to get worse
in the 1880s and 1890s. Marie Mallet left when she got
married, only to return five years later in 1895, when she
noted that, 'everything is so exactly the same as when I left
five years ago ... the same plum cake, even the same number
of biscuits on the plate and their variety absolutely identical,
the same things said and the same done, only some of the
old faces gone and a selection of new dogs follow the pony
chair'.[25] It was made more obvious by Victoria's habit of
surrounding herself with physical mementos of people –
and animals – she had loved and lost, and which lent all of
the palaces a certain air of mausoleum at times. At Windsor,
the room where Albert had died was kept preserved as it was
on the day he breathed his last, while the Victorian habit of
collecting locks of hair from the dead meant that the Queen
collected hairy broaches and lockets at a rate of knots. She
slept with Albert's possessions around her, including his
clothes and a sculpture of his hand.[26] One of her

grandchildren recalled the 'mysterious photographs of dead people, even of little dead children, which, although they made us feel creepy, we always furtively looked at again and again', while one of her great-grandchildren explained that at nearly all of the palaces she 'had surrounded herself with countless monuments commemorating her past associations ... as one walked around the grounds, every turn of the paths brought one face to face with a statue erect or recumbent, an inscribed granite drinking fountain, or a granite seat dedicated to the memory of a relation, or a faithful retainer, or even a pet dog'.[27]

Meals at court had always been relatively predictable, with certain foods appearing day after day: in the 1840s to 1860s it was lamb or mutton chops, in the 1870s and 1880s roast beef, and from the 1890s the sideboard laden with hot and cold fowls, roast beef and tongue was ever-present. Marie Mallet wrote of the unfailing routine at Balmoral:

> breakfast at a quarter to ten, then general conversation till about eleven, when we repair to our respective dens and do what writing we have ... When the Queen goes out about twelve, we all emerge and walk for an hour, weather permitting ... at one we write again or read ... at two we have a sociable meal and have coffee afterwards in the Billiard Room where we all gossip and wait for driving orders, by three thirty to a quarter to four we all drive out or on our own; tea at five thirty, more talk, then to our rooms again or we pay each other friendly visits, finally dinner at nine (if with the Queen), quarter to nine if with the Household. At eleven the Queen leaves the Drawing Room and I wait in my

bedroom till I am summoned at twenty or a quarter to twelve and go to the Queen in her Sitting Room where I talk and read and take orders till about twelve thirty, then 'Good night' and I fly to my bed and hot water bottle! I do not keep up my maid. This routine never varies by a hair's breadth, as soon a revolution as to drive in the morning and walk after lunch, and boiled beef on Thursday and 'mehlspeise mit ananas' on Friday recur with unfailing regularity.[28]

The dining ledger entries for this period are erratic, but certainly seem to bear out Mallet's despair, especially at Osborne, and presumably Balmoral (for which no records exist beyond a few menus). That said, the meals aren't quite as monotonous as she makes out, and while certain dishes – celery in cream, and the dreaded mehlspeise (a generic German word for sweet) – do crop up repeatedly, there is still significant variation between menus, both across days and weeks, and a great deal of choice upon the table. In any case, some people found the random German puddings extremely tasty. Mehlprei, which was another favourite, comes up in the memoirs of Alfred's daughter Marie, who barely contains her joy at the gustatory memory: 'Every Sunday Grandmamma had more or less the same menu served, which had roast beef as pièce de resistance, and "mehlbrei" as a sweet dish.' She's exaggerating: on four consecutive Sundays in January 1897 roast beef with Yorkshire pudding was indeed served for every second course remove, but the roasts were woodcocks and golden plovers, twice each, and the sweet entremets were asparagus, boudoir pudding, iced soufflés on one day; chicory in cream, orange parfait and – admittedly the same – dish of iced soufflés on another; celery in cream, cardinal pudding, plum pudding and orange jelly on the third; and green beans, orange soufflé tartelettes and a light gingerbread on the last. Marie goes on, describing the mehlprie of her memory:

> This was almost a nursery dish and when it had to receive an elegant French name the cooks would call it bouillie de farine à la vanille, but Grandmamma, who was sentimental about all things pertaining to Germany, admitted German names on her menu, so plain 'mehlbrei' was allowed. The deliciousness of this 'mehlbrei' was heightened by little diamond shaped pieces of brown skin which floated on top. The taste of these little squares of skin, which were simply the top part of the bouillie slightly burnt, belonged to those things that for some reason gave my palate exquisite satisfaction. I would shut my eyes and let the wee morsel lie for a moment on my tongue so as to taste it to the utmost. The tragedy was that there were so few of these floating little squares in each dish, and as I was very young I was of course served one of the last and it more than once happened that when my turn came, the squares had all been already consumed by those luckier and more privileged than I. In fact, to be accurate, I think only once did I taste of this ambrosial food, but the memory has remained for ever, so it must have been especially exquisite.[29]

Francatelli gives a recipe for it, which is a simple batter mix elevated to dizzying heights. The 'skin' of Marie's memory was a carefully constructed delicacy, made by spreading thin layers of the batter sauce on a baking sheet to crisp up before cutting them up with biscuit cutters. The quality of the food remained superb, and another of the grandchildren (there were 42 in the end), Moretta (christened Victoria, the same as her mother, the Queen's eldest daughter), commented repeatedly in her letters home on the 'good food': 'For dinner last night we had to my great joy whitebait – & how awfully good they were – only I had too few!'[30]

Marie, meanwhile, also had fond memories of the equally set routine of breakfast, which, weather permitting – and the Queen's definition of permitting was, as ever, rather looser than that of her Household – took place in what Victoria called 'the tent'. Marie described it as a 'large ecru green-lined and green-fringed parasol which had been fixed to the ground', under which the Queen would sit, surrounded by cups, plates, coffee pots and teapots, as well as the breakfast food itself. Along with the meats sometimes listed on the dining ledgers, there were breakfast breads and biscuits, and she remembered, 'a delicious fragrance of coffee, or of a certain brown biscuit which came in flat round tins from Germany, was characteristic of Grandmamma's breakfast. Our greedy little noses sniffed it in longingly, but it was not always that we were invited to have a taste.' Photographs and prints survive of Victoria in her tent, taking breakfast, or tea, or signing papers, attended by 'grey-kilted Highlanders or white-turbaned Indians', along with 'tall monumental footmen'.[31] The tea-taking rituals of the holidays abroad were also now a fixed part of the domestic regime and the apparently impromptu roadside teas of the Riviera were repeated at Balmoral and Osborne, where the Queen usually took tea while out excursing, often popping into Swiss Cottage or one of the various buildings on the Balmoral estate to sit down. At Windsor in 1870 the architecturally muddled Tudor-Gothic summerhouse, with its huge Hampton Court-inspired chimneys, was converted into a teahouse with a kitchen constructed off to one side. It and the larger Adelaide Lodge, which was a fake rustic cottage, were useful stopping-off places for tea and a wee, and even Buckingham Palace had a beautifully decorated pavilion with an attached kitchen. Most country houses had a scattering of buildings in their grounds which served both as interesting features on a gentle walk, and places under shelter in which to take tea. In many ways such gardens were the private equivalent of the once-popular tea gardens, which had been aristocratic spaces of sociability in the eighteenth century but by the nineteenth were popular and rowdy places for working-class entertainment including, at Vauxhall in the 1820s, a nightly re-enactment of the battle of Waterloo. The tea didn't get there by itself, however, and hot water either had to be carted out in the nineteenth-century equivalent of a thermos, or heated on a fire in situ. Likewise, china tea-wares, picnic baskets of food, and tables and chairs all had to appear somehow. Victoria frequently remarked in her journals that she and her party 'found' tea, or simply 'took' tea: something of an over-simplification of what was often quite a convoluted process with a fair degree of planning and catering involved. She certainly enjoyed her tea-taking, including the cake, which invariably accompanied it, commenting ruefully to Lady Lytton in 1897 that 'I'm afraid I must not have anymore', after consuming two scones, two bits of toast and several biscuits at one sitting.[32]

By the 1870s, afternoon tea was an established part of upper- and middle-class Victorian life, and cookery manuals were quick to offer advice, although even as late as 1888 the revised *Beeton's Book of Household Management* did not call it afternoon tea, preferring instead the term 'at home' tea. Indeed, although the idea of tea and a snack in the afternoon had been established since the late eighteenth century, and although tea had been associated with women almost since its introduction in the mid-seventeenth century, the idea of the highly feminised, cake-heavy afternoon tea, with the inevitable plethora of specialist equipment, was very much a late Victorian one (there is no substance to the oft-told story that the Duchess of Bedford somehow 'invented' it in 1842), and as a rule-ridden, etiquette-led ceremony, it was decidedly middle class.[33] The upper classes tended to ignore the angst of those below them, and behave exactly as they wished, and the Queen, with her love of outdoor, apparently impromptu kettle boiling, was very much an individual tea-drinker. She even dunked her cake, according to another granddaughter: 'The queen had many German ways – for example she liked to soak cake, and things of that sort, in her coffee, which in England is absolutely forbidden.'[34] Tea was inextricably linked with femininity, described as 'the most feminine and most domestic of all occupations',[35] and it therefore carried connotations of privacy and domesticity, reflecting the side of Victoria which was very human, over the bit that was always Queen. State visitors did not come to tea, but in contrast she did used to drive to Cliveden from Windsor and take tea with the housekeeper, wearing a bonnet, which, one commentator bitchily remarked, 'couldn't have cost five shillings'.[36]

Tea wasn't the only drink to find favour with Victoria in the 1880s and 1890s. The taste for whisky, which she'd developed since visiting Begg's distillery in 1848, had grown into a daily habit. It was regarded as at least partly medicinal, as a grandchild testified: 'Her table beverage was seltzer-water with a little whisky, ordered by the doctor.' But it was also tasty, and Moretta wrote to her mother that, 'I was so amused this morning – at what Francis Clark gave me to drink, because I was thirsty – it was lemon squash, & whisky & how delicious it did taste. Do try it when you are thirsty, at 11 o clock.'[37] Moretta had inherited the troubled family relationship with food, and when she came to stay with the Queen in 1889, her mother wrote a sort of covering letter:

> You would indeed make me most happy & do me the greatest favour, if you could induce Moretta not to be so foolish about her food! Her one craze is to be thin! She starves completely – touches no milk – no sugar – no bread – no sweets – no soup – no butter – nothing but a scrap of meat & apples, – which is not enough! She will ruin her health! – & she has a fine strong constitution. She goes to bed too late, & takes almost too much exercise – I have begged & prayed – ordered & threatened all to no effect, – she is quite fanatical on the subject! Her pretty figure is quite spoilt from being too thin!![38]

The food at Victoria's palaces, along with the Queen's encouragements, clearly did the trick. Although Moretta was doubtless aware of her mother's scrutiny, and, therefore, may have been protesting a little too much in her letters home, she put on weight, lamenting that, 'my appetite is tremendous, & my belts are beginning to get <u>very</u> tight alas! What is to be done, when all is so good.' Like the young Victoria, she was eventually weighed and 'it was a lot – 10 stone 10 ½. I am miserable & don't know what to do – it's this <u>horrid good food</u>.' She sent edible gifts back to Germany: an eclectic mix of oatmeal for porridge and Scottish shortbread, melons and tea. Like her grandmother, she revelled in the fruit, commenting on the strawberries that they were, '<u>quite</u> too beautiful in size, colour and taste'.[39]

The Queen's own love of fruit had not abated either, and Marie Mallet found herself supplying fruit from the family estate, including grapes which 'arrived safely and in first-rate condition yesterday and were beautifully arranged on a golden platter and duly presented to the Queen at lunch. Her Majesty ordered the bunch to be weighed before she touched it. The weight was 5lbs, at which there was great astonishment and when I dined with the Queen and they reappeared praise was simply lavished on them ... in fact no present could have been more appreciated, and no one likes little attentions better than the Queen.'[40] In Mallet's view, grapes from the Windsor kitchen gardens were far inferior, as they were grown for quantity, not quality. She also provided apples, writing to her stepfather, 'I dined with the Queen last night and beheld her peel and eat a Ledbury apple with evident relish and many expressions of admiration as to size, beauty and flavour. Her Majesty wished me to tell you how very much pleased she is with the fruit and I had to answer many questions on apple growing etc. Presently the Queen said, I have never tasted perry and only cider once or twice in my life do you think your mama will send me some?' Naturally, both were immediately dispatched, and a few days later, 'the cider and perry arrived yesterday and the Queen partook of both for lunch and thought them quite delicious, but she preferred the perry'.[41] It was typical of Victoria that she continued to seek out new eating experiences, not just in the relatively undemanding areas of fruit and alcohol, but also more challenging foods. In 1884, when the International Health Exhibition was on in London, she drafted in her own version: 'At luncheon, we had some very extraordinary dishes, which the Chinese cooks from the Health Exhibition prepared. The Bird's Nest Soup, I thought very good, some salmon excellent, but the other dishes less "appetitlich". The 2 nice looking men, with their long pigtails, wearing their national dress, came in & served the dishes, each kneeling down to do so. At the end of luncheon they brought in tea on a very pretty tray, with covered cups, each cup having been made separately. Its fragrance is quite extraordinary & most delicious, & it is taken without milk or cream, & very little, or no sugar. It is made from fresh tea leaves.'[42]

In 1877 Victoria was declared Empress of India, a position of which she was very proud (not least because it put her on an equal footing, status-wise, with all the other Empresses in the world – Empresses beat Queens in the title ranks). For the Golden Jubilee in 1887, she acquired a set of Indian servants, to join her kilted Highlanders to wait on her every whim. The first of what would eventually be a procession of Indians, Mohammed Buksh and Abdul Karim, were employed specifically to act as attendants upon the Queen. Their duties were 'to attend the Queen's breakfast in and out of doors and also the Queen's luncheon, tea and dinner [and to make themselves] useful in any way that the Queen may require'.[43] They were joined by four others in 1888. They wore special livery, and waited at table, as well as attending the Queen as she wrote letters and greeted visiting dignitaries. Eventually, Abdul Karim was picked out to become one of Victoria's closest personal attendants: known as the Munshi, he taught her Hindustani, and gradually rose to a position of prominence within the Household. The Queen found his company stimulating, and decided that he was far too grand to act as a servant. The Household absolutely loathed him, and a heady mix of racism, class snobbery and personal dislike was exacerbated by his own heavy-handed dealings with other people (including the other Indian servants, who regularly complained about him). Given that in 1901 his salary was a staggering £992, including various allowances, a hefty measure of not unwarranted jealousy was doubtless also involved. He wasn't quite the scoundrel that the Household imagined him to be, but nor was he quite the devoted servant, and when he contracted gonorrhoea in 1897 at the end of a year during which the Household was veritably consumed with Munshi-related angst, it proved all too much. There were explosive arguments between the Queen and Dr Reid, the Queen and the Prince of Wales, the Queen and the Munshi himself, until eventually, helped by Karim's departure on an extended trip to India, things calmed down. One of her ministers, Lord Salisbury, expressed the view that, 'she really likes the emotional excitement, as being the only form of entertainment she can have'.[44] He was probably right.

The Indian attendants were lodged separately to the rest

of the Establishment, and had their own cook. Muni Kahan was listed in the 1901 census as an 'Indian cook', and prior to that at least five others had filled the role. It was a lower position and slightly apart from the other Indian servants, and described as a 'man of all work [and] cook', but 'in the absence of Indian attendants he agrees to wait at table, accepting any temporary increase of pay ... for extra duty'.[45] At least two cooks were later promoted to full attendant status, and replacements brought over, and the turnover among the Indian servants was remarkably high. The new attendants generally cooked, and ate, separately to the rest of the Household (and the proposal that Karim should join their table on holiday in Nice brought the Household to outright mutiny). Gabriel Tschumi recalled that, 'for religious reasons they could not use the meat which came to the kitchens in the ordinary way, so they killed all their own sheep and poultry for the curries. Nor would they use the curry-powder in stock in the kitchens, though it was of the best imported kind, so a part of the Household had to be given to them for their special use and there they worked Indian-style, grinding their own curry powder between two large stones.' The dining ledgers confirm part of this, listing meat (not necessarily still alive) for the 'Indian servants' on several occasions.[46] The meals that they cooked were largely for their own consumption, and were prepared away from the royal kitchens. The Queen was no stranger to curry: she'd been eating it throughout her life, but the curries she was used to were of the Anglo-Indian variety that had been popular since the eighteenth century – delicious, but very different to the food eaten by her Indian subjects.[47] However, she was not one to miss an opportunity for something different, and in August 1887 remarked in her journal, 'we had some excellent curry, made by one of my Indian servants'.[48] From then on, the dining ledgers show that she had dishes cooked by the Indian cook on a relatively regularly basis – they appear in the menus as 'Indian dish'. By 1897 they'd become part of the weekly routine: 'Indian dish – chicken curry' or variants thereof were served as one of the luncheon dishes on most Sundays, and 'Indian fish dish' was added to the other two fish choices for many of the Tuesday dinners. They were not served to the Household, and the pattern did not continue indefinitely.[49]

In many ways it's not surprising that Victoria felt the need to seek novel experiences or create unnecessary (but fun) rows with her Household, for by the mid-1890s she was beginning to slow down, albeit mainly due to her eyesight and the second injury to her knee. From 1894 she wore false teeth and she was by now locked into a semi-permanent battle with her doctors about her eating habits, having long suffered from indigestion, along with nervous headaches and a cough. She was very open with her doctors, and, in an echo of her youthful prescriptions for rhubarb pills and gastric upsets, in 1885 Dr Reid wrote, 'the Queen has had a headache and flatulence in the last two days, but is somewhat better again. She had salt both yesterday and today, and her bowels were acting well; she thinks the podophyllin pill has upset her.'[50] (Podophyllin was a purgative.) Trapped wind plagued her, and later that year she convinced herself that she was having a heart attack, with Reid writing wearily, 'I fancy her majesty had flatulence, and that she is a little nervous.' He was writing to another of her doctors, Jenner, who replied, 'it is really flatulence from indigestion. I remember once an attack of indigestion from cranberry tart and cream when Sir James Clark's only remark to Her Majesty was "don't eat it again" whereat Her Majesty was very much annoyed.'[51] She didn't learn, and in 1889 Reid recorded that he'd been up until 5.30 a.m. as she was racked in pain and felt sick. He said, 'It was caused, I believe, by her eating among other things a very heavy indigestible sweet at dinner; and I trust she will be more careful in future.'[52] She also had issues sleeping, exacerbated by going to bed late, usually after 1.30 a.m., getting up early and guilt-ridden about her late night, worrying about getting to sleep, taking sleeping powders, and waking up her maids to help her do a bit more worrying whenever she woke in the night. In 1897 she took to eating Cytos, a health bread known for its anti-flatulent properties.[53]

Despite these issues, she continued to get on with her duties, and gave every impression of indefatigability. In 1899 Marie Mallet wrote, 'we had a most cheerful Ladies' Dinner last night, the Queen in excellent spirits, making jokes about her age and saying she <u>felt</u> quite young and that had it not been for an unfortunate accident she would have been <u>running</u> about still!'[54] She also continued to eat new foods, including an ostrich-egg omelette in France in 1899, which she pronounced delicious and asked why they couldn't have them at Windsor – after all, 'we have an ostrich'. 'Yes mama,' replied Beatrice, 'a male one.'[55] She still launched herself enthusiastically at fruit, with Mallet noting that 'her favourite fruits were oranges and pears and monster indigestible apples which would have daunted most people half her age but she enjoyed them, sometimes sharing a mammoth specimen with Princess Beatrice, but more often coping with it alone. Oranges were treated in a very convenient manner: a hole cut in the top and the juice scooped out with a spoon.'[56] As usual, her manners were her own, and in sharp contrast to the excruciating (but brilliant) advice meted out by one etiquette guide:

> The Orange. First, let me advise you to avoid embarking upon an orange, unless you are an adept. It requires long experience, a colossal courage, any amount of cool self-possession, and a great skill to attack and dispose of one without harm to yourself or your neighbour. No amount of care can prevent the juice from besprinkling your own shirt or your neighbour's gown, be she opposite or beside you. In fact, no gown, no spotless shirt front within range is safe, while there seems to be in the human eye some uncanny magnetism whereby it attracts itself to the juice of this pungent fruit. Tangerines are more manageable. But if after this you feel drawn to an orange or urged by a spirit of defiance to try your fortune, here is the safest and most correct mode of attack. The issue lies between you and the fruit. Cut the orange in two, then in four pieces, afterwards cutting the pulp from the skin and conveying it on the fork to the mouth. It sounds simple![57]

In July 1900, when stormy foreign affairs prevented the usual French jolly, she decided to go to Ireland instead, declaring, 'I expect to enjoy myself.' Marie Mallet wrote that 'this, at eighty-one, beats the record. With such intense vitality and power of enjoyment there can be no serious decay of mind or body. I feel bursting with admiration and loyalty.'[58]

However, by 1900 age was finally taking its toll. Even in February she was looking older, and, despite the success of the Irish trip in April, by July she was starting to visibly struggle. Her cough had got worse, and her digestion was now a real issue. Mallet, in waiting during July, wrote exasperated letters back to her husband: 'The Queen is certainly less vigorous and her digestion is becoming defective after so many years of hard labour! If she would follow a diet and live on Benger's Food and chicken all would be well, but she clings to roast beef and ices! And what can you then expect? Sir James has at last persuaded her to try Benger's and she likes it and now to his horror, instead of substituting it for other foods she adds it to her already copious meals just as poor Princess Mary thought it banting to eat biscuits as well as bread. She is very sleepy in the evenings and goes to bed early although not early enough.'[59] (Benger's was an indigestion remedy.) As usual, the Queen went on regardless: 'This hot weather does try her and there is no denying it, and of course when she devours a huge chocolate ice followed by a couple of apricots washed down with iced water as she did last night she ought to expect a dig from the indigestion fiend.'[60] She hosted a garden party at Buckingham Palace on 11 July, doing the rounds of the guests in her carriage, and taking tea in her tent. It was the last major public occasion at which she was present, and her family started to become concerned. Bertie wondered out loud whether she was eating enough and drinking enough wine, but when Reid tackled her about her diet she put him down firmly.[61] In November she turned out to review the troops, recording that she met 'an old Australian Chaplain, who lost his leg, by the bite of a mad horse', and lunched with the Mayor and

Corporation of Windsor.[62] She put on a brave face, for it's clear from her journals that was in daily pain, and felt very ill. It was a long way from the eighteen-year-old who declared that she'd 'felt for the first time like a man, as if I could fight myself at the head of my troops' as she reviewed the troops on horseback, in her new general's outfit.[63]

By November it was clear to those who cared to see it that all was not well. Reid recorded that she had a 'foul tongue, no appetite, digestion very bad, much emaciated, bad nights etc'.[64] In her own journals she charted the decline of her appetite from the beginning of the month with annoyance: 'Had again not a good night & slept on rather late. My lack of appetite worse than ever. It is very trying.' It was especially so when it meant that she had to eat dinner with Beatrice in private.[65] She had good and bad days, rejoicing when she was 'able to take a little breakfast', and dining in company whenever she could.[66] On 14 November she was visited by Helena and her daughter Thora, and the latter, 'kindly mixed what is called "lait de poule", which I was able to take and liked'.[67] She was frustrated and exhausted, writing, 'this sitting through meals, unable to eat anything is most trying'.[68] She was also well aware what this loss of appetite, so rare, and its accompanying symptoms, might mean, saying to Marie Mallet in a private moment that 'after the Prince Consort's death I wished to die, but <u>now</u> I wish to live and do what I can for my country and those I love'.[69] Although no one was aware of it, she was also suffering from a ventral hernia and a prolapsed uterus, ailments uncharacteristically kept from her doctors, probably because she feared an operation. Though the hernia probably only caused intermittent pain, symptoms of a prolapsed uterus can include problems going to the loo, mild incontinence when coughing, and back pain.

Lait de poule was hard-core invalid food, intended to alleviate throat problems, including coughing and difficulty swallowing. Feeding the sick was a whole branch of cookery, occupying significant space in most cookery books, and the remedies suggested ranged from the sensible – the omni-present beef tea – to the bizarre – water imbued with tar and mixed with claret was a blood purifier according to Jules Gouffé.[70] The general advice was to prepare easily digested food, present it in a delicate and appetising fashion, and remove it when the person was done so that the smell and sight of food didn't make them nauseous. In this time of need, the royal kitchens for once proved surprisingly less than able, and a furious Marie Mallet recorded: 'I could kill the cooks who take no pains whatsoever to prepare tempting little dishes and would be a disgrace to any kitchen. How I should like to work a sweeping reform, we are abominably served just now. The footmen smell of whisky and are never prompt to answer the bell and although they do not speak rudely, they stare in such a supercilious way. As for the Queen's dinner it is more like a badly arranged picnic.' It was not a one-off incident, and two days later: 'The ser-vants here are too irritating. The Queen only ordered one small dish – nouilles – for her dinner last night and it was entirely forgotten, so she had nothing. The cooks should be drawn and quartered and the Clerks of the Kitchen strung from the Curfew Tower; their indifference makes me boil with rage.'[71] The Queen continued to have good and bad days, though, enjoying coffee and omelette for breakfast on 13 November, and attending a luncheon on the 14th. She apparently shouted to the Princess of Wales throughout, and felt dreadful again after it, and Mallet wrote that, 'she resents being treated as an invalid and as soon as she feels a tiny bit better she overtires herself and collapses. She is less meek now and that is a good sign.'[72] Marie's husband Bernard, the recipient of many of her letters, noted sadly that 'one fears it may be the beginning of the end'.[73]

In December the Household moved to Osborne as usual for Christmas. The Queen continued to feel terrible, though on the 29th she recorded that she 'managed to eat a little cold beef, which was the first I have had for weeks, & I really enjoyed'.[74] As the New Year dawned she wrote, 'I am feeling so weak and unwell, that I enter upon it sadly.'[75] It was increasingly clear that she would not recover, although her children managed to remain in denial for a remarkably long time, the Prince of Wales writing hopefully of her 'vitality and pluck'. She was more realistic and self-aware, confiding in her granddaughter Thora that 'you know I sometimes feel that when I die I shall be a little, just a little, nervous about meeting Grandpapa for I have taken to doing a good many things that he would not quite approve of'.[76] Her last journal entry, on 13 January, included a drive, some work, and a drink of milk. On the 15th, Reid was shocked to note that 'nothing annoyed her and she took apathetically things that formerly would have irritated her'. On the 16th she had a stroke, and, apart from a short time in a dressing gown in a wheelchair, was from now on confined to bed. She was now taking only liquid food, and the first official bulletin, advising the public that she was suffering 'great physical prostration', went out on the 19th. That evening she told Reid that 'I should like to live a little longer, as I have still a few things to settle. I have arranged most things, but there are still some left, and I want to live a little longer.' She hung grimly on, although she was now virtually unable to move. On the 20th 'during the day she took food fairly well, but was very apathetic', but by the evening 'the Queen was almost quite unconscious and had much difficulty in swallowing'.[77] By now the gravity of the situation was finally apparent to her family, as well as the public, and *The Times* printed the news of her illness, and all of the rather mealy-mouthed official bulletins, in horrified tones, as well as repeating the most doom-laden writings of the global press: 'The news of the Queen's illness has caused the deepest distress in both the European and native communities. Every telegram is anxiously awaited, and the newspapers issue them the moment they are received. The first reports came so unexpectedly that not until last night was the grave danger of the illness fully understood.'[78] On the 22nd it was more upbeat: 'A gleam of hope has pierced the dark shadow which yesterday hung over the spirit of the nation. The latest reports from Osborne show that the QUEEN has not only rallied from the almost desperate condition indicated in the bulletin issued on Sunday, but that the improvement, if only a "slight" one, has been maintained. Last night the news was that food had been taken fairly well, and some tranquil sleep secured. This is not much to go upon, considering the other factors in the situation, but it is something.'[79] At 9.30 a.m. that morning, the whole family had been summonsed, ready for the end, but she rallied. One of the other doctors in attendance noted that 'her vitality was phenomenal'. She took some food, and Reid wrote a very hasty note to his wife, Susan, saying, 'she does not look like dying just now'.[80] By 3 p.m. the family were gathered around the bed again, however, and the 4 p.m. court bulletin sent out the message that 'the Queen is slowly sinking'. Again she struggled back to life, and this time the Bishop of Winchester, who was present, was asked if he could stop reciting prayers until she was actually dying, as it was not really adding to the atmosphere. She eventually died at 6.30 p.m., and the official notice went out half an hour later.

Epilogue: how to end an age

t was fitting, perhaps, that the Queen's body lay in state for the next ten days in the Osborne dining room, which was hastily refitted as a chapel, with the family portraits covered up, and a Union Jack hanging on one wall. The funeral, on 2 February, was, in accordance with Victoria's wishes, a white one: the coffin was draped in a white and gold pall, white horses pulled the carriages, and instead of black drapes in the London streets, purple with white trimming was used instead. Even the weather helped, when, at the end of the bitterly cold day, the falling sleet turned to white snow. She was buried in the Frogmore mausoleum, next to Albert, in a coffin filled with trinkets and mementos of the previous 81 years. After some hasty investigation, the marble statue she'd had commissioned to match that of Albert in 1861 was dug out from where it had been temporarily mislaid, and put in place.

The new King, Victoria's eldest son Albert Edward, rejected firmly his mother's choice of name, saying he could never be King Albert – there could really only be one Albert and he had died in 1861. He declared he would rule as Edward VII. It was a firm break with his mother's desires, and a declaration of intent. His accession, in his view, had come twenty years too late, and at 59 he was already showing signs of bad health. Dr Reid commented that 'he eats far too much, and drinks to match!'[1] He was also a chain-smoker, rarely without a cigar in his mouth. Unlike Victoria, however, he largely escaped censure, at least to his face. Bertie could eat like a King and be accepted in ways that his mother never could.

And eat Bertie did. Victoria had despaired of him early on. Her own and Albert's expectations of their eldest son had always been too high for any mere mortal, and when, as a child, he proved more interested in pranks and playing than study and abstinence, he was immediately put on a regime of study and diet which had reflections of Victoria's own childhood. It didn't work, and Bertie grew into a fully fledged glutton, philanderer and good-time party guy. In other words, he was a lot like his mother, had she been freed of gender constraints, in her brief pre-Albert phase. He was thought of as jolly lovely but a bit dim, with nicknames including Tum-Tum and, as he acceded to the throne, Edward the Caresser.[2] No one expected a great deal from him in 1901: he was a smart dresser, but obese, a delightful man but with a scandalous past, and his love of fine living defined him. He'd had little experience of what ruling Britain meant, for Victoria, believing him to be foolish and feckless, refused to let him help her. Even he once remarked that he'd rather have been a landscape gardener.[3]

But Bertie, as Edward VII, surprised everyone. Although most of his life had been spent canoodling, shooting, gambling and eating, he had also deputised for his mother abroad, and all that partying was founded on a genuine love of company, which meant that he was effortlessly charming. As a king, he was a skilled diplomatist at home and abroad. His efforts to calm the increasingly febrile atmosphere in Europe, and to promote the Anglo-French entente cordiale, went hand-in-hand with his work to manage the political scene at home. Victoria had democratised the monarchy, in a certain sense, putting out pictures of family life, publishing homely extracts from her journals, and working hard to make people forget her ghastly Georgian forebears. Her jubilees had been masterclasses in polite pageantry. Bertie went one step further and now made the institution relevant in a new century, building on the ceremonial displays of pomp and patriotism engendered by the jubilees (and Victoria's funeral), and reworking the monarchy as a repository of tradition, and that indefinable thing, British values. As a result, he is often credited with ensuring the survival of the monarchy into the twentieth century.

At home, Bertie was brutal in the changes he wrought, sweeping away the creaking edifice of the late Victorian court and making his own, Edwardian age, quite distinct from what had come before. He kept the good bits, and destroyed what he saw as the bad. Since the glory days of the 1840s and 1850s, when Victoria and Albert had pumped money into the physical structures of the monarchy, there had been little or no real investment. A report into the Windsor kitchen gardens, left to run themselves since the 1850s, concluded that they were, 'strangely unworthy in equipment and methods of cultivation ... altogether discreditable to those who have been responsible for [them]'. What had been cutting edge 60 years ago was now hopelessly out of date: the plant houses had 'none ... which conform with the position of modern gardening'; the heating was 'a most extravagant system both in fuel and labour', and the potting sheds were 'in keeping with the needs of the moderate horticultural practice of the early years of the last century, but ... quite inadequate to modern requirements'.[4] The same was true of the palaces as well, which, apart from the installation of electric lighting, and the addition of bike sheds as the new craze for cycling swept the court in the 1890s, had undergone little real modernisation since 1861. Bertie swept into action: Osborne was turned into a convalescent home, and Sandringham replaced it in the convenient country home stakes; Balmoral was kept, as it was politically important, but the whisky allowance was drastically cut, and habitual drunkenness now banned; Buckingham Palace was wholly revamped and became the major royal palace of the era; and at both Buckingham Palace and Windsor the creepy, unchanged rooms where Albert had passed his last days were torn apart, the ornaments and holiday souvenirs flung out, and the dusty old books packed up and removed.

The kitchens weren't left alone either, although they were less in need of modernisation, such was the slow pace of technological change at an aristocratic level. However, by 1907, Windsor finally had gas ovens, supplied by William Sugg & Co. (and which remain in use, at least in the pastry room). Staffing changes were drastic: Louis Chevriot, who'd been chief cook for a mere four years, was replaced, and left to run a small hotel in London (where he employed his own cook). Great swathes of the kitchen staff were pensioned off, including the first three master cooks (George Malsch was now listed as having completed 45 years in service, so he was, admittedly, a tad superannuated), the chief confectioner and his assistant, and the first pastry assistant.[5] The apprenticeship scheme was abolished altogether, with the new chief chef, Juste Alphonse Menager, dismissing it as a waste of money, for they struggled to get the quality, and if they did, the newly trained cooks left and went to work for more money elsewhere. Menager had been part of Bertie's separate kitchen establishment since 1888, and he was one of a number of staff who crossed over from Marlborough House, which was the Prince of Wales' official London residence. The reshuffle was substantial, with maids and cooks joining in various positions, to be promoted hastily into others when vacancies occurred, and it took several years for the dust to settle properly. Bertie was used to a different type of food, the very high-end French *cuisine classique*, which at the time was being elaborated and codified by one of the icons of French cooking, the chef at the Carlton Hotel in London, Auguste Escoffier. There was no more room for garbled German puddings, or sideboards full of good British roast meat, and service *à la Russe* was now fully adopted, in its most elaborate and show-off form, its seven courses cooked by a team handpicked for their ability to show the world that Edward VII had arrived.

Elsewhere in the Establishment, there were other changes. Whisky-sodden footmen were out, and a smart new regime was in. It permeated everything: even the dining ledgers became more ordered and a great deal more legible after 1901. For a few months, the Indian servants stayed on, and continued to wait on the royal table, but in July 1901 they, too, were awarded pensions and shipped back to Agra. Instead, an Egyptian, Amin Ibrahim, was brought over from Hamburg. He was prized for his excellent coffee-making skills, and 'the ladies were very fond of the thick, sweetish brew'.[6] He appeared kitted out in full eastern-style garb, paid for by the privy purse and which included blue and red silk suits, shot with gold and silver embroidery, white gaiters and shoes, and an 'eastern fez'.[7]

Bertie was a gourmet, but he was also a glutton who, like his mother, yo-yo dieted and had a troubled relationship with food.[8] After his accession he ate even more, using food as a crutch to cope with all the work he so desperately wanted to do, and do well. He drank heavily, bolted his meals, and used food as an escape mechanism.[9] He had more in common with Victoria than she (or he) may have cared to recognise. From the teenage years, when she gobbled and gorged on fruit, through early queenship when she gained and lost weight with terrifying speed, and from the restraint or distraction that came with her marriage, food had been a fundamental way in which she asserted control. In mourning, and afterwards, as she rediscovered her zest for life, it was a comfort, and as she outlived her friends, her servants and, eventually, some of her children, it was left as one of her few pleasures. Food was the only true constant in her life: it didn't judge, it didn't moan, it rarely disappointed, and there was always something new to discover just around the corner.

Human lives are marked out by meals: the everyday routine of breakfast, lunch and dinner (and/or tea); the yearly rituals of birthdays, Easter and Christmas; and the life stages of christenings, weddings and funerals. Any life can be defined by food, but with Victoria it seems especially true. She ate like only a queen could, ignoring the people who told her what to do or suggested that women shouldn't have large appetites, retaining control over that one element even as she lost control of her children, or her ladies, and as the balance of power between monarch and Parliament shifted decisively away from her. Although she presided over a period of massive culinary change, her own meals became monotonous and, like the palaces in which she lived, unchanging in the face of outside influences. They were not anachronistic, but they were old-fashioned. When Bertie swept the old away, the new was still recognisable. A greedy Queen was replaced by a greedy King, but the culinary legacy of Victoria would live on. British cuisine, like Victoria's menus, is a mishmash of different cultures and styles made coherent by use. Like Victoria the Queen, it can be complicated, and time-consuming and awe-inspiring, and some of the best chefs in the world are British. But it can also be, like Victoria the person, down-to-earth, honest and delightful. She ate bustard and turtle, and mutton chops and giant apples. She drank milk, and tea, and champagne and whisky, and all with equal delight. She embraced, whole-heartedly, all that the world had to offer her to eat, for all of her life, and for that she deserves respect. She had a lot of flaws – after all, she was human – but her greed for food reflected a wider appetite for life, and for experiences so often denied to her. So she was greedy, yes, but just some-times greedy can also be good.

Appendix: annotated and modernised recipes

CHAPTER 2
Brussels Biscuits or Rusks[1]

*Ingredients required – One pound of flour, ten ounces of
butter, half an ounce of German-yeast, four ounces of sugar,
four whole eggs, and four yolks, a teaspoonful of salt, and a
gill of cream. Mix the paste (in the manner described for
Compiegne cake, excepting that this must be beaten) with the
hand upon the slab until it presents an appearance of elasticity:
the sponge should then be added, and after the whole has been
well worked once more, the paste must be placed in long
narrow tins [about 2 inches deep, and of about the same width,
preparatory to placing the paste in the moulds: these should
first be well buttered and floured inside (to prevent the paste
from sticking), then the paste rolled out to their own lengths,*

*and about one inch and a half thick, dropped into them] and
set in a warm place to rise … when the paste has sufficiently
risen, it must be gently turned out [on a baking sheet,
previously spread with butter. Then] egged [all over with a
soft paste brush,] and baked [of a bright, deep yellow colour.
When done,] cut it up into slices [about a quarter of an inch
thick] place them flat on a baking-sheet, and put them again
in the oven to acquire a light-yellow colour on both sides.*

These biscuits were beloved of Victoria as a teenager recovering from a serious illness in 1835. This recipe is from a book by Charles Elmé Francatelli, who was chief cook to her in 1840. He wrote several books, and this recipe appears in one aimed solidly at the middle classes. Interestingly it is not included in his high end cookery book, which is in general more reflective of the kind of dishes which he would have been cooking at Windsor and Buckingham Palace.

I have halved the ingredients – it still makes quite a lot of biscuits, so by all means halve them again. You can buy 'fresh' yeast in blocks from the bakery counter at many supermarkets: it is the equivalent of the processed German-yeast mentioned here.

8oz plain flour
5oz unsalted butter
½ oz fresh yeast or ½ tsp of dried yeast
2oz caster sugar
1 whole large egg
1 large egg yolk
½ tsp salt
5fl oz single cream

Crumble the yeast into about 2tbsp of tepid water, and mix to dissolve. Put 2oz of the flour into a bowl. Make a well in the centre, and add the yeast mixture. Sprinkle with a little flour from round the edges. Leave for about 10 minutes, at which point the yeast should be bubbling through the flour. Mix, adding a little more water if necessary, and form it into a loose and rather sticky ball. Cover with a damp teatowl or clingfilm, and leave in a warm place to double or triple in size. This is your sponge.

Meanwhile, mix the other ingredients well. Knead them, and, when the sponge has risen, add this in and mix everything thoroughly. Knead again. Francatelli now uses long, thin moulds as a way of shaping the dough which will be rather sticky and hard to handle. If you don't have any, you can use plastic food containers, mini loaf tins, or half a kitchen roll inner tube, lined with greaseproof paper or clingfilm – whatever comes to hand is fine – just be aware that this will dictate the size of your final biscuits. Butter and flour whatever you are using, and put the dough in, to about ⅔ the height of your mould. Leave, covered with clingfilm or a damp cloth, for a couple of hours until it has risen and quite probably overflowed. Heat the oven to 180°c (170°c fan). Turn the dough out fast onto a greased baking sheet and bake for about 15–20 minutes. You can egg wash the whole thing for extra authenticity if you have a soft enough brush not to tear the rather delicate dough.

Leave to cool slightly, and cut your cakes into thin slices. Egg wash them if you can be bothered, and spread on a greased baking sheet. Re-bake for 10–15 minutes until they are golden brown. Store in an airtight container and eat with everything you can think of (especially orange jelly and beef tea).

CHAPTER 3
Sir-Loin of Beef[2]

The noble Sirloin of about fifteen pounds, will require to be before the fire about four hours: take care to spit it evenly, that it may not be heavier on one side than the other; put a little clean dripping into the dripping pan, (tie a sheet of paper over it to preserve the fat), baste it well as soon as it is put down, and baste it every quarter of an hour all the time it is roasting; then take off the paper, and make some gravy for it ... to brown and froth it, sprinkle a little salt over it, baste it with butter, and dredge it with flour; let it go a few minutes longer, till the froth rises, take it up, put it on the dish, &c.

William Kitchener, who wrote this recipe, was a true Regency man: involved in everything, and a great gourmand. His recipes are well-researched and from the heart. Roasting was always done in front of a fire in the past: first on spits turned by people, and, from the seventeenth century, with a variety of mechanisms, including weight driven, clockwork and a fan-driven smoke-jack. The Windsor roasting ranges still exist, and one of them retains most of the system of cogs which originally turned the spit. It is impossible to replicate the taste of spit-roast beef when it is, as now roasted (the Victorians would have deemed it baked) in an oven. However, if you have a spit on your barbeque, you can have a go!

The principle here is simple – you tie paper loosely

over any bits of the joint which might burn, spit the meat and get it turning. Baste it with the juices which drip into the drip-pan beneath it, and, when it is almost cooked, remove the paper, and sprinkle the joint with a mixture of salt and flour, plus a bit of melted butter. As Kitchener suggests, a froth will emerge from the joint, which then cooks and browns and forms a gorgeous crispy coating. It was served as a joint, whole, unadulterated and in-your-face. Beef was emblematic of Britishness. It was usually served with plum pudding and potatoes.

CHAPTER 4
Chicken consommé[3]

Put 2 chickens, or hens, having first removed their fillets, and 6lbs of fillet of veal, in a stockpot, with 5 quarts of General Stock, and ½ oz of salt: put in the fire to boil; then skim, and add 2 onions, with 2 cloves stuck in one; 4 leeks, and a head of celery; simmer on the stove corner for three hours; strain the broth; take off the fat, and clarify the consommé with the fillets of chicken, or hen ... and strain once more, through a broth napkin, into a basin.

Observation: Chicken consommé should be colourless; by following the indications given, it will be obtained perfectly white and clear.

There is not much to add to this. There's a tremendous quantity of meat, entirely appropriate for the royal kitchens, and an equally tremendous amount of work. It is, however, delicious. If you should fancy doing it at home, scaling things down somewhat is probably the order of the day. Once you've simmered your meats and strained the liquid off, leave it to cool completely, and then add two crushed egg whites, along with their crushed shells, and the diced or minced chicken breasts. Stir well, and very, very gradually bring it to the boil. Once it gets there, turn the heat down and boil gently for about 5–10 minutes. The whites, shells and chicken will form a sort of nasty, scummy omelette on top, which will cook through as you simmer it. Take the pan off the heat and pour ever-so-gently through a sieve, preferably a conical one, lined with muslin. It'll take a while, but the second you rush, the stock will go cloudy.

Heston Blumenthal, incidentally, has a slightly different method, where you simply freeze the (strained but unclarified) stock in small quantities, and then defrost it overnight in a coffee filter or sieve lined with muslin so that the impurities remain behind.

CHAPTER 5
Albert Sauce

Grate three large sticks of horse-radish, put them into a stewpan with a pint of good broth; let this simmer gently on a moderate fire for half-an-hour, then add a little white sauce and half a pint of cream; reduce the whole over a brisk fire, and pass the sauce through a tammy as you would a purée, and put it into a bain marie. Just before using the sauce, make it hot, and mix in a little French vinegar, a dessert-spoonful of mixed mustard, some salt, a tablespoonful of chopped and blanched parsley, and two yolks of eggs.

This sauce is well adapted to be eaten with braised fillet of beef, garnished with potatoes cut into the shape of olives, and fried in butter.[4]

This is one of the hottest things I have ever eaten, and preparing the root is not for the faint-hearted, but it is strangely compelling with red meat.

1 horseradish root, peeled and grated or minced in a food
    processor
½ pt beef or chicken stock
3–4 fl oz of white sauce (butter and flour to make a roux,
    mix with hot milk and whisk till smooth)
5 fl oz cream – it doesn't matter what kind
1 level tsp mustard, heat depending on personal taste
1 tbsp white wine vinegar
generous pinch of salt
½ tbsp finely chopped parsley
The yolk of 1 small egg (or ½ a large one)

Simmer the horseradish in the stock until it is very soft (approx. 30 minutes). While doing this, make the white sauce. Add the sauce and cream to the horseradish and blitz in a blender. Allow to cool slightly and add the rest of the ingredients. Return to a very gentle heat, and stir until it thickens. Do not allow to boil (or the egg will curdle). Keeps well in the fridge, good hot or cold.

CHAPTER 6
Haggis Royal

Three pounds of leg of mutton chopped; a pound of suet

chopped; a little, or rather as much beef marrow as you can spare; the crumb of a penny loaf (our own nutty flavoured, browned oatmeal is, by the way, far better) the neat yolks of four eggs; a half-pint of red wine; three mellow fresh anchovies boned: minced parsley, lemon grate, white pepper ... cayenne to taste ... blend the ingredients well: truss them neatly in a veal-caul; bake in a deep dish, in a quick oven, and turn out. Serve hot as fire, with brown gravy or venison sauce.[5]

The book that this is from, Margaret Dod's *Cook and Housewife's Manual*, is a culinary curiosity in some ways. It's author is fictional, named after a celebrated innkeeper and cook in Walter Scott's *St Ronan's Well*. It was actually written by a popular author, journalist and magazine editor, Christian Isobel Johnstone. It was one of the first cookbooks to include explicitly Scottish dishes, part of the growing celebration and commensurate creation of, modern Scottish national identity. The book was very popular, both for its refreshingly tongue-in-cheek approach, and because the recipes were very good. It is an excellent recipe, especially if you don't like the stuff sold as haggis today.

1 ½ lb of mutton, goat or lamb leg, chopped finely with a knife

½ lb suet

1–2tbsp bone marrow (optional)

About a cup of oatmeal

2 small or one large egg yolk

2.5 fl oz red wine

2 anchovies, minced

Finely chopped parsley, to taste (be generous)
Grated rind of one small lemon
1 tsp salt
1 tsp cayenne pepper
½ tsp white pepper, ground
Caul fat (optional)

Mix all the ingredients, adding enough oatmeal to soak up all the liquid. Put into a well-greased pudding basin and sprinkle oatmeal on the top or, if you have caul fat, wrap it up in this, and then put it into a greased pudding basin. Bake at 180°c for 45 minutes and serve hot, possibly with with redcurrant jelly.

CHAPTER 7
Pancake with marmalade

Put a quarter of a pound of sifted flour into a basin, with four eggs, mix them together very smoothly, then add half a pint of milk or cream, and a little grated nutmeg, put a piece of butter in your pan, (it requires but a very little), and when quite hot put in two tablespoonfuls of the mixture, let spread all over the pan, place it upon the fire, and when coloured upon the one side toss it over, then turn it upon your cloth; proceed thus til they are all done, then spread apricot or other marmalade all over, and roll them up neatly, lay them upon a baking sheet, sift sugar all over, glaze nicely with the salamander, and serve upon a napkin; the above may be served without the marmalade, being then the common pancake.[6]

Alexis Soyer was the leading chef of his day, and one of

London's most flamboyant culinary figures. Like Francatelli, he published cookery books aimed at the upper,
middle and lower classes, and he also put his ideas into
action, going out to the Crimea to work out whether the
food had anything to do with the appalling death rate in
the Scutari field hospital (it did). He subsequently invented
a military stove which remained in use well into the latter
half of the twentieth century, and was lauded as a hero by
The Times. This recipe is from his middle class *Cook's
Guide*, which is written as letters from an experienced
hostess to her protégé. It's refreshingly odd, but the
recipes are brilliant.

4oz flour
2 large eggs
10 fl oz single cream or whole milk
Nutmeg
Butter
Jam or marmalade
Icing sugar (to finish)

Mix the eggs and flour until there are no lumps, then whisk
in the cream or milk, adding a little grated nutmeg. Melt the
butter in a pan, and pour in two ladles-full of batter, spreading it out across the pan. Flip or toss the pancake when it is
just cooked on the top, and cook the bottom until it is
brown. To be properly Victorian, spread each pancake with
a thin layer of jam or marmalade, roll it up, and put it on a
baking sheet. When the sheet is full of pancakes, sprinkle
with icing sugar and put them under a grill to brown the
sugar. Serve on a doily, stacked neatly in a pyramid.

CHAPTER 8
Curry of Chickens, à l'Indienne[7]

*Fry the pieces of chicken or fowl in butter, until they are brightly browned all over, and remove them into a stewpan; then slice up three large onions and two heads of celery, and put these into a stewpan, together with a clove of garlic, a garnished faggot of parsley, a blade of mace, and four cloves. Fry the whole over a slow fire until they acquire a light brown colour; add a large tablespoonful of Cook's meat-curry-paste, and a similar proportion of flour; mix all the above together and moisten with a pint of good broth or gravy; stir the sauce over the fire, and keep it boiling for about twenty minutes, then rub the whole through a hair sieve or tammy, and afterwards pour it to the pieces of chicken. Set the curry to simmer gently over a slow fire until the pieces of chicken become tender, when the *éntree* may be served as in the former case [with the sauce poured over, and plain boiled rice on the side].*

750g ish chicken pieces (or a chicken, jointed, or pieces, etc)
50g butter
2–3 onions
6–8 stalks of celery
1 clove of garlic
A bouquet garni
1 blade of mace
4 cloves
1 heaped tbsp. of curry paste (see note)
1 heaped tsp rice flour or plain flour
1pt stock

Melt half of the butter and fry the chicken. Remove from the pan and put in the rest of the butter. Turn down the heat and fry the chopped vegetables until the onions go translucent and the celery is tender. Put in the curry paste and flour and give a good stir. Add the stock and simmer the whole lot for about 20 minutes. It should now be relatively thick: you should puree it in a blender. You don't have to. Add the chicken pieces to the sauce and simmer until the chicken is done (you can also do this stage in the oven or a slow cooker).

Note: This relies, as do many Victorian recipes, on a branded sauce. A bewildering variety of proprietary pastes and powders were available in Victorian England (and had been since the late Georgian period, when curry first became popular). You can either buy a modern meat curry paste, or put together a suitably Victorian curry powder.

A suitably Victorian curry powder (from Eliza Acton, Modern Cookery): 8oz turmeric, 4oz coriander seed, 2oz cumin seed, 2oz fenugreek seed, ½oz cayenne (or more, to taste – Acton also suggests going easy on the turmeric). Dry the seeds (fry or bake), grind them and mix. She also suggests adding desiccated coconut to most curries – it works well as a garnish. Be warned that this recipe makes a lot more curry powder than you will need, so it's probably best to quarter the recipe, or substitute ounces for teaspoons.

CHAPTER 9
Boar's Head, with aspic jelly[8]

Procure the head of a bacon hog which must be cut off deep into the shoulders; bone it carefully, beginning under the throat, then spread the head out upon a large earthenware dish, and rub it with the following ingredients: Six pounds of salt, four ounces of saltpetre, six ounces of moist sugar, cloves, mace, half an ounce of juniper berries, four cloves of garlic, six bay leaves, a handful of thyme, marjoram, and basil. When the head has been well rubbed with these, pour about a quart of port-wine lees over it, and keep in a cool place for a fortnight; observing that it must be turned over in its brine every day, during that period.

When about to dress the head, take it out of the brine, and wash it thoroughly in cold water; then absorb all the exterior moisture from it with a clean cloth, and spread it out upon the table. Next, pare off all the uneven pieces from the cheeks, &c., cut these into long narrow fillets, and put them with the tongue, fat bacon, and truffles, prepared as directed for the galantine; then, line the inside of the head with a layer of force-meat (the same kind as used for galantines), about an inch thick, and lay thereon the fillets of tongue, bacon, truffles, and here and there some pistachio kernels (the skin of which must be removed by scalding); cover these with a layer of force-meat, and then repeat the rows of tongue, &c., and when the head is sufficiently garnished to fill it out in its shape, it should be sewn up with a small trussing-needle and twine, so as thoroughly to secure the stuffing. The head must then be wrapped up in a strong cloth, previously well spread with butter, and sewn up in this, so as to preserve its original form: it should next be put into a large oval braising-pan, covered with any carcasses of game (especially of grouse, from its congenial flavour) or any trimmings of meat there may be at hand, and also four cow-heels, or six calves' feet;

then moisten with a copious wine mirepoix, in sufficient quantity to cover the surface of the head. Set the brazier on the stove-fire; as soon as it boils up, skim it thoroughly, then remove it to a slow fire (covered with the lid containing live embers), that the head may continue to simmer or boil very gently, for about five hours; as soon as it appears to be nearly done, remove the brazier from the fire, and when the heat of the broth has somewhat subsided, let the head be taken up on a large dish : if it appears to have shrunk considerably in the wrapper, this must be carefully tightened, so as to preserve its shape : it should then be put back into its braise, there to remain, until the whole has become set firm by cooling. The head must next be taken out of the braise or stock, and put in the oven, upon a deep baking-dish, for a few minutes, just to melt the jelly which may adhere to the wrapper; it must then be taken out quickly, and the wrapper carefully removed, after which, glaze the head with some dark-coloured glaze; place it on its dish, ornament it with aspic-jelly, and serve.

Note. On the Continent it is usual to decorate boars' heads with coloured gum-paste, and sometimes with natural flowers: the latter produce a very pretty effect, when arranged with taste; the former method is objectionable, from the liability of the gum-paste to give way, and run down the sides of the head: it has, moreover, a vulgar and gaudy look.

As I doubt anyone reading this will be desperate to dash off to the kitchen and replicate it, I have not modernised it fully. However, I *have* cooked it, and it is a very fine thing indeed. If you do wish to replicate it, allow a good few hours for the boning, and ensure you have a range of sharp knives of different shapes. The snout is the most challenging part, as the bone is very close to the skin there. It is essential to buy your pig's head from a butcher where you can specify what you need: off-the-peg heads are cut off just behind the ears, but you really need one cut off a couple of vertebrae back, so that you have some skin to form the back of your stuffed piggie parcel (otherwise you will need to wrap it in caul fat and, while you can make it work, it's a bit messy). Allow at least ten days, preferably two weeks, for the brining stage and don't forget to turn it every day.

Once boned, brined and ready to stuff, arm yourself with a gloving needle, a thimble, and at least 5 spare hours (and another 5 for cooking). You'll need to sew closed the mouth, eyes, any splits in the flesh and the bolt hole which you will find in the centre of the forehead if your pig was killed in an abattoir. You can use any meat-based stuffing: mine is usually 50:50 fatty veal and pork, with generous amounts of ham, mushrooms, pistachios and anything I fancy. The forcemeats used in the Victorian period were often pounded until they resembled very fine pâté, but I usually opt for mince. You can layer in other things – like the tongue that Francatelli suggests – as you desire. Once stuffed, you can use the extra skin to close off the back, sew it tightly, and swaddle it tightly in muslin. It looks like a hamster with well-stuffed cheeks at this stage. Stock, roughly chopped vegetables, bones, lots of feet and a couple of bottles of red wine are an adequate braising liquid – you need the wine for the colour and the feet for the gelatine, and the rest is for flavour. It'll take at least 5 hours to cook and do not underestimate the size of pan you need. You may need to do a bit more wrapping to reshape it when it's cooked, and it needs to cool fully.

When you unswaddle it (the next day, and I'd suggest judicious use of scissors), the head will resemble a stonking great haemorrhoid, and you'll wonder why you bothered. However, since you've got this far, you might as well try and wrench victory from the jaws of defeat. Strain and clarify your boiling liquid, and reduce it so that it will set into decent, thick, reddish jelly. As it cools and thickens you can set it in trays to cut up for jellied decoration and brush it onto your head to even out the colour and make it shine. The rest of the decoration is only determined by your own imagination – Edwardian boar's heads sometimes had veritable forests of holly and mistletoe poking out of their ears, as well as scenes of rural Christmas hunting and gambolling in pastry, sugar or marzipan romping across their brows. You can make eyes from radishes, sculpt tusks from potatoes, and pipe lard designs on every surface which will take it. When you stand back, you will be awed by your creation.

Serve cold (!). It will feed a large number of people and fill a freezer drawer. If you merely want a snifter of the experience, might I suggest a nice boar sausage cooked in red wine.

CHAPTER 10
Toad in the hole[9]

To make this a cheap dinner, you should buy 6d or 1s worth of bits or pieces of any kind of meat, which are to be had cheapest at night when the day's sale is over. The pieces of meat should be fist carefully overlooked, to ascertain if there be any necessity to pare away some tainted part, or perhaps a

*fly-blow, as this, if left on any one piece of meat, would tend
to impart a bad taste to the whole, and spoil the dish. You then
rub a little flour, pepper, salt all over the meat, and fry it
brown with a little butter or fat in the frying-pan, and when
done, put it with the fat it has been fried in into a baking dish
containing some Yorkshire or suet pudding batter, made as
directed at nos. 57 and 58, and bake the toad-in-the-hole for
about an hour and a half, or else send it to the baker's.*

Yorkshire pudding batter
*To one pound of flour add three pints of skim milk, two eggs,
nutmeg and salt; mix smoothly.*

Suet pudding batter
*To one pound of flour add six ounces of chopped suet, three
pints of skim milk, nutmeg and salt; mix thoroughly.*

Toad-in-the-hole was originally a much more versatile and
varied dish than the modern sausage-based versions. Any
meat can be used, raw or cooked (leftover roast beef works
very well indeed), and in any quantity which you have. It's
designed to eke out small quantities of meat with cheap
ingredients: I often pack it full of meat, but I am not a
struggling urban worker in 1861, and meat is a lot cheaper
now. Either batter mix works well (the suet one is a revela-
tion. Both were intended to be baked as batter puddings in
an oven or under a joint as it roasted on the fire, and,
again, to provide cheap filler for small quantities of meat.
Whole milk is fine in a modern context – skim would often
have been bought by workers as it was cheaper, since it
lacked the cream. Sadly it was also less nutritional, and

lacked calories which they desperately needed. Alexis Soyer, incidentally, suggests fillings for toad-in-the-hole which range from sparrows wrapped in bacon through to pretty much an entire roast dinner, vegetables and all.

Some meat, equivalent to 8–10 fat sausages, seasoned with
    pepper
½lb / 500g plain flour
3oz / 75g beef suet or 1 small egg
1½ pts / 750ml milk
generous pinch or two of nutmeg
½ tsp salt

Fry the meat briefly in hot fat of some form (unless you are using pre-cooked leftovers). Use the fat to grease a pie dish, and add the meat. Mix all of the batter ingredients and stir very vigorously until frothy and well mixed. Pour the batter on the meat and bake in an oven at 180°c conventional (160°c fan) for 45–60 minutes until cooked. The top should be brown and crispy, and the inside fluffy but cooked through.

CHAPTER 11
Lait de Poule[10]

Put the yolks of two new laid eggs in a basin; beat them up with 10z of pounded sugar and a teaspoonful of orange flower water, and stir in ½ pint of boiling water or milk.

Lait de Poule should be taken very hot, and will be found very soothing for coughs and colds.

Although the name is off-putting – translating literally as chicken's milk – this is not nearly as bad as it sounds (unless you make it with water, in which case it is pretty grim). It is essentially outrageously sweet thin custard and perfectly pleasant, unless you have a sore throat, in which case it's really quite good.

1 medium egg yolk
1oz/25g sugar
½ pint whole milk
1tsp orange flower water

Whisk the yolk up with the sugar and bring the milk to boil with the orange flower water. Pour the milk scalding hot onto the yolk, whisking. Cool enough to drink.

A slightly more useful alternative is to keep aside a tablespoon of the cold milk, and mix it with a teaspoon of cornflour or arrowroot. Once you've mixed the hot milk with the yolk, pour the lot back into a pan and add the cornflour mix, heating gently until the yolk and cornflour work their magic to give you a proper custard. This is then very nice as a sweet, served with tart fruit.

Select bibliography

ABBREVIATIONS

ILN – *Illustrated London News*

QVJ – Queen Victoria's Journals (online), full reference RA VIC/MAIN/QVJ/ (W) and accessible at http://www. queenvictoriasjournals.org/ from within the UK and some Commonwealth libraries.

RA – The Royal Archives, Windsor

RC – The Royal Collection, Windsor

TNA – The National Archives, Kew

'A Lady' (1840) *Anecdotes, Personal Traits and Characteristic Sketches of Victoria*. London

Anon. (1874) *Buckmaster's Cookery*. London: Routledge

Anon. (1897) *The Private Life of the Queen*

Anon. (Arthur G. Payne) (1886) *The Housekeeper's Guide to Preserved Meats, Fruits, Condiments, Vegetables &c*. London: Crosse & Blackwell

Arengo-Jones, Peter (1995) *Queen Victoria in Switzerland*. London: Robert Hale

Arnstein, Walter (1998) 'Queen Victoria's Other Island', in *More Adventures with Britannia: Politics, Personalities and Culture in*

Britain, edited by William Roger Louis. Austin & London: University of Texas & Tauris, 45–66

Barratt, Carrie (2000) *Queen Victoria and Thomas Sully*. New York: Princeton University Press/The Metropolitan Museum of Art

Bartley, Paula (2016) *Queen Victoria*. Abingdon: Routledge

Beeton, Isabella (1861) *The Book of Household Management*. London: S. O. Beeton

Benson, Arthur, and Viscount Esher (1908) *A Selection from Her Majesty's Correspondence between the Years of 1837 and 1861, vol 1: 1837–1843*. London: John Murray

Benson, Arthur, and Viscount Esher (1908) *The Letters of Queen Victoria*, vol. 2. London: John Murray

Braddon, Mary Elizabeth (1862) *Lady Audley's Secret*

Braddon, Mary Elizabeth (1875) *Hostages to Fortune*. London

Broomfield, Andrea (2007) *Food and Cooking in Victorian England*. Westport: Praeger

Brown, Peter (1990) *Pyramids of Pleasure: Eating and Dining in the Eighteenth Century*. York: York Civic Trust

Burnett, John (1989) *Plenty and Want: A Social History of Food in England from 1815 to the Present Day*. London: Routledge

Buxeoveden, Sophie (Baroness) (1928) *The Life and Tragedy of Alexandra Feodorovna, Empress of Russia*. London: Longmans

Campbell, Susan (1984) 'The Genesis of Queen Victoria's Great New Kitchen Garden', in *Garden History* 12, no. 2: 100–19.

Charlot, Monica (1991) *Victoria, the Young Queen*. London: Blackwell

Clark, Ronald (1981) *Balmoral: Queen Victoria's Highland Home*. London: Thames & Hudson

Collingham, Linda (2006) *Curry: A Tale of Cooks and Conquerers*. London: Vintage

Cowen, Ruth (2006) *Relish: The Extraordinary Life of Alexis Soyer, Victorian Celebrity Chef*. London: Weidenfeld & Nicolson

Critchell, James, and Joseph Raymond (1912) *A History of the Frozen Meat Trade*. London: Constable

Davidson, Alan (2006) *The Oxford Companion to Food*. 2nd edn. Oxford: OUP

De La Noy, Michael (1990) *Windsor Castle: Past and Present*. London: Headline

Dennison, Matthew (2007) *The Last Princess*. London: Weidenfeld & Nicolson

Devereux, G. (1904) *Etiquette for Men*. London: C. Arthur Pearson, Ltd

Dods, Margaret (Christian Isobel Johnstone) (1862) *The Cook and Housewife's Manual*. Edinburgh: Oliver and Boyd

Duff, David (1968) *Victoria in the Highlands*. London: Frederick Muller

Duff, David (1970) *Victoria Travels*. London: Frederick Muller

Duff, David (1972) *Victoria and Albert*. New York: Taplinger

Erskine, Beatrice (writing as Mrs Steuart Erskine) (1916) *Twenty Years at Court, 1842–1862: From the Correspondence of the Hon. Eleanor Stanley, Maid-of-Honour to Her Late Majesty Queen Victoria*. London: Nisbet & Co.

Francatelli, Charles Elmé (1855) *The Modern Cook*. 9th edn. London: Richard Bentley

Francatelli, Charles Elmé (1861) *A Plain Cookery Book for the Working Classes*. London

Francatelli, Charles Elmé (1862) *The Cook's Guide*. London: Richard Bentley

Fulford, Roger (1964) *Dearest Child: Letters between Queen Victoria and the Princess Royal, 1858–1861*. London: Evans Brothers

Fulford, Roger (1968) *Dearest Mama: Letters between Queen Victoria and the Crown Princess of Prussia, 1861–1864*. London: Evans Brothers

Fulford, Roger (1971) *Your Dear Letter: Private Correspondence of Queen Victoria and the Crown Princess of Prussia, 1865–1871*. London: Evans Brothers

Garrett, Theodore (c.1895) *The Encyclopedia of Practical Cookery*. 8 vols, vol. 7, London: L. Upcott Gill

Gaskell, Elizabeth (1854) *North and South*

Gill, Gillian (2010) *We Two: Victoria and Albert: Rulers, Partners, Rivals*. New York: Ballantine Books

Gouffé, Jules (1893) *Le Livre de Cuisine*. Paris: Hachette

Gouffé, Jules, and Alphonse Gouffé (trans.) (1871) *The Book of Preserves (Le Livre de Conserves)*. London: Sampson, Low, Son and Marston

Gray, Annie (2009) ' "Man Is a Dining Animal": The Archaeology of the English at Table, c.1750–1900'. Unpublished PhD thesis, University of Liverpool.

Gray, Annie (2013) '"The Proud Air of an Unwilling Slave": Tea, Women and Domesticity, c.1700–1900', in *Historical and Archaeological Perspectives on Gender Transformations: From Private to Public*, edited by Suzanne Spencer-Wood. New York: Springer

Gray, Peter (2000) 'National Humiliation and the Great Hunger: Fast and Famine in 1847', in *Irish Historical Studies* 32, no. 126: 193–216

Grey, Charles (1867) *The Early Years of the Prince Consort*. London

Groom, Suzanne (2013) *At the King's Table: Royal Dining through the Ages*. London: Merrell/Historic Royal Palaces

Hare, Augustus (1900) *The Story of My Life*, vol. 4. London: George Allen

Hassall, Arthur Hill (1855) *Food and Its Adulterations*. London: Longmans

Hibbert, Christopher (1981) *Greville's England: Selections from the Diaries of Charles Greville, 1818–1860*. London: The Folio Society

Hibbert, Christopher (1982) *The Court at Windsor: A Domestic History*. London: Penguin

Hibbert, Christopher (2001) *Queen Victoria, a Personal History*. London: HarperCollins

Hone, William (1825) *The Every Day Book*. London: William
   Hone

Horn, Pamela (1975) *The Rise and Fall of the Victorian Servant*.
   Dublin: Gill & Macmillan

Horn, Pamela (1991) *Ladies of the Manor: Wives and Daughters in
   Country House Society, 1830–1918*. Stroud: Sutton

HRH the Duchess of York, and Benita Stoney (1991) *Victoria and
   Albert: Life at Osborne House*. London: Weidenfeld &
   Nicolson.

Hubbard, Kate (2012) *Serving Victoria: Life in the Royal
   Household*. London: Chatto & Windus

Huxley, Gervas (1965) *Lady Elizabeth and the Grosvenors: Life in
   a Whig Family, 1822–1839*. London: OUP

Jagow, Kurt (ed.), and E. T. S. Dugdale (trans.) (1938) *Letters of
   the Prince Consort, 1831–1861*. London: John Murray

Jones, Kathryn (2008) *For the Royal Table: Dining at the Palace*.
   London: Royal Collection Enterprises

Kerr, Robert (1871) *The Gentleman's House; or, How to Plan
   English Residences, from the Parsonage to the Palace*. 3rd edn.
   London: John Murray

King, Greg. *Twilight of Splendor: The Court of Queen Victoria
   During Her Diamond Jubilee Year*. Hoboken: John Wiley, 2007

Kitchener, William (1818) *The Cook's Oracle*. London

Krout, Mary (1898) *A Looker on in London*

Leapman, Michael (2001) *The World for a Shilling: How the Great
   Exhibition of 1851 Shaped a Nation*. London: Headline

Lister, Thomas (Lord Ribblesdale) (1927) *Impressions and
   Memories*. London: Cassell

Longford, Elizabeth (2011) *Victoria*. London: Abacus

Lutyens, Mary, ed. (1961) *Lady Lytton's Court Diary, 1895–1899*.
   London: Rupert Hart-Davis

Mallet, Victor, ed. (1968) *Life with Queen Victoria: Marie Mallet's
   Letters from Court, 1887–1901*. London: John Murray

Mars, Valerie (1994) 'A la Russe: The New Way of Dining', in *Luncheon, Nuncheon and Other Meals: Eating with the Victorians*, edited by C. Ann Wilson, 117–44. Stroud: Sutton

Mason, Laura (1994) 'Everything Stops for Tea', in *Luncheon, Nuncheon and Other Meals: Eating with the Victorians*, edited by C. Ann Wilson, 71–90. Stroud: Sutton

Mayhew, Henry (1861) *London Labour and the London Poor*. London: Dover

Millar, Delia (1985) *Queen Victoria's Life in the Scottish Highlands*. London: Philip Wilson

Mundy, Harriot, ed. (1885) *The Journal of Mary Frampton, from the Year 1779, until the Year 1846*. London: Sampson Low, Marston, Searle, & Rivington

Murray, Hugh (1994) 'Queen Victoria, York and the Royal Myths'. *York Historian* 11: 56–68.

Murray, John (1867) *A Handbook for Travellers to France*. 10th edn. London: John Murray

Nelson, Michael (2007) *Queen Victoria and the Discovery of the Riviera*. London: Tauris Parke

Paoli, Xavier, and Alexander Teixeira de Mattos (trans.) (c.1911) *My Royal Clients*. London: Hodder & Stoughton

Ponsonby, Arthur (1942) *Henry Ponsonby, Queen Victoria's Private Secretary: His Life from His Letters*. London: Macmillan

Pope-Hennessy, James. *Queen Victoria at Windsor and Balmoral: Letters from Her Granddaughter Princess Victoria of Prussia, June 1889*. London: George Allen & Unwin, 1959

Qajar, Nasir al-Din Shah, and J. W. Redhouse (trans.) (1874) *The Diary of H.M. The Shah of Persia During His Tour through Europe in A.D. 1873*. London: John Murray

Rappaport, Helen (2012) *Magnificent Obsession: Victoria, Albert, and the Death That Changed the Monarchy*. London: Windmill

Reid, Michaela (1987) *Ask Sir James: The Life of Sir James Reid, Personal Physician to Queen Victoria*. London: Eland

Ridley, Jane (2012) *Bertie: A Life of Edward VII*. London: Chatto & Windus

Roberts, Jane (1997) *Royal Landscape: The Gardens and Parks of Windsor*. New Haven: Yale University Press

Roumania, Queen Marie of (1934) *The Story of My Life*, vol. 1. London: Cassell

Rundell, Maria (1806) *A New System of Domestic Cookery*. London: John Murray; reissued edition (2009) London: Persephone Books

Sambrook, Pamela (2005) *Keeping Their Place: Domestic Service in the Country House*. Stroud: Sutton

Senn, Charles Herman (1904) *The Century Cookbook: Practical Gastronomy and Recherché Cookery*. London: Ward, Lock & Co.

Smythe, Colin (2014) 'Charles Elmé Francatelli, Crockford's and the Royal Connection', in *Petits Propos Culinaires* 101: 42–67

Smythe, Colin (2015) 'Charles Elmé Francatelli, Additions and Supplementations', in *Petits Propos Culinaires* 102: 100–18

Soyer, Alexis (1849) *The Modern Housewife*. London

Soyer, Alexis (1860) *A Shilling Cookery Book for the People*. London: Routledge

Stocks, Christopher (2009) *Forgotten Fruits*. London: Windmill

Stoney, Benita, and Heinrich Weltzien, eds (1994) *My Mistress the Queen: The Letters of Frieda Arnold, Dresser to Queen Victoria*. London: Weidenfeld & Nicolson

Strange, William (1848) *Sketches from Her Majesty's Household: A Guide to Situations in the Queen's Domestic Establishment*. London: William Strange

Sultan Muhammed Shah, Sir (1954) *The Memoirs of the Aga Khan*. London: Cassell & Co.

Surtees, Virginia (1975) *Charlotte Canning: Lady in Waiting to Queen Victoria and Wife of the First Viceroy of India, 1817–1871*. London: John Murray

Suzanne, Alfred (1904) *La Cuisine Et Pâtisserie Anglaise Et Américaine*. Paris

The Dean of Windsor, and Hector Bolitho (1927) *Letters of Lady Augusta Stanley: A Young Lady at Court, 1849–1863*. London: Gerald Howe

Tschumi, Gabriel, and Joan Powe (1954) *Royal Chef: Forty Years with Royal Households*. London: William Kimber

Uglow, Jenny (2005) *A Little History of British Gardening*. London: Pimlico

Vallone, Lynne (2001) *Becoming Victoria*. New Haven: Yale

Van der Kiste, John (2003) *Childhood at Court, 1819–1914*. Stroud: Sutton

Wake, Jehanne (1998) *Princess Louise: Queen Victoria's Unconventional Daughter*. London: HarperCollins

Watson, Vera (1952) *A Queen at Home*. London: W. H. Allen

Whittle, Tyler (1980) *Victoria and Albert at Home*. London: Routledge & Kegan Paul

Wickes, Ian (1953) 'A History of Infant Feeding, Part III: Eighteenth and Nineteenth Century Writers', in *Archives of Diseases in Children* 28

Wilson, Bee (2008) *Swindled: From Poison Sweets to Counterfeit Coffee – the Dark History of the Food Cheats*. London: John Murray

Duke of Windsor (1998) *A King's Story*. London: Prion

Woodham-Smith, Cecil (1972) *Queen Victoria: Her Life and Times: 1819–1861*. London: Hamish Hamilton

Wright, Patricia (1996) *The Strange History of Buckingham Palace*. Stroud: Sutton

Wyndham, Maud (1912) *The Correspondence of Sarah Spencer, Lady Lyttelton, 1787–1870*. London: John Murray

Zu Erbach-Schönberg (Princess of Battenberg), Marie (1925) *Reminiscences*. London: George Allen & Unwin

Notes

CHAPTER 2: CHILDHOOD

1. Duke of Kent to Baron de Mallet, 26 May 1819, cited in Christopher Hibbert, *Queen Victoria, a Personal History* (London: HarperCollins, 2001), 12.
2. Charles Francatelli, *The Cook's Guide* (London: Richard Bentley, 1862), 309.
3. Cecil Woodham-Smith, *Queen Victoria: Her Life and Times: 1819–1861* (London: Hamish Hamilton, 1972), 15.
4. Ibid., 14. The boys, all of whom were supported by the state, largely ended up in long-term relationships with women they were not permitted to marry, which of course allowed them to wiggle out of any financial commitment to their hordes of illegitimate children when the relationships broke down. The girls either married in accordance with their father's wishes, or entered into embittered spinsterhood with an occasional secret pregnancy.
5. Woodham-Smith, *Queen Victoria*, 40; Royal Archive (henceforth RA) Geo/add/7/1393, Duke of Kent to General Weatherall, 19 April 1819.
6. *The Times* (London, England), Wednesday, 26 May 1819.

7. Ian Wickes, 'A History of Infant Feeding, Part III: Eighteenth and Nineteenth Century Writers', *Archives of Diseases in Children*, 28 (1953).

8. RA VIC/M3/6, cited in Lynne Vallone, *Becoming Victoria* (New Haven: Yale, 2001), 4.

9. Woodham-Smith, *Queen Victoria: Her Life and Times: 1819–1861*, 55.

10. Anon., *The Royal Kalendar and Court and City Register* (1819); *The Royal Kalendar and Court and City Register* (London, 1825).

11. The National Archives (henceforth TNA) WORK 19/16/1, report on the general state of Kensington Palace. The Duke's apartments were better than some, as they'd been hollow-drained, which had alleviated the damp.

12. She was made a Baroness (of Hanover), in 1827, despite her fairly humble beginnings. The Duke of York had just died, making Victoria second in line to the throne after the Duke of Clarence, and it sounded rather better to have Victoria surrounded by nobles, rather than just plain Frauleins.

13. For more on tea and feminism, see Annie Gray, '"The Proud Air of an Unwilling Slave": Tea, Women and Domesticity, c.1700–1900', in *Historical and Archaeological Perspectives on Gender Transformations: From Private to Public*, Suzanne Spencer-Wood, ed. (New York: Springer, 2013), 23–44.

14. Hibbert, *Queen Victoria, a Personal History*; Vallone, *Becoming Victoria*; Woodham-Smith, *Queen Victoria: Her Life and Times: 1819–1861*; Gillian Gill, *We Two: Victoria and Albert: Rulers, Partners, Rivals* (New York: Ballantine Books, 2009); Monica Charlot, *Victoria, the Young Queen* (London: Blackwell, 1991).

15. Arthur Benson and Viscount Esher, *A Selection from Her Majesty's Correspondence between the Years of 1837 and 1861*, vol. 1: *1837–1843*, (London: John Murray, 1908).

16. Andrea Broomfield, *Food and Cooking in Victorian England* (Westport: Praeger, 2007), 46–48; Mrs Frederick Pedley,

Nursing and the Management of Young Children (London: Routledge, 1866).

17. RA VIC/MAIN/Y/61/12, Leopold to Victoria, 13 December 1831.

18. RA VIC/MAIN/Y/61/14, Leopold to Victoria, 23 January 1832.

19. Royal Collection (henceforth RC) 929653, plans and elevations of the new kitchen at Kensington.

20. TNA WORK 19/16/1.

21. Benson and Esher, *A Selection from Her Majesty's Correspondence between the Years of 1837 and 1861*, Vol. 1: *1837–1843*.

22. TNA WORK 19/16/2, concerning works to repair structures at Kensington kitchen gardens.

23. Gervas Huxley, *Lady Elizabeth and the Grosvenors: Life in a Whig Family, 1822–1839* (London: OUP, 1965), 64.

24. Charlot, *Victoria, the Young Queen*, 51.

25. It is available online at http://www.queenvictoriasjournals.org/home.do. The full Royal Archives reference is RA VIC/MAIN/QVJ (W) followed by the date. I have used the simple form: QVJ (date) throughout this book. Until 1 January 1837 references are taken from Victoria's own entries, and thereafter either Lord Esher's typescript (where available) or Princess Beatrice's edited copies have been used.

26. They stayed there on 4 September 1835. A brief history is at http://www.yeoldebell-hotel.co.uk/theres-more/hotel-history

27. 'A Lady', *Anecdotes, Personal Traits and Characteristic Sketches of Victoria* (London, 1840).

28. Staffordshire Record Office, D615/PS/6/5/4, Sir John Conroy to Lady Lichfield, Sat. evening, the 20th.

29. Anon., *The Royal Kalendar and Court and City Register*.

30. QVJ 6 November 1833.

31. 'A Lady', *Anecdotes, Personal Traits and Characteristic Sketches of Victoria*.

32. QVJ 29 July 1833.
33. QVJ 18 July 1832 and 5 August 1832; 'A Lady', *Anecdotes, Personal Traits and Characteristic Sketches of Victoria*, 262.
34. QVJ 28 October 1832.
35. QVJ 3 November 1832; 'A Lady', *Anecdotes, Personal Traits and Characteristic Sketches of Victoria*, 217.
36. QVJ 31 July 1833.
37. QVJ 20 October 1832.
38. Gervas Huxley, *Lady Elizabeth and the Grosvenors: Life in a Whig Family, 1822–1839* (London: OUP, 1965), 44.
39. Vallone, *Becoming Victoria*, 157. Very few biographers have made this leap. (Most biographers have been men.)
40. Bangor Archives, Plâs Bodafon Papers, Bangor 4661: notebook belonging to Dr William Mason.
41. RA VIC/MAIN/Y/61/38, Leopold to Victoria, 22 December 1834.
42. RA VIC/MAIN/Z/493/30, Victoria to Leopold, 28 December 1834.
43. Woodham-Smith, *Queen Victoria: Her Life and Times: 1819–1861*, 116–18.
44. Huxley, *Lady Elizabeth and the Grosvenors: Life in a Whig Family, 1822–1839*, 38.
45. QVJ 7 September 1832, 18 September 1832, 21 September 1832 and 22 September 1832; 'A Lady', *Anecdotes, Personal Traits and Characteristic Sketches of Victoria*, 368–73.
46. Gill, *We Two: Victoria and Albert: Rulers, Partners, Rivals*, 72.
47. QVJ 31 October 1835.
48. QVJ 25 January 1836; Francatelli, *The Cook's Guide*, 309.
49. Woodham-Smith, *Queen Victoria: Her Life and Times: 1819–1861*, 133.
50. QVJ 19 January 1836.
51. Woodham-Smith, *Queen Victoria: Her Life and Times: 1819–1861*, 142.
52. Ibid.

53. Helen Rappaport, *Magnificent Obsession: Victoria, Albert, and the Death That Changed the Monarchy* (London: Windmill, 2012), suggests that these stomach problems were caused by Crohn's Disease, and that this, aggravated by stress, was part of what killed him.

54. Huxley, *Lady Elizabeth and the Grosvenors: Life in a Whig Family, 1822–1839*; Christopher Hibbert, *Greville's England: Selections from the Diaries of Charles Greville, 1818–1860* (London: The Folio Society, 1981), 134.

55. QVJ 17 June 1837; QVJ 18 June 1837.

56. RA MRH/MRHF/MENUS/MAIN/WC/1837, dining ledger for Windsor Castle.

CHAPTER 3: DINING STYLE

1. Cecil Woodham-Smith, *Queen Victoria: Her Life and Times: 1819–1861* (London: Hamish Hamilton, 1972), 240.

2. QVJ, 20 June 1837.

3. William Kitchener, *The Cook's Oracle* (London, 1818), 160–61.

4. It still does: as of 2015 no one had yet challenged the law, and daughters of titled families still can't inherit. It was only in 2014 that the royal system of descent changed to allow the first-born child to succeed to the throne regardless of gender: prior to that the male claim always trumped that of the female.

5. Woodham-Smith, *Queen Victoria: Her Life and Times: 1819–1861*, 171.

6. 'A Lady', *Anecdotes, Personal Traits and Characteristic Sketches of Victoria* (London, 1840), 472.

7. Carrie Barratt, *Queen Victoria and Thomas Sully* (New York: Princeton University Press/The Metropolitan Museum of Art, 2000), 45. Later writers have taken off a few inches, and estimated anything down to 4 feet 11 inches. This seems to be based on the slightly odd idea that 5 feet 1 inch isn't that short, so if everyone said she was short, then she must have

been shorter than she said she was (and shorter than the height recorded by all the contemporaries who mentioned it, as well as by the tape measure).

8. John Burnett, *Plenty and Want: A Social History of Food in England from 1815 to the Present Day* (London: Routledge, 1989), 187.

9. RA MRH/MRHF/MENUS/MAIN/BP/1837, dining ledger entry for 13 July 1837.

10. Kathryn Jones, *For the Royal Table: Dining at the Palace* (London: Royal Collection Enterprises, 2008).

11. Maud Wyndham, *The Correspondence of Sarah Spencer, Lady Lyttelton, 1787–1870* (London: John Murray, 1912), 287.

12. Peter Brown, *Pyramids of Pleasure: Eating and Dining in the Eighteenth Century* (York: York Civic Trust, 1990), 14.

13. Beatrice Erskine (writing as Mrs Steuart Erskine), *Twenty Years at Court, 1842–1862: From the Correspondence of the Hon. Eleanor Stanley, Maid-of-Honour to Her Late Majesty Queen Victoria* (London: Nisbet & Co., 1916), 228.

14. Woodham-Smith, *Queen Victoria: Her Life and Times: 1819–1861*, 210.

15. Monica Charlot, *Victoria, the Young Queen* (London: Blackwell, 1991), 101.

16. Christopher Hibbert, *Greville's England: Selections from the Diaries of Charles Greville, 1818–1860* (London: The Folio Society, 1981), 147.

17. Ibid., 153.

18. QVJ 25 September 1834; QVJ 23 September 1834.

19. Hibbert, *Greville's England: Selections from the Diaries of Charles Greville, 1818–1860*, 145.

20. Ibid., 156.

21. Ibid., 159.

22. Christopher Hibbert, *The Court at Windsor: A Domestic History* (London: Penguin, 1982), 172.

23. Woodham-Smith, *Queen Victoria: Her Life and Times: 1819–1861*, 96.

24. Suzanne Groom, *At the King's Table: Royal Dining through the Ages* (London: Merrell/Historic Royal Palaces, 2013), 130.

25. Wyndham, *The Correspondence of Sarah Spencer, Lady Lyttelton, 1787–1870*, 285.

26. QVJ 17 August 1839.

27. Woodham-Smith, *Queen Victoria: Her Life and Times: 1819–1861*, 196.

28. Erskine, *Twenty Years at Court, 1842–1862: From the Correspondence of the Hon. Eleanor Stanley, Maid-of-Honour to Her Late Majesty Queen Victoria*, 57.

29. Woodham-Smith, *Queen Victoria: Her Life and Times: 1819–1861*, 196.

30. QVJ 17 December 1838.

31. Harriot Mundy, *The Journal of Mary Frampton, from the Year 1779, until the Year 1846* (London: Sampson Low, Marston, Searle, & Rivington, 1885), 403–04.

32. QVJ 4 August 1839.

33. Woodham-Smith, *Queen Victoria: Her Life and Times: 1819–1861*, 218.

34. Charles Grey, *The Early Years of the Prince Consort* (London, 1867), 138–39.

35. Charlot, *Victoria, the Young Queen*, 188.

36. Wyndham, *The Correspondence of Sarah Spencer, Lady Lyttelton, 1787–1870*, 334.

37. RA MRH/MRHF/MENUS/MAIN/WC/1857, dining ledger entry for 8 June 1857. The menu is in French, and the entremets are given as 'Schaum Torte' and 'Pains à la Duchesse'. These are my translations and explanations.

38. Virginia Surtees, *Charlotte Canning: Lady in Waiting to Queen Victoria and Wife of the First Viceroy of India, 1817–1871* (London: John Murray, 1975), 175.

39. QVJ 26 August 1861.

40. Valerie Mars, 'A la Russe: The New Way of Dining', in *Luncheon, Nuncheon and Other Meals: Eating with the*

Victorians, C. Ann Wilson, ed. (Stroud: Sutton, 1994), 131.
For a (very) detailed look at dining change, see Annie Gray,
'"Man Is a Dining Animal": The Archaeology of the English
at Table, c.1750–1900' (University of Liverpool, 2009,
unpublished).

41. Michael De La Noy, *Windsor Castle: Past and Present*
(London: Headline, 1990), 112.

CHAPTER 4: KITCHENS

1. Jules Gouffé and Alphonse Gouffé (trans.), *The Royal
Cookery Book* (London: Sampson, Low, Son and Marston,
1869).

2. RA MRH/MRHF/GOODSREC/KITCHEN/MIXED.
This figure is for Windsor Castle.

3. RA MRH/MRHF/MENUS/MAIN/WC/1857 7 June. The
term used for waffles is an impossible to read 'hollipen',
which was a nineteenth-century culinary term for *gaufres* or
waffles.

4. Patricia Wright, *The Strange History of Buckingham Palace*
(Stroud: Sutton, 1996), 162. The full quote is in *Waldie's
Select Circulating Library*, 15 (3 February 1841).

5. Monica Charlot, *Victoria, the Young Queen* (London:
Blackwell, 1991), 102.

6. Wright, *The Strange History of Buckingham Palace*, 160.

7. TNA WORK 19/7 (2201).

8. TNA WORK 19/7 (2272).

9. TNA WORK 19/7 (2099).

10. TNA WORK 19/7 (2236); Wright, *The Strange History of
Buckingham Palace*, 165–67.

11. TNA WORK 19/7 (2230)

12. TNA WORK 19/8 (2594).

13. Jan Bondeson, *Queen Victoria's Stalker: The Strange Story of
The Boy Jones* (Stroud: Amberley, 2010). Some earlier authors
suggested that there were two boys who broke in – Tom
Cotton and Edward Jones. However, this is incorrect. Jones

gave a false name at his initial hearing – hence Tom Cotton – but it was always him.

14. Anon., *The Private Life of the Queen* (1897), 115.

15. Christopher Hibbert, *Queen Victoria, a Personal History* (London: HarperCollins, 2001), 138.

16. Wright, *The Strange History of Buckingham Palace*.

17. TNA WORK 19/9. Letters from Cubitt et al. concerning kitchen fit-out and reuse of materials. Folio 3408 concerns the lack of air in the new areas.

18. David Duff, *Victoria and Albert* (New York: Taplinger, 1972), 213–14.

19. RA MRH/MRHF/GOODSREC/DAIRY/WC, supply mesnil for 1842.

20. Gabriel Tschumi and Joan Powe, *Royal Chef: Forty Years with Royal Households* (London: William Kimber, 1954), 62. This book, which has been used as a major source on Victoria's kitchens, is very shaky on the details. It's quite clear that Tschumi is remembering the Edwardian era in his general reminiscences about the kitchens, and, while the specifics of some anecdotes are almost certainly true, he misremembers a lot of non-event-specific details, and he cannot be used as a reliable source for how the kitchens functioned in the late Victorian era. For example, the chef in 1898 was called Chevriot, not Menager, and Christmases under Victoria were spent at Osborne, not Sandringham. Additionally, he is the source for the oft-quoted 'fact' that the Queen ate a boiled egg from a golden cup for breakfast. Even he says that this is only a rumour.

21. Pamela Horn, *Ladies of the Manor: Wives and Daughters in Country House Society, 1830–1918* (Stroud: Sutton, 1991).

22. RA MRH/MENUS/MAIN/WC/1855.

23. Tschumi and Powe, *Royal Chef: Forty Years with Royal Households*, 95.

24. Ibid., 39–40.

25. Benita Stoney and Heinrich Weltzien, eds, *My Mistress the Queen: The Letters of Frieda Arnold, Dresser to Queen Victoria* (London: Weidenfeld & Nicolson, 1994), 42.

26. *Illustrated London News* (henceforth *ILN*) 28 December 1850.

27. Anon., *The Private Life of the Queen*, 35.

28. Ibid., 34–35.

29. Vera Watson, *A Queen at Home* (London: W. H. Allen, 1952), 82; Robert Kerr, *The Gentleman's House; or, How to Plan English Residences, from the Parsonage to the Palace*, 3rd edn. (London: John Murray, 1871), 211.

30. Anon., *The Private Life of the Queen*, 36.

31. Watson, *A Queen at Home*, 238–39.

32. Michael De La Noy, *Windsor Castle: Past and Present* (London: Headline, 1990), 76–77.

CHAPTER 5: COOKS

1. Charles Elmé Francatelli, *The Modern Cook*, 9th edn. (London: Richard Bentley, 1855), 12.

2. William Strange, *Sketches from Her Majesty's Household: A Guide to Situations in the Queen's Domestic Establishment* (London: William Strange, 1848).

3. TNA LS2/67 gives salary details for 1837. RA MRH/MRH/ EB/2 contains the Establishment lists for the 1840s, listing all the positions in the Household, again with salary details. Some of the Establishment books are also available via findmypast.co.uk.

4. RA MRH/MRH/EB/2 for the 1840s, and RA MRH/MRH/ EB/4 for 1900.

5. *The Western Times*, 29 January 1842.

6. *The Chelmsford Chronicle*, 2 September 1842.

7. Edmund Burke, *The Annual Register, or a View of the History, and Politics, of the Year 1840* (London, 1841), 14.

8. *The Morning Post*, 7 February 1840.

9. RA VIC/MAIN/Z/202/123, Sir John Cowell to Queen Victoria, 20 June 1867.

10. The position was usually known as first yeoman to the confectionery.

11. The details are given on his death certificate.

12. Eric Parker, *Eton in the 'Eighties* (London: Smith, Elder & Co., 1914), 63–64.

13. RA VIC/MAIN/Z/202/59, Colonel Biddulph (then master of the Household) to Queen Victoria, 1 May 1866.

14. Gabriel Tschumi and Joan Powe, *Royal Chef: Forty Years with Royal Households* (London: William Kimber, 1954), 18.

15. RA MRH/MRH/EB/2 includes the letter of reference; RA PPTO/PERSO/EB/6 gives details of his retirement date and pension.

16. In RA MRH/MRH/EB/4 both are listed as having 'reentered' service. No sign of Malsch in the 1861 census, but his long service medal is for 33 years, dating to 1859, so either he didn't leave, or they ignored the four years out (he may well have been working for another royal).

17. RA MRH/MRH/EB/2. In 1871 he was still in London, still a cook, but either living out or freelance, as he was head of his own household (and renting out rooms in his house to two other French chefs). In 1881 he was listed as a domestic cook, with his wife as his assistant, at the Langleybury Estate in Abbots Langley.

18. *The Spectator*, 6 June 1874.

19. Colin Smythe, 'Charles Elmé Francatelli, Crockford's and the Royal Connection', *Petits Propos Culinaires* 101 (2014), 42–67.

20. Ibid., and Colin Smythe, 'Charles Elmé Francatelli, Additions and Supplementations', *Petits Propos Culinaires* 102 (2014), 100–18.

21. RA VIC/MAIN/Z/202/11, Colonel Biddulph to Queen Victoria, no date, c.1864–65.

22. RA MRH/MRH/EB/2.

23. RA VIC/MAIN/Z/203/21, Anon. letter, 13 July 1868. He is eventually (letter 23) made a messenger in the Lord Chamberlain's department at Buckingham Palace.

24. Also spelt Kraeusslach (on his death certificate) and Kraeufslach (in other documents).

25. RA MRH/MRH/EB/2/86.

26. Tschumi and Powe, *Royal Chef: Forty Years with Royal Households*, 33.

27. RA MRH/MRH/EB/2/23, list of recipients of the Queen's Bounty.

28. RA VIC/MAIN/Z/203/102.

29. Helen Rappaport, *Magnificent Obsession: Victoria, Albert, and the Death That Changed the Monarchy* (London: Windmill, 2012), 234–35; Christopher Hibbert, *Queen Victoria, A Personal History* (London: HarperCollins, 2001), 495.

30. Victor Mallet, ed., *Life with Queen Victoria: Marie Mallet's Letters from Court, 1887–1901* (London: John Murray, 1968), 44.

31. Court Circular, 9 April 1878 (Osborne House).

32. RA VIC/MAIN/Z/202/22, Colonel Biddulph to Queen Victoria.

33. RA VIC/MAIN/Z/202/23. Letter 24 contains the actual menus, which can be compared to the rather sparser details given in the ledgers.

34. RA VIC/MAIN/Z/202/162, from Sir John Cowell, 5 January 1868.

35. RA VIC/MAIN/Z/202/168, ditto, 2 March 1868.

36. RA MRH/MRHF/MENUS/MAIN/WC, 29 December 1837. There were 24 diners at the royal table; 8 equerries and a 30-strong military band were also listed. The numbers, and number of groups, went up with time.

37. RA F&V/PRFF/MENU/Undated, but c.1875.

38. Thomas Lister (Lord Ribblesdale), *Impressions and Memories* (London: Cassell, 1927), 119.

CHAPTER 6: PRIVATE PALACES

1. QVJ 11 February 1840.

2. Margaret Dods (Christian Isobel Johnstone), *The Cook and Housewife's Manual* (Edinburgh: Oliver and Boyd, 1862), 399.

3. HRH the Duchess of York and Benita Stoney, *Victoria and Albert: Life at Osborne House* (London: Weidenfeld & Nicolson, 1991), 18.

4. Charles Grey, *The Early Years of the Prince Consort* (London, 1867), 138–39.

5. Ibid., 170.

6. Gillian Gill, *We Two: Victoria and Albert: Rulers, Partners, Rivals* (New York: Ballantine Books, 2010), 325.

7. Grey, *The Early Years of the Prince Consort*, 235.

8. Gill, *We Two: Victoria and Albert: Rulers, Partners, Rivals*, 373. Letter to Princess Victoria (Empress Frederick) 18 December 1861.

9. QVJ 18 August 1839.

10. Based on a height of 5 feet 1 inch, as shown by Thomas Sully's measuring tape (the only real piece of evidence surviving), and her stated weight in her journal of 7 stone 2 lb.

11. Maud Wyndham, *The Correspondence of Sarah Spencer, Lady Lyttelton, 1787–1870* (London: John Murray, 1912), 354.

12. Monica Charlot, *Victoria, the Young Queen* (London: Blackwell, 1991), 171.

13. Gill, *We Two: Victoria and Albert: Rulers, Partners, Rivals*, 232.

14. Christopher Hibbert, *Queen Victoria, a Personal History* (London: HarperCollins, 2001), 161.

15. Tyler Whittle, *Victoria and Albert at Home* (London: Routledge & Kegan Paul, 1980), 10. The payment records are in TNA LS8/314 – list of creditors not paid by salary for 1854.

16. Benita Stoney and Heinrich Weltzien, eds, *My Mistress the Queen: The Letters of Frieda Arnold, Dresser to Queen Victoria* (London: Weidenfeld & Nicolson, 1994), 33.

17. Wyndham, *The Correspondence of Sarah Spencer, Lady Lyttelton, 1787–1870*, 364.

18. RA VIC/MAIN/Z/204/67.

19. RA PP/OSB/MAIN/OS/45 is a plan of the dormitory block with annotations; RA PPTO/PP/OSB/MAIN/OS/839 is a list of servants in 1888 and 1894; the 1861 census for Osborne House provides the other details.

20. This section draws on various internal English Heritage documents, including conservation plans, contents summaries and architectural surveys, all consulted for an unpublished research report: Annie Gray (2009), 'The Royal Kitchens at Osborne House'.

21. RA PPTO/PP/OSB/OS/557, letters from Capt. Mann to Capt. Fleetwood Evans, 3 July 1880 and 8 July 1880; HRH the Duchess of York and Stoney, *Victoria and Albert: Life at Osborne House*, 83.

22. Ibid., 66.

23. Stoney and Weltzien, eds, *My Mistress the Queen: The Letters of Frieda Arnold, Dresser to Queen Victoria*, 31.

24. HRH the Duchess of York and Stoney, *Victoria and Albert: Life at Osborne House*, 67.

25. Delia Millar, *Queen Victoria's Life in the Scottish Highlands* (London: Philip Wilson, 1985), 31.

26. QVJ, 8 September 1848.

27. Quoted in Ronald Clark, *Balmoral: Queen Victoria's Highland Home* (London: Thames & Hudson, 1981), 30.

28. Rt Hon. The Earl of Malmesbury, *Memoirs of an ex-Minister* (London: Longmans Green & Co., 1885), 345.

29. Millar, *Queen Victoria's Life in the Scottish Highlands*, 25.

30. RC 921293 and RC 921285: ground floor and first floor plans of Balmoral.

31. RA F&V-PRFF1819–1900: menus for Balmoral, n.d. but probably 1870s.

32. David Duff, *Victoria in the Highlands* (London: Frederick Muller, 1968), 45.

33. Millar, *Queen Victoria's Life in the Scottish Highlands*, 91.

34. Gill, *We Two: Victoria and Albert: Rulers, Partners, Rivals*, 207.

35. Stoney and Weltzien, eds, *My Mistress the Queen: The Letters of Frieda Arnold, Dresser to Queen Victoria*, 127.

36. Ibid., 47, 134.

37. Clark, *Balmoral: Queen Victoria's Highland Home*, 31.

38. Ibid., 91.

39. Stoney and Weltzien, eds, *My Mistress the Queen: The Letters of Frieda Arnold, Dresser to Queen Victoria*, 134.

40. Ibid., 182. Frieda Arnold again, expressing delight that a farmer was so hospitable, only to be told that the 'old fox' supplied butter and flour to the estate and would well have known who she was.

41. Duff, *Victoria in the Highlands*, 166.

42. Ibid., 182.

43. Helen Rappaport, *Magnificent Obsession: Victoria, Albert, and the Death That Changed the Monarchy* (London: Windmill, 2012), 199; Millar, *Queen Victoria's Life in the Scottish Highlands*, 77; Duff, *Victoria in the Highlands*, 14.

44. Duff, *Victoria in the Highlands*, 31, 211, 311 and 50.

45. Rappaport, *Magnificent Obsession: Victoria, Albert, and the Death That Changed the Monarchy*, 249–60. Albert's death is usually attributed to typhoid, and this was certainly the belief at the time, but as Rappaport points out, typhoid was rare at that point in history, and there's no real medical evidence as to what killed him. She argues convincingly that Crohn's was what brought him down, and pneumonia was what finished him off.

46. Anon., *The Private Life of the Queen* (1897), 211.

47. Paula Bartley, *Queen Victoria* (Abingdon: Routledge, 2016), 180, Lord Halifax to Lord Ponsonby.

CHAPTER 7: MOTHERHOOD

1. Roger Fulford, *Dearest Child: Letters between Queen Victoria and the Princess Royal, 1858–1861* (London: Evans Brothers, 1964), 77–78.

2. Kurt Jagow, ed., and E. T. S. Dugdale (trans.) *Letters of the Prince Consort, 1831–1861* (London: John Murray, 1938), 272.

3. Alexis Soyer, *The Modern Housewife* (London, 1849), 346.

4. QVJ 1 December 1840.

5. Michaela Reid, *Ask Sir James: The Life of Sir James Reid, Personal Physician to Queen Victoria* (London: Eland, 1987), 68.

6. Fulford, *Dearest Child: Letters between Queen Victoria and the Princess Royal, 1858–1861*, 115.

7. Roger Fulford, *Your Dear Letter: Private Correspondence of Queen Victoria and the Crown Princess of Prussia, 1865–1871* (London: Evans Brothers, 1971), 18.

8. Paula Bartley, *Queen Victoria* (Abingdon: Routledge, 2016), 133.

9. HRH the Duchess of York and Benita Stoney, *Victoria and Albert: Life at Osborne House* (London: Weidenfeld & Nicolson, 1991).

10. QVJ 14 December 1846.

11. Gabriel Tschumi and Joan Powe, *Royal Chef: Forty Years with Royal Households* (London: William Kimber, 1954), 71.

12. QVJ 20 April 1848.

13. QVJ 19 December 1848.

14. QVJ 24 May 1850.

15. HRH the Duchess of York and Stoney, *Victoria and Albert: Life at Osborne House*, 107; Jehanne Wake, *Princess Louise: Queen Victoria's Unconventional Daughter* (London: HarperCollins, 1998). The information about Swiss Cottage and its gardens is largely drawn from an unpublished research report written by the author for English Heritage in 2009, as part of the process of reinterpreting Swiss Cottage to the public, and uses information taken from letters written by the

children, conversations with English Heritage curatorial and conservation staff, and various internal reports.

16. QVJ 26 October 1850.

17. QVJ 5 May 1853.

18. Prince of Wales, 'Lettes Diary', 1853, cited in an unpublished internal English Heritage research document.

19. Cited in an unpublished internal English Heritage report on activities at Swiss Cottage.

20. Swiss Cottage Quarter, Osborne House, Conservation Management Plan (2012, unpublished).

21. QVJ 19 September 1881.

22. RA VIC/MAIN/Z/204/144.

23. QVJ 15 May 1856.

24. Roger Fulford, *Dearest Mama: Letters between Queen Victoria and the Crown Princess of Prussia, 1861–1864* (London: Evans Brothers, 1968), 210.

25. RA PPTO/PP/QV/PP2/6/4622.

26. Alice to Prince Albert, 29 May 1858, cited in an unpublished English Heritage research report.

27. Lenchen to Prince Albert, 3 June 1858, cited in an unpublished English Heritage research report.

28. RA VIC/MAIN/Y34/10, Feodora to Princess Victoria, 21 October 1834.

29. QVJ 11 July 1861.

30. Elizabeth Craig, *Court Favourites: Recipes from Royal Kitchens* (London: Andre Deutsch, 1953).

31. Report on Activities at the Swiss Cottage Quarter, unpublished internal English Heritage report, n.d.

32. Affie to Bertie, 6 January 1855, cited in an unpublished English Heritage research report.

33. QVJ 18 December 1857.

34. Fulford, *Dearest Child: Letters between Queen Victoria and the Princess Royal, 1858–1861*, 73.

35. *Dearest Mama: Letters between Queen Victoria and the Crown Princess of Prussia, 1861–1864*, 207–08; *Your Dear Letter:*

Private Correspondence of Queen Victoria and the Crown Princess of Prussia, 1865–1871, 159.

36. Arthur Ponsonby, *Henry Ponsonby, Queen Victoria's Private Secretary: His Life from His Letters* (London: Macmillan, 1942), 85.

37. Fulford, *Dearest Child: Letters between Queen Victoria and the Princess Royal, 1858–1861*, 40, 44.

38. Ibid., 211.

39. *Your Dear Letter: Private Correspondence of Queen Victoria and the Crown Princess of Prussia, 1865–1871*, 125.

40. *Dearest Child: Letters between Queen Victoria and the Princess Royal, 1858–1861*, 125.

41. Augusta Stanley's letters of 18 July 1860 and 15 January 1861, cited in Matthew Dennison, *The Last Princess* (London: Weidenfeld & Nicolson, 2007), 19.

42. Fulford, *Your Dear Letter: Private Correspondence of Queen Victoria and the Crown Princess of Prussia, 1865–1871*, 99.

CHAPTER 8: ORDINARY EATING

1. Peter Arengo-Jones, *Queen Victoria in Switzerland* (London: Robert Hale, 1995), 44.

2. I can manage two inches with ease, and swan about all day feeling pretty comfortable, and she would have worn them from the age of eight and been well used to them. They would also have been made for her, which helps.

3. Brown Windsor Soup, which is often cited as a favourite dish of the Queen, did not exist at all in the nineteenth century. The earliest references are from the 1930s, and by the time it became well known, in the 1950s, it was as a music-hall joke, and there are suggestions that the term came into being as a typically punning mixture of an established, upper-class soup and a type of soap, known as brown Windsor. These dubious connotations notwithstanding, it did become a real soup, largely associated with shabby boarding houses trying to sound posh. There was a soup called Windsor Soup (not

brown), which Francatelli included in his section, in *The Modern Cook*, on 'English Soups', but it rarely appeared on the royal menus.

4. Charles Elmé Francatelli, *The Modern Cook*, 9th edn. (London: Richard Bentley, 1855), 983.

5. QVJ 20 September 1838.

6. RA MRH/MRHF/MENUS/MAIN/BP/1847 (10 June 1848); RA MRH/MRHF/MENUS/MAIN/BP/1888 (5 March 1890); RA MRH/MRHF/MENUS/MAIN/BP/1898 (10 May 1898). All of the menu details in this chapter are taken from these ledgers, along with RA MRH/MRHF/MENUS/MAIN/WC/1837, RA MRH/MRHF/MENUS/MAIN/WC/1847, RA MRH/MRHF/MENUS/MAIN/BP/1837, RA MRH/MRHF/MENUS/MAIN/WC/1856, RA MRH/MRHF/MENUS/MAIN/BP/1856, RA MRH/MRHF/MENUS/MAIN/BP/1876, RA MRH/MRHF/MENUS/MAIN/BP/1853, the menus in the Royal Archive under RA MRH/MRHF/F&V/PRFF/1819–1900 and MRH/MRHF/F&V/ENGT/1760–1884, and the dining ledger for Osborne House for 1897 which is in the collection of English Heritage.

7. RA MRH/MRHF/MENUS/MAIN/BP/1847.

8. Mrs de Salis, *À La Mode Cookery* (London: Longmans, 1902).

9. Anon., *The Private Life of the Queen* (1897), 140.

10. RA MRH/MRHF/GOODSREC/KITCHEN/MAIN/1837.

11. Gabriel Tschumi and Joan Powe, *Royal Chef: Forty Years with Royal Households* (London: William Kimber, 1954), 43. Tschumi says that this was for the Diamond Jubilee in 1897: it may have been, in which case he has got the name of the chief cook wrong, and it doesn't appear on the menu for the banquet (!). As usual, he's probably remembering a later occasion, but the principle of correctly clarified stock in this case remains the same.

12. TNA LS8/298 list of creditors not paid by salary (1838).

13. Charles Herman Senn, *The Century Cookbook: Practical Gastronomy and Recherché Cookery* (London: Ward, Lock & Co., 1904), 255.

14. TNA LS8/298.

15. RA MRH/MRHF/F&V/PRFF/1819–1900. The recipes are taken from Jules Gouffé, *Le Livre de Cuisine* (Paris: Hachette, 1893).

16. For the 1840s, RA MRH/MRHF/GOODSREC/ KITCHEN/MAIN, and for a full list of exactly what was supplied and by whom, TNA LS8/314. The National Archives only hold this information up to 1854.

17. RA VIC/MAIN/Z/203/111, obituary from *Land and Water*, 25 December 1869.

18. Vera Watson, *A Queen at Home* (London: W. H. Allen, 1952), 115.

19. Susan Campbell, 'The Genesis of Queen Victoria's Great New Kitchen Garden', *Garden History* 12, no. 2 (1984): 112.

20. Jenny Uglow, *A Little History of British Gardening* (London: Pimlico, 2005).

21. Campbell, 'The Genesis of Queen Victoria's Great New Kitchen Garden'.

22. Ibid., 116.

23. RA MRH/MRH/H/H/2/16, Vails distribution list, 1895. The head gardener at the time was called Owen Thomas.

24. TNA LS8/314 – list of creditors not paid by salary, 1854.

25. Francatelli, *The Modern Cook*, 17.

26. Benita Stoney and Heinrich Weltzien, eds., *My Mistress the Queen: The Letters of Frieda Arnold, Dresser to Queen Victoria* (London: Weidenfeld & Nicolson, 1994), 55.

27. Anon., *The Private Life of the Queen* (1897), 117.

28. TNA LS8/312 – there were also orders for various border moulds, all of which were in addition to the enormous batterie de cuisine already at the palace.

29. Stockmar quote, and wine consumption figures, in Charles Ludington, 'Drinking for Approval: Wine and the British

Court from George III to Victoria and Albert', in Danielle de Vooght, ed., *Royal Table: Food, Power and Status at the European Courts after 1789* (Farnham: Routledge, 2016), 57–86.

CHAPTER 9: EXTRAORDINARY EATING

1. QVJ 29 September 1837.
2. Charles Elmé Francatelli, *The Modern Cook*, 9th edn. (London: Richard Bentley, 1855), 377–79.
3. Christopher Hibbert, *Queen Victoria, a Personal History* (London: HarperCollins, 2001), 346.
4. QVJ 2 June 1844.
5. QVJ 4 June 1844.
6. QVJ 7 June 1844.
7. QVJ 7 June 1844; RA F&F/SVIN/1844: dinner party account.
8. QVJ 9 June 1844.
9. RA F&V/SVIN: state visits to England 1841–1899.
10. QVJ 9 October 1844.
11. RA MRH/MRHF/GOODREC/KITCHEN/MAIN.
12. Arthur Benson and Viscount Esher, *The Letters of Queen Victoria*, vol. 2 (London: John Murray, 1908), 22–23.
13. QVJ 13 April 1855.
14. QVJ 21 April 1855.
15. RA MRH/MRHF/MENUS/MAIN/BP/1838; RA MRH/MRHF/MENUS/MAIN/BP/1871; RA MRH/MRHF/MENUS/MAIN/BP/1855.
16. Peter Arengo-Jones, *Queen Victoria in Switzerland* (London: Robert Hale, 1995), 17–18.
17. QVJ 13 July 1867.
18. Kathryn Jones, *For the Royal Table: Dining at the Palace* (London: Royal Collection Enterprises, 2008), 105.
19. Augustus Hare, *The Story of My Life*, vol. 4 (London: George Allen, 1900).

20. Vera Watson, *A Queen at Home* (London: W. H. Allen, 1952), 221.

21. QVJ 20 June 1873.

22. Nasir al-Din Shah Qajar and J. W. Redhouse (trans.), *The Diary of H.M. The Shah of Persia During His Tour through Europe in A. D. 1873* (London: John Murray, 1874), 179.

23. TNA LC2/92: Bills from the visit of the Shah in 1873; Watson, *A Queen at Home*, 121.

24. TNA LC2/119: Correspondence regarding the Shah's visit in 1889.

25. Virginia Surtees, *Charlotte Canning: Lady in Waiting to Queen Victoria and Wife of the First Viceroy of India, 1817–1871* (London: John Murray, 1975), 95.

26. Ibid., 97.

27. Ibid., 96.

28. QVJ 2 September 1843.

29. Surtees, *Charlotte Canning: Lady in Waiting to Queen Victoria and Wife of the First Viceroy of India, 1817–1871*, 96.

30. QVJ 9 September 1843.

31. QVJ 6 September 1843.

32. Surtees, *Charlotte Canning: Lady in Waiting to Queen Victoria and Wife of the First Viceroy of India, 1817–1871*, 102; *ILN* 16 September 1843.

33. QVJ 15 August 1845.

34. Annie Gray, '"The Proud Air of an Unwilling Slave": Tea, Women and Domesticity, c.1700–1900', in *Historical and Archaeological Perspectives on Gender Transformations: From Private to Public*, Suzanne Spencer-Wood, ed. (New York: Springer, 2013). Afternoon tea appears in the eighteenth century, but it takes a long time to be accepted and then, inevitably, is codified by advice book writers.

35. QVJ 19 August 1845; QVJ 21 August 1858.

36. Surtees, *Charlotte Canning: Lady in Waiting to Queen Victoria and Wife of the First Viceroy of India, 1817–1871*, 113, 158.

37. Ibid., 112, 114.

38. Ibid., 158; QVJ 23 August 1845.
39. Surtees, *Charlotte Canning: Lady in Waiting to Queen Victoria and Wife of the First Viceroy of India*, 155.
40. Benita Stoney and Heinrich Weltzien, eds., *My Mistress the Queen: The Letters of Frieda Arnold, Dresser to Queen Victoria* (London: Weidenfeld & Nicolson, 1994), 99–108.
41. The Dean of Windsor and Hector Bolitho, *Letters of Lady Augusta Stanley: A Young Lady at Court, 1849–1863* (London: Gerald Howe, 1927), 68, 75.
42. QVJ 18 August 1855, 22 August 1855, 25 August 1855.
43. David Duff, *Victoria Travels* (London: Frederick Muller, 1970), 146; Kurt Jagow (ed.) and E. T. S. Dugdale (trans.), *Letters of the Prince Consort, 1831–1861* (London: John Murray, 1938), 306.
44. Surtees, *Charlotte Canning: Lady in Waiting to Queen Victoria and Wife of the First Viceroy of India, 1817–1871*, 90.
45. Kate Hubbard, *Serving Victoria: Life in the Royal Household* (London: Chatto & Windus, 2012), 88; Surtees, *Charlotte Canning: Lady in Waiting to Queen Victoria and Wife of the First Viceroy of India, 1817–1871*, 93.
46. Surtees, *Charlotte Canning: Lady in Waiting to Queen Victoria and Wife of the First Viceroy of India, 1817–1871*, 109.
47. QVJ 21 January 1845, QVJ 1 December 1843.
48. Beatrice Erskine (writing as Mrs Steuart Erskine), *Twenty Years at Court, 1842–1862: From the Correspondence of the Hon. Eleanor Stanley, Maid-of-Honour to Her Late Majesty Queen Victoria* (London: Nisbet & Co., 1916), 261; Hugh Murray, 'Queen Victoria, York and the Royal Myths', *York Historian* 11 (1994).
49. Arengo-Jones, *Queen Victoria in Switzerland*, 20.
50. RA VIC/ADDC40. He calls Jungbleeth 'Jungbluth', which was a common alternative spelling of his name.
51. Arengo-Jones, *Queen Victoria in Switzerland*, 47.
52. Blair Castle Account Book vol. 5/44.
53. Arengo-Jones, *Queen Victoria in Switzerland*, 74.

54. QVJ 9 August 1868; 12 August 1868; 17 August 1868; 31 August 1868 and 13 September 1868.

55. QVJ 6 April 1879.

56. QVJ 27 March 1889.

57. QVJ 23 April 1887.

58. Mary Lutyens, ed., *Lady Lytton's Court Diary, 1895–1899* (London: Rupert Hart-Davis), 94.

59. John Murray, *A Handbook for Travellers to France*, 10th edn. (London: John Murray, 1867), 544–48.

60. Xavier Paoli and Alexander Teixeira de Mattos (trans.), *My Royal Clients* (London: Hodder & Stoughton, c.1911), 338; RA MRH/MRHF/EB/4: Lord Steward's department to 1900; 1871 UK census; Lutyens, ed., *Lady Lytton's Court Diary, 1895–1899*, 99.

61. Paoli and Teixeira de Mattos, *My Royal Clients*, 346.

62. Michael Nelson, *Queen Victoria and the Discovery of the Riviera* (London: Tauris Parke, 2007), 84.

63. Elizabeth Longford, *Victoria* (London: Abacus, 2011), 563–64.

64. Paoli and Teixeira de Mattos, *My Royal Clients*, 352.

65. *ILN* 24 April 1897.

66. Anon., *The Private Life of the Queen* (1897), 182.

67. QVJ 24 December 1862.

68. QVJ 24 December 1866.

69. William Hone, *The Every Day Book* (London, 1825), 24–25.

70. QVJ 6 January 1880; QVJ 6 January 1892. For some inexplicable reason the internet has decided that Victoria 'banned' Twelfth Cakes in the 1870s. She didn't.

71. RA VIC/MAIN/Y/203/78.

72. Victor Mallet, ed., *Life with Queen Victoria: Marie Mallet's Letters from Court, 1887–1901* (London: John Murray, 1968), 126.

73. John Van der Kiste, *Childhood at Court, 1819–1914* (Stroud: Sutton, 2003), 57.

CHAPTER 10: THE WIDER WORLD OF FOOD

1. QVJ 22 June 1897.
2. Charles Elmé Francatelli, *A Plain Cookery Book for the Working Classes* (London, 1861), 36.
3. Mary Krout, *A Looker on in London* (1898), republished by Dodo Press, 2009.
4. RA PPTO/PP/OSB/OS/910.
5. QVJ 25 June 1897.
6. Benita Stoney and Heinrich Weltzien, eds., *My Mistress the Queen: The Letters of Frieda Arnold, Dresser to Queen Victoria* (London: Weidenfeld & Nicolson, 1994), 55; Alfred Suzanne, *La Cuisine et Pâtisserie Anglaise et Américaine* (Paris, 1904), 84.
7. Alexis Soyer, *A Shilling Cookery Book for the People* (London: Routledge, 1860), 97.
8. John Burnett, *Plenty and Want: A Social History of Food in England from 1815 to the Present Day* (London: Routledge, 1989).
9. Pamela Horn, *The Rise and Fall of the Victorian Servant* (Dublin: Gill & Macmillan, 1975), 24. See also P. Sambrook, *Keeping Their Place: Domestic Service in the Country House* (Stroud: Sutton, 2005).
10. Maria Rundell, *A New System of Domestic Cookery* (London: John Murray, 1806), reissued edition (London: Persephone Books, 2009), 312–13. The same menus are repeated in the edition of 1861.
11. Elizabeth Gaskell, *North and South* (1854).
12. Laura Mason, 'Everything Stops for Tea', in *Luncheon, Nuncheon and Other Meals: Eating with the Victorans*, C. A. Wilson, ed. (Stroud: Sutton, 1994).
13. QVJ 3 August 1832; QVJ 1 January 1837; QVJ 29 December 1836.
14. Elizabeth Longford, *Victoria* (London: Abacus, 2011), 383.
15. 'Tamworth Agricultural Dinner', report in *The Examiner*, 28 October 1865, 680.

16. Jane Roberts, *Royal Landscape: The Gardens and Parks of Windsor* (New Haven: Yale University Press, 1997), 93.

17. Walter Arnstein, 'Queen Victoria's Other Island', in *More Adventures with Britannia: Politics, Personalities and Culture in Britain*, William Roger Louis, ed. (Austin & London: University of Texas & Tauris, 1998); https://mikedashhistory.com/2014/12/29/queen-victorias-5-the-strange-tale-of-turkish-aid-to-ireland-during-the-great-famine/

18. RA MRH/MRHF/MENUS/MAIN/BP/1842, 26 May.

19. Peter Gray, 'National Humiliation and the Great Hunger: Fast and Famine in 1847', *Irish Historical Studies* 32, no. 126 (2000): 200.

20. Ibid.

21. QVJ 24 March 1847.

22. QVJ 1 September 1849.

23. QVJ 22 April 1854.

24. QVJ 7 July 1855.

25. Mary Elizabeth Braddon, *Hostages to Fortune* (London, 1875). It's a great read.

26. For more on Soyer, see Ruth Cowen, *Relish: The Extraordinary Life of Alexis Soyer, Victorian Celebrity Chef* (London: Weidenfeld & Nicolson, 2006).

27. *ILN* 2 November 1850.

28. Michael Leapman, *The World for a Shilling: How the Great Exhibition of 1851 Shaped a Nation* (London: Headline, 2001), 143.

29. Isabella Beeton, *The Book of Household Management* (London: S. O. Beeton, 1861), 956.

30. Ibid., 944–45.

31. Henry Mayhew, *London Labour and the London Poor* (London: Dover, 1861). A fully searchable version of this, with many other very useful sources, is at http://www.victorianlondon.org/index-2012.htm

32. QVJ 29 August 1861.

33. Burnett, *Plenty and Want: A Social History of Food in England from 1815 to the Present Day*, 216–39; Arthur Hill Hassall, *Food and Its Adulterations* (London: Longmans, 1855). This section also draws on research done for the 2016 BBC TV series, *Victorian Bakers*.

34. Anon., *Buckmaster's Cookery* (London: Routledge, 1874), 105.

35. James Critchell and Joseph Raymond, *A History of the Frozen Meat Trade* (London: Constable, 1912). Online via archive. org

36. RA MRH/MRHF/GOODREC/SPICES/WC/1888

37. RA MRH/MRHF/GOODREC/SPICES/WC/1853; Bee Wilson, *Swindled: From Poison Sweets to Counterfeit Coffee – the Dark History of the Food Cheats* (London: John Murray, 2008), 138.

38. Anon. (Arthur G. Payne), *The Housekeeper's Guide to Preserved Meats, Fruits, Condiments, Vegetables &c* (London: Crosse & Blackwell, 1886), 51, 116.

39. The hot meat whatever the weather continued until at least the 1950s, but a modern compromise has been reached whereby some Australians hold 'Christmas in July', sitting down to turkey and tinsel on 25 July, when it's a bit more likely to be snowing or at least raining, as per the usual British Christmas.

40. QVJ 1 December 1851.

41. QVJ 30 March 1853; 24 January 1873; 28 December 1874.

42. Mary Lutyens, ed., *Lady Lytton's Court Diary, 1895–1899* (London: Rupert Hart-Davis, 1961), 142.

CHAPTER 11: THE AGEING QUEEN

1. Queen Marie of Roumania, *The Story of My Life*, vol. 1 (London: Cassell, 1934), 74.

2. Duke of Windsor, *A King's Story* (London: Prion, 1998), 11–12. The mid-twentieth century saw a rash of memoirs from Victoria's grandchildren and the children of her courtiers, the best of which used letters or diary entries

written at the time, but many of which peddled similar stories reliant on the hazy memories of a far-off childhood, and containing tell-tale phrases along the lines of 'I heard it said … '.

3. Michaela Reid, *Ask Sir James: The Life of Sir James Reid, Personal Physician to Queen Victoria* (London: Eland, 1987), 107.

4. Jules Gouffé and Alphonse Gouffé (trans.), *The Book of Preserves (Le Livre de Conserves)* (London: Sampson, Low, Son and Marston, 1871), 299.

5. QVJ 19 August 1871.

6. QVJ 16 October 1871.

7. QVJ 2 September 1871.

8. QVJ 18 October 1871.

9. QVJ 31 December 1871.

10. Carrie Barratt, *Queen Victoria and Thomas Sully* (New York: Princeton University Press/The Metropolitan Museum of Art, 2000), 45.

11. Reid, *Ask Sir James: The Life of Sir James Reid, Personal Physician to Queen Victoria*, 57.

12. Arthur Ponsonby, *Henry Ponsonby, Queen Victoria's Private Secretary: His Life from His Letters* (London: Macmillan, 1942), 120.

13. RA VIC/MAIN/Y/34/9 Feodora to Victoria, 2 October 1834.

14. Greg King, *Twilight of Splendor: The Court of Queen Victoria During Her Diamond Jubilee Year* (Hoboken: John Wiley, 2007), 74–75.

15. Victor Mallet, ed., *Life with Queen Victoria: Marie Mallet's Letters from Court, 1887–1901* (London: John Murray, 1968), 34, 37.

16. Ibid., 106.

17. She had not stopped wearing them entirely, however. Norwich Castle Museum has a gown given by the Queen to one of her attendants which dates from *c.* 1895. It is boned,

368 THE GREEDY QUEEN

shaped and intended for wearing over corsets, and in an
indication of how much weight she'd put on since the 1860s,
it has a waist measurement of 45 inches (114.5 cm). The gown
and its waist is not directly comparable to earlier garments:
she would have reduced her waist much more in earlier years
than in later life, and the waistline itself had changed as
fashion altered throughout the nineteenth century. However,
even allowing for a certain leeway, she was certainly very
obese.

18. Sir Sultan Muhammed Shah, *The Memoirs of the Aga Khan*
(London: Cassell & Co., 1954), 45, 47.

19. Mary Lutyens, ed., *Lady Lytton's Court Diary, 1895–1899*
(London: Rupert Hart-Davis, 1961), 71.

20. Ibid., 77; *The Times*, 24 September 1896.

21. QVJ 24 September 1896; Sophie Baroness Buxeoveden, *The
Life and Tragedy of Alexandra Feodorovna, Empress of Russia*
(London: Longmans, 1928), 7.

22. Mallet, ed., *Life with Queen Victoria: Marie Mallet's Letters
from Court, 1887–1901*, 5; Lutyens, ed., *Lady Lytton's Court
Diary, 1895–1899*, 128.

23. Thomas (Lord Ribblesdale) Lister, *Impressions and Memories*
(London: Cassell, 1927), 119–20.

24. Reid, *Ask Sir James: The Life of Sir James Reid, Personal
Physician to Queen Victoria*, 37, 44.

25. Mallet, ed., *Life with Queen Victoria: Marie Mallet's Letters
from Court, 1887–1901*, 71–72.

26. Helen Rappaport, *Magnificent Obsession: Victoria, Albert, and
the Death That Changed the Monarchy* (London: Windmill,
2012), 142, 50.

27. Roumania, *The Story of My Life*, vol. 1, 20; Windsor, *A
King's Story*, 14.

28. Mallet, ed., *Life with Queen Victoria: Marie Mallet's Letters
from Court, 1887–1901*, 66. Mehlspiese is a generic German
term for pudding.

29. Roumania, *The Story of My Life*, vol. 1, 25–26. The recipe is in Francatelli's *Modern Cook*.

30. James Pope-Hennessy, *Queen Victoria at Windsor and Balmoral: Letters from Her Granddaughter Princess Victoria of Prussia, June 1889* (London: George Allen & Unwin, 1959), 34, 48.

31. Roumania, *The Story of My Life*, vol. 1, 21–22.

32. Lutyens, ed., *Lady Lytton's Court Diary, 1895–1899*, 124.

33. For more on tea, specifically its feminisation and the development of tea in the late nineteenth century, see A. Gray, '"The Proud Air of an Unwilling Slave": Tea, Women and Domesticity, c.1700–1900', in *Historical and Archaeological Perspectives on Gender Transformations: From Private to Public*, Suzanne Spencer-Wood, ed. (New York: Springer, 2013).

34. Marie Zu Erbach-Schönberg (Princess of Battenberg), *Reminiscences* (London: George Allen & Unwin, 1925), 236.

35. Mary Elizabeth Braddon, *Lady Audley's Secret* (1862), 222.

36. Elizabeth Longford, *Victoria* (London: Abacus, 2011), 88.

37. Zu Erbach-Schönberg (Princess of Battenberg), *Reminiscences*, 237; Pope-Hennessy, *Queen Victoria at Windsor and Balmoral: Letters from Her Granddaughter Princess Victoria of Prussia, June 1889*, 44.

38. Pope-Hennessy, *Queen Victoria at Windsor and Balmoral: Letters from Her Granddaughter Princess Victoria of Prussia, June 1889*, 26.

39. Ibid., 37, 64, 90.

40. Mallet, ed., *Life with Queen Victoria: Marie Mallet's Letters from Court, 1887–1901*, 33.

41. Ibid., 23, 25.

42. QVJ 18 July 1884.

43. PPTO/PP/INDHH/CSP/22: letter setting out duties of Ahmed Hussain (one of the later Indian servants).

44. Reid, *Ask Sir James: The Life of Sir James Reid, Personal Physician to Queen Victoria*, 154.

45. PPTO/PP/INDHH/CSP/INDEX; PPTO/PP/INDHH/ CSP/27. The cooks were paid from the Privy Purse until 1891, after which they were directly under Abdul Karim, and part of his £992 salary was a £60 allowance for paying them.

46. Tschumi and Powe, *Royal Chef: Forty Years with Royal Households* (London: William Kimber, 1954), 69. An example entry in the ledgers can be found on 26 July 1889. These entries are not particularly regular, which suggests that meat was either brought in live, as Tschumi suggests, or, more likely given the lack of butchery facilities anywhere in any of the palaces by the 1880s, not listed in the ledgers which, after all, deal primarily with dining, and not supplies. The supply books don't shed any further light on the question.

47. For example, curry de poulet appears on the dinner menu for Windsor on 29 December 1847.

48. QVJ 20 August 1887. For an excellent discussion on curry in all its forms, see Linda Collingham, *Curry: A Tale of Cooks and Conquerers* (London: Vintage, 2006).

49. Dining ledger for 1897 at Osborne House (English Heritage); RA MRH/MRHF/MENUS/MAIN/BP/1888.

50. Reid, *Ask Sir James: The Life of Sir James Reid, Personal Physician to Queen Victoria*, 74.

51. Ibid., 77–78.

52. Ibid., 81.

53. RA MRH/MRHF/GOODSREC/BREAD/WC: accounts from 1889.

54. Mallet, ed., *Life with Queen Victoria: Marie Mallet's Letters from Court, 1887–1901*, 148.

55. Ibid., 161–62.

56. Ibid., 5.

57. G. R. M. Devereux, *Etiquette for Men* (London: C. Arthur Pearson, Ltd, 1904), 61–62.

58. Mallet, ed., *Life with Queen Victoria: Marie Mallet's Letters from Court, 1887–1901*, 192.

59. Ibid., 195. 'Banting' means jolly good fun.

60. Ibid., 197.
61. Reid, *Ask Sir James: The Life of Sir James Reid, Personal Physician to Queen Victoria*, 195–96.
62. QVJ 16 November 1900.
63. Gillian Gill, *We Two: Victoria and Albert: Rulers, Partners, Rivals* (New York: Ballantine Books, 2010), 78.
64. Reid, *Ask Sir James: The Life of Sir James Reid, Personal Physician to Queen Victoria*, 197.
65. QVJ 12 November 1900.
66. QVJ 13 November 1900.
67. QVJ 14 November 1900.
68. QVJ 19 November 1900.
69. Mallet, ed., *Life with Queen Victoria: Marie Mallet's Letters from Court, 1887–1901*, 213.
70. Jules Gouffé and Alphonse Gouffé (trans.), *The Book of Preserves (Le Livre de Conserves)* (London: Sampson, Low, Son and Marston, 1871), 291.
71. Mallet, ed., *Life with Queen Victoria: Marie Mallet's Letters from Court, 1887–1901*, 214–15.
72. Ibid., 218.
73. Ibid., 219.
74. QVJ 29 December 1900.
75. QVJ 1 January 1901.
76. Kate Hubbard, *Serving Victoria: Life in the Royal Household* (London: Chatto & Windus, 2012), 354.
77. Reid, *Ask Sir James: The Life of Sir James Reid, Personal Physician to Queen Victoria*, 200–07.
78. *The Times*, 21 January 1901.
79. *The Times*, 22 January 1901.
80. Reid, *Ask Sir James: The Life of Sir James Reid, Personal Physician to Queen Victoria*, 211.

EPILOGUE: HOW TO END AN AGE

1. Michaela Reid, *Ask Sir James: The Life of Sir James Reid, Personal Physician to Queen Victoria* (London: Eland, 1987), 225.

2. Jane Ridley, *Bertie: A Life of Edward VII* (London: Chatto & Windus, 2012).

3. HRH the Duchess of York and Benita Stoney, *Victoria and Albert: Life at Osborne House* (London: Weidenfeld & Nicolson, 1991), 111.

4. RA VIC/ADDQ/1448: Professor Isaac Bayley Balfour to Viscount Esher, 15 November 1901.

5. Samuel Ponder and Lucy Pell, and Jane Macdonald. RA PPTO/PP/CL/MAIN/EVII – List of pensions, 1901, accessed via findmypast.com

6. Gabriel Tschumi and Joan Powe, *Royal Chef: Forty Years with Royal Households* (London: William Kimber, 1954), 122.

7. RA PPTO/PP/EVII/MAIN/A/4335.

8. Suzanne Groom, *At the King's Table: Royal Dining through the Ages* (London: Merrell/Historic Royal Palaces, 2013), 181.

9. Ridley, *Bertie: A Life of Edward VII*, 364.

APPENDIX: ANNOTATED AND MODERNISED RECIPES

1. Charles Elmé Francatelli, *The Cook's Guide* (London: Richard Bentley, 1861), p. 309.

2. William Kitchener, *The Cook's Oracle* (London: John Hatchard, 1818), pp. 160–61.

3. Jules Gouffé, *Royal Cookery* (London: Sampson, Low and Marston, 1868), p. 228.

4. Charles Elmé Francatelli, *The Modern Cook* (London: Richard Bentley, 1855), p. 12.

5. Margaret Dods (Christian Isobel Johnstone), *The Cook and Housewife's Manual* (Edinburgh: Oliver and Boyd, 1862), p. 399.

6. Alexis Soyer, *The Modern Housewife* (London: Simpkin, Marshall and Co, 1849), p. 346.

7. Francatelli, *Modern Cook*, p. 983.

8. Ibid., 377–79.

9. Charles Elmé Francatelli, *A Plain Cookery Book for the Working Classes* (London: Bosworth and Harrison, 1861), p. 36.

10. Jules Gouffé, translated by Alphonse Gouffé, *The Book of Preserves (Le Livre De Conserves)* (London: Sampson, Low, Son and Marston, 1871), p. 299.

List of Illustrations

1. Princess Victoria, self-portrait, 1835; Royal Archives/© Her Majesty Queen Elizabeth II 2017: RA VIC/MAIN/M/5/85

2. Prince Leopold's christening banquet, 28 June 1853, painted by Louis Haghe: Royal Collection Trust/© Her Majesty Queen Elizabeth II 2017: RCIN 919917

3. Queen Victoria attending the Lord Mayor's Banquet, 9 November 1837 © Pictorial Press Ltd/Alamy Stock Photo

4: The Queen's Dinner, Tuesday 25 December, 1894, held at Osborne House © Private Royal Menu collection of Jake Smith

5: 'Evening at Balmoral', 1854. Painted by Carl Haag: Royal Collection Trust/© HM Queen Elizabeth II 2017: RL 22033

6. Windsor Castle kitchen, 1878: Royal Collection Trust/© HM Queen Elizabeth II 2017: RCIN 2100721

7. Windsor Castle Kitchen, 1886. Painted by Frank Watkins © Gavin Graham Gallery, London, UK/Bridgeman Images

8. The Kitchens and Offices, Osborne House, 1867. Photograph by André Disderi: Royal Collection Trust/© HM Queen Elizabeth II 2017: RCIN 2102593

9. Gottlob Waetzig, c. 1867: Royal Collection Trust/© HM Queen Elizabeth II 2017: RCIN 2910362

10. George Dessaulles in c. 1865: Royal Collection Trust/© HM Queen Elizabeth II 2017: RCIN 2910361

11. Portrait of Victoria and Albert © Mayall/Getty Images

12. Swiss Cottage, Osborne House, 1855. Painted by William Leitch: Royal Collection Trust/© HM Queen Elizabeth II 2017: RCIN 919867

13. Swiss Cottage kitchen. Photograph by André Disderi: Royal Collection Trust/© HM Queen Elizabeth II 2017: RCIN 2102589

14. Prince Albert, the British Farmer, 1843 © The Print Collector/Print Collector/Getty Images

15. Queen Victoria in 1875. Painted by Heinrich Von Angeli © Her Majesty Queen Elizabeth II, 2017/Bridgeman Images

16. Taking tea. *The Illustrated London News*, 24 April 1897: © Look and Learn/Illustrated Papers Collection/Bridgeman Images

17. Victorian dishes in all their glory. Picture sources: Gouffé, *Royal Cookery*; Frederick Vine, *Savoury Pastry*; Francatelli, *Modern Cook*; Theodore Garrett, *Encyclopedia of Practical Coookery*; George Cox, *The Art of Confectionery*; Alexis Soyer, *The Gastronomic Regenerator*, Katherine Mellish, *Cookery and Domestic Management* and John Kirkland, *The Modern Baker, Confectioner and Caterer*.

18. Queen Victoria's wedding dress © Miguel Medina/AFP/Getty Images

19. Black silk and net gown worn by Victoria in the 1890s ©Fashion Museum, Bath and North East Somerset Council, UK/Bridgeman Images

20. The Queen lying in State, January 1901. Painting by Robert Pritchett (1828–1907)/Private Collection © Christie's Images/Bridgeman Images

Index

Pigeons à l'Anglaise

Iced Cake, à la Stanley

Chartreuse, à la Cardinal

Chickens, à la Montmorency

Apples and Rice, ornamented

Filet de Bœuf Jardinière